MW01626969

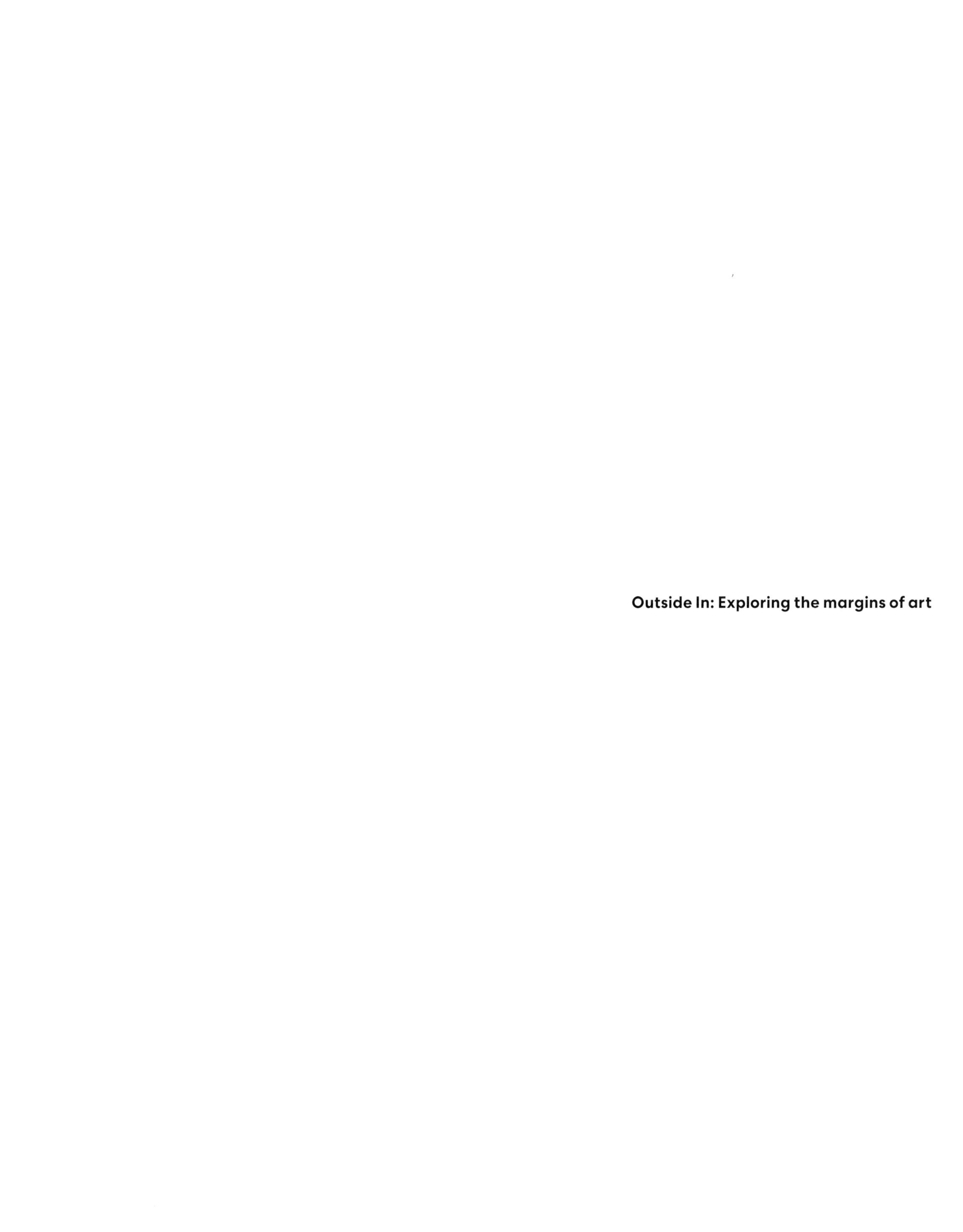

Outside In: Exploring the margins of art

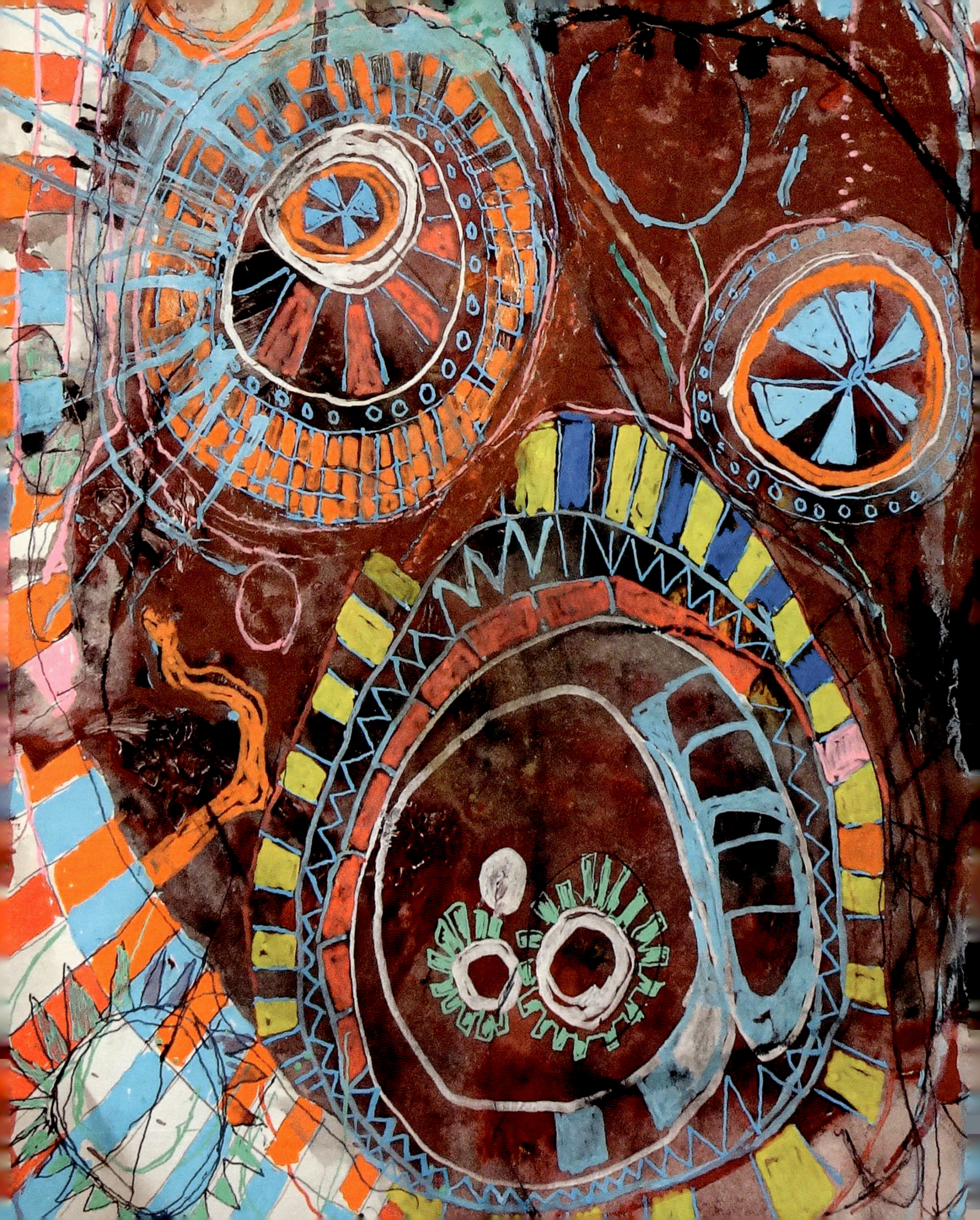

Outside In

Marc Steene

Exploring the margins of art

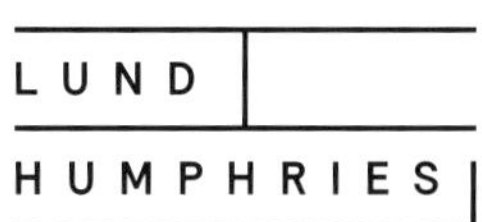

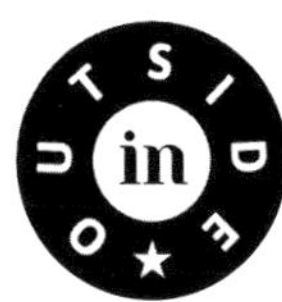

For my mother Luana who first introduced me to art, my wife Emily for her steadfastness, and my daughters, Saskia, Molly and Flora.

First published in 2023 by Lund Humphries
in association with Outside In

Lund Humphries
Huckletree Shoreditch
Alphabeta Building
18 Finsbury Square
London EC2A 1AH
UK

www.lundhumphries.com

Outside In: Exploring the margins of art

ISBN: 978-1-84822-455-1

A Cataloguing-in-Publication record for this book is available from the British Library

Designed by Paul Arnot
Set in Centra No2
Printed in Bosnia and Herzegovina

Cover
Tyrome Jordan
United States Overlook Me 1, 1995
Pencil, ink and crayon on paper
56.5 × 44.5 cm

Page 2
David Puttick
Untitled (detail), 2022
Mixed media
40 × 30 cm

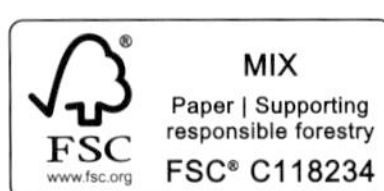

Acknowledgements

My sincere thanks go to all who have helped and supported me in the writing of this book. In particular, I would like to thank: Lucy Clark for her patience; Lucy Macmillan for enabling the almost impossible task of organising the images; James Peto for his gentle words of advice and guidance; Charles Rolls for believing in the cause and for his contributions; and Frances Christie for her endless enthusiasm. I am also extremely thankful for the generous support provided by Nigel Farrow and David Macmillan.

The book, and a lot of the work Outside In undertakes, would not be possible without the many arts organisations and their staff who do such incredible work in supporting artists, in particular: Laurence Ward from the Community Art Project in Darlington, Sheryll Catto from ActionSpace, Sarah Ballard from Barrington Farm in Norfolk and Sophie Leighton from the Bethlem Gallery.

I am fortunate to work with a talented and committed team at Outside In. The charity would not be what it is without them. I am indebted to team members, past and present, and all they have achieved – and continue to achieve. My heartfelt thanks to: Clair Montier, Kate Davey, Cornelia Marland, Charlotte Hanlon, Hannah Whitlock, Beth Hopkins, Beth Troakes, Laura Miles, Matt Forbes-Dale, Aoife Dunphy, José Sunshine-Okoro and Ellie Page. I have also never experienced a more dedicated board of trustees who give tirelessly to the mission, so my thanks to Charles Rolls, Trevor James, Scott Greenhalgh, Dannielle Hodson, Charles Martin and Frances Christie, as well as former trustee Rose Knox-Peebles.

I'd like to thank all the organisations that have helped with providing images, particularly the Prinzhorn Collection, West Sussex Record Office and Pallant House Gallery.

Finally, and most importantly, I'd like to express my gratitude to all the artists who have trusted me and Outside In with their work and words. The world will be a richer place if they are enabled to take the place they deserve – at the heart of our art world.

Carlo Keshishian
Picture Worth a Thousand Words
(detail)
1998–9
Spray and gloss paint on canvas
151 × 116 cm

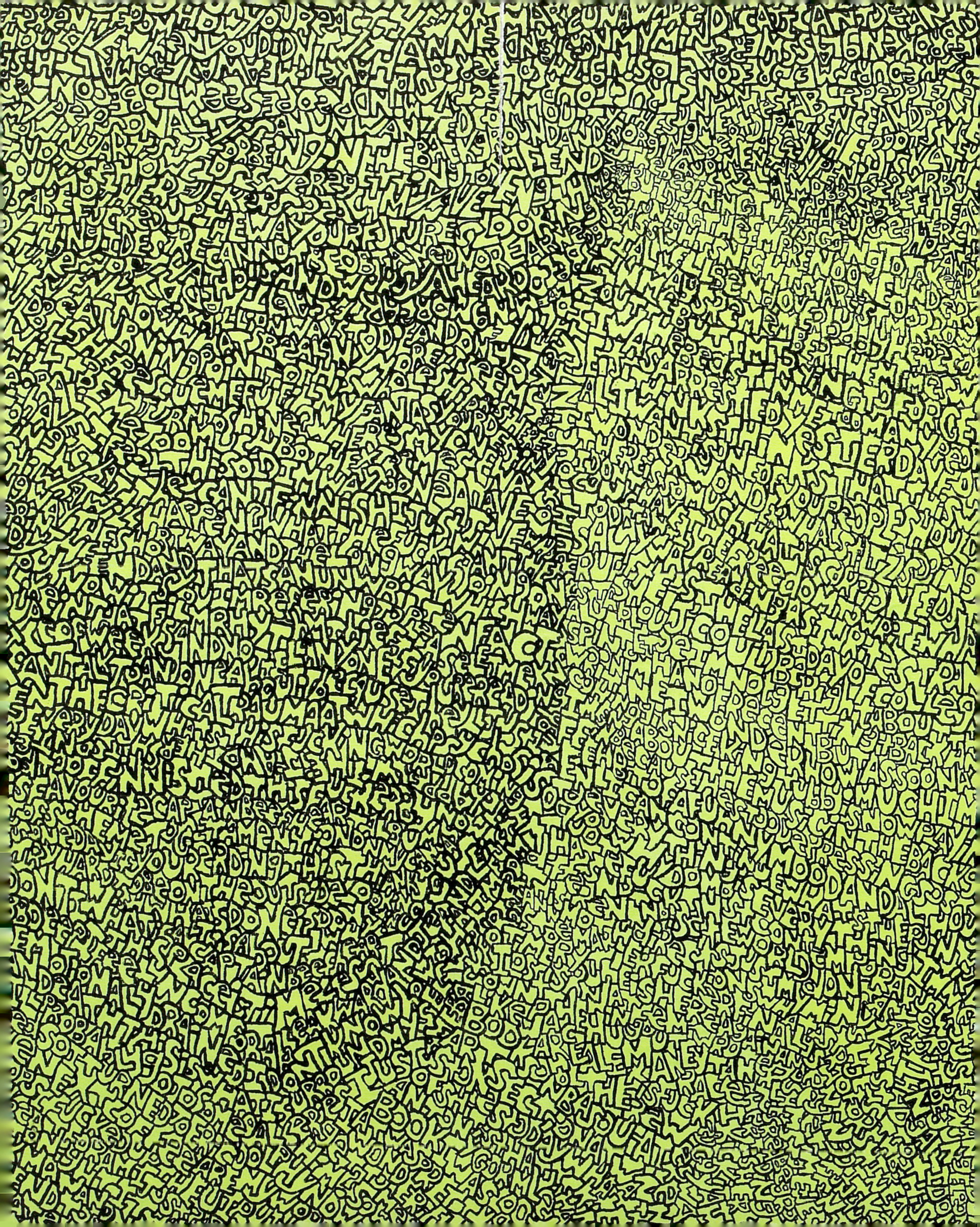

Foreword

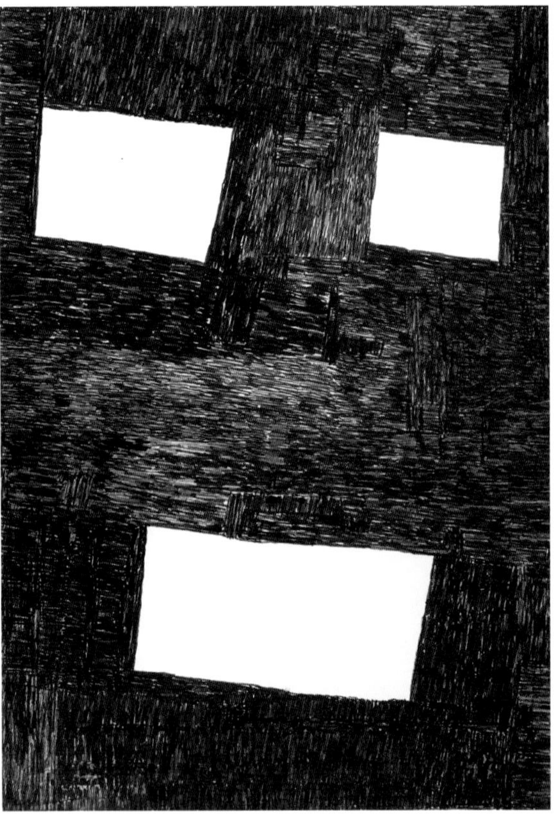

Alan Liddle
Untitled (Black)
2012
Felt pen on paper
84 × 59 cm

The global art market is immense, estimated to have a value of over US$60 billion in 2021. But as almost any aspiring artist will attest, it can seem an extraordinarily daunting task to try to break into any part of that market. Consider then how hard it would be for a creative person with virtually no arts engagement, maybe with mental or other significant health issues, disability, or difficult social circumstances. That is the issue that Marc Steene, the founder and director of Outside In, has been addressing since conceiving the idea for the charity in 2006.

His approach was based on his own experiences of the difficulties and injustices faced by many excluded artists. His account of this revelation in this book's introduction is poignant and defines the core of a man who over the past 12 years I have grown to know as a person of external gentleness, but with great inner strength and determination. It initially started as part of the Community Programme at Pallant House Gallery, and Marc continued to push his idea, finding supporters and backers until, in 2017, it became a stand-alone charity. Outside In is now helping an increasingly diverse group of artists right across the UK to find their way (and is part of a wider European network of similar organisations[1]). Some 3500 artists have worked with, and been helped by, the charity since 2006.

As this book demonstrates, it is the artists themselves who are at the heart of the charity. Their interests are always at the forefront of the strategy, a position assured by the integration of artists within the board of trustees. The ingenious use of Outside In trained artist ambassadors helps to spread the word and to deliver much of the further training and support. The quality of the art is of course what makes the output so interesting. At their best, the works are sublime, matching in resonance with many modern masterpieces.

Sometimes challenging, often unique, so much of the work that I admire is driven by a compulsion to express creatively. Marc and his team are rigorous in letting the artists define themselves in their own narrative. As a result, the art stands alone. Always trying to avoid stigmatising or pigeonholing any individual artist, the team adhere to the charity's stated objectives of supporting individuals to find their creative voice, unimpeded by outside influence or direction. This is refreshing and facilitates truly original pieces, as this book testifies.

From my first involvement with Outside In, I was struck by meeting several artists who made it clear that the charity is a lifeline, vital to them in the most profound way possible. The mission of the charity is that important. There is also a growing Outside In collection helping to demonstrate the rich diversity of work created by the artists, and the widening possibilities for a movement of art and artists. With the assistance of Sotheby's, and galleries such as Paradise Row

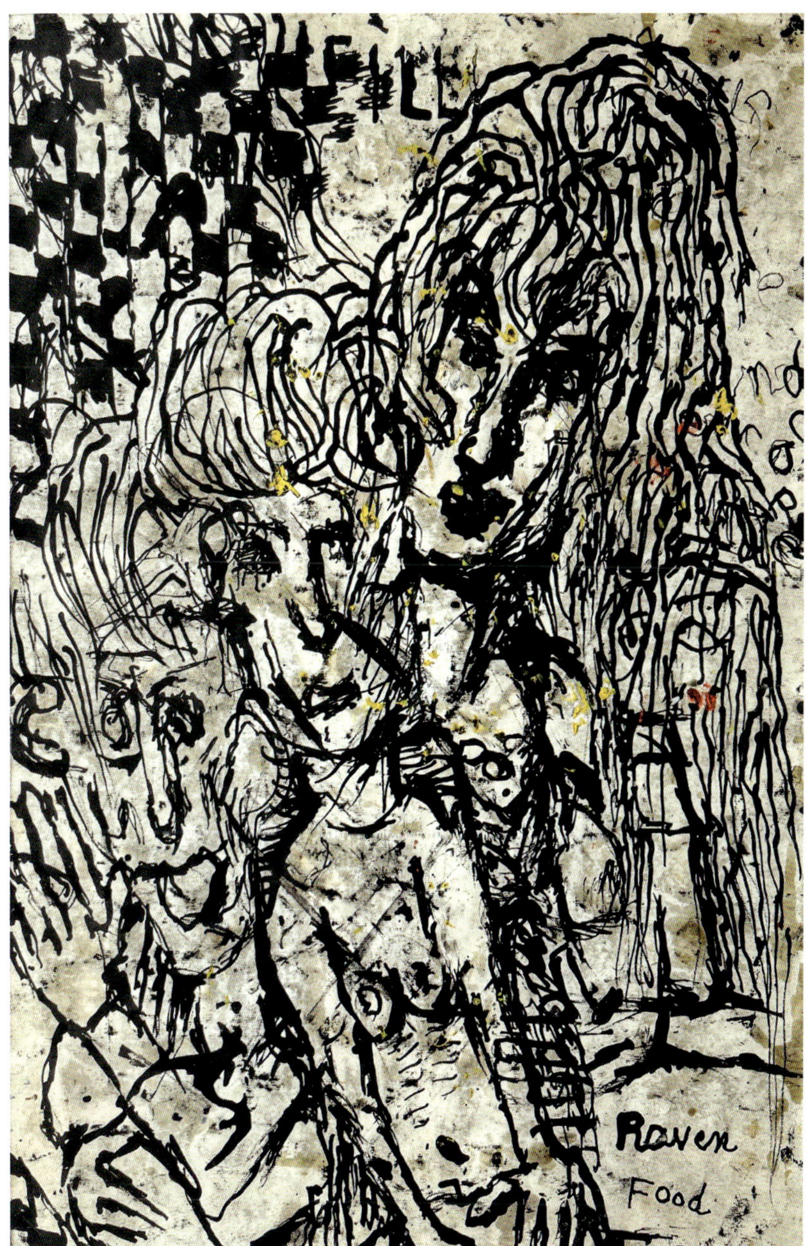

and the Harley Gallery, and in partnership with the Ingram and Jerwood Collections, some of the collection and the works of Outside In artists have now been displayed in the most exalted locations in London, elsewhere in the UK and on occasion on the continent.

In time, a part of what the Outside In collection might achieve is the bringing together of the work of a valuable group of loosely associated artists from the marginalised sectors of our society. Since my involvement in the charity, I have added works of British Outsider artists such as Madge Gill and Scottie Wilson, alongside some recently acquired European works and Outside In artists, to my own collection. The UK has been poorly served when compared to continental Europe and the US, with limited gallery space dedicated to non-traditional art and, apart from the Musgrave Kinley Outsider Art Collection at the Whitworth, no public collection. This book celebrates the work of artists championed by Outside In and will hopefully help in the charity's continuing aims to reach out to and encourage those with artistic talent, but the least opportunity – to acknowledge their artistic voice and to afford everyone who has a talent the chance to use it to enjoy a better creative life.

Charles Rolls

Louis Soutter (1871–1942)
Raven Food
c.1930–37
Ink on paper (double sided work)
42 × 28 cm

Preface

This book is not seeking to address the multiple issues associated with art created outside of the mainstream, or what has been commonly known as outsider art, such as how to define or label the artists and their work within a traditional art historical context. Instead, it aims to highlight and celebrate the diversity of talent often hidden in our communities. Overlooking this diversity of creativity means that the art world is not truly representative of our whole artistic community. Given the amount of public funding accorded to the arts, it seems there is a moral imperative that we reach out and understand creativity in its wider context. As Martin Herbert so perfectly described in *ArtReview*: 'But mostly "the artworld" is a piece of divisive, defining, this-not-that nomenclature, a portcullis that's generally up unless there's money in it and/or the exclusion is no longer tenable. What we call contemporary art at any given time certainly doesn't contain all new art of worth.'[1] Elsewhere, Max Lakin commented in *The New York Times Style Magazine*: 'The bitter flavor of exclusion, the willful ignorance of art's gatekeepers manicuring the pasture of a well-mannered in-group, is a very real history that the art world continues to reckon with.'[2]

By challenging the status quo, as Outside In aims to do, we can bring vital change to the sector, ensuring that art institutions meaningfully reflect the creative diversity of their communities. Not in the time-worn way of engaging marginalised groups in workshops and peripheral learning spaces, but by according the disempowered the same opportunity as any other contemporary practitioners. By embracing a wider understanding of creativity, and changing the language and methodology that the art world uses, a humanising and inclusive approach can be facilitated so ensuring that these spaces maintain and build a relevance for existing and future artists and audiences.

Labels are always problematic, and I have sought to highlight individual achievement rather than defaulting to any collective descriptors, whether societal or cultural, in this book. It is not within the scope of this publication to address the history of outsider art, or the many other associated terms used to describe art from the margins, the Disability Arts Movement, or other related areas. This book acknowledges that without the attention brought to work of this kind by Hans Prinzhorn, Jean Dubuffet, Roger Cardinal and many others, important artistic contributions would be hidden from public view or perhaps not even exist. But the term outsider art is loaded with meaning. In its art-historical context it is used to describe art that has been created independently of accepted contemporary practice, outside the established canon. The challenge in discussing outsider art is that the only common denominator is often the artist's life situation, frequently a disability or mental health issue, and their individualised approach to making their work. There are no stylistic comparisons, or shared techniques or subject matter. This is very different to other art movements such as Expressionism, for example, where artists have often come together to create collectives which they choose to align with, sharing similar values and approaches.

Interestingly, some of the artists included in this book define themselves as 'outsider' artists. Kept at arm's length from the art world, they have proudly reclaimed the term. Also of interest is that many of the existing collectors and dealers of 'outsider art' seem reluctant to let go of the label or the need to show this art differently. It seems that there is a value in selling and promoting art that is produced by artists seemingly removed from 'normal' society. Perhaps this creation of an exotic species of 'others' provides a fetishistic pleasure; rather like paying visitors viewing patients at an asylum in times past. It is my hope that this book goes some way towards opening the door to lasting change and inclusion of a broader set of creators and their work, no longer a labelled side show, but sharing centre stage simply as 'artists'.

Marc Steene

Jean Dubuffet
Body of a Woman
1950
Oil on canvas
116 × 89 cm

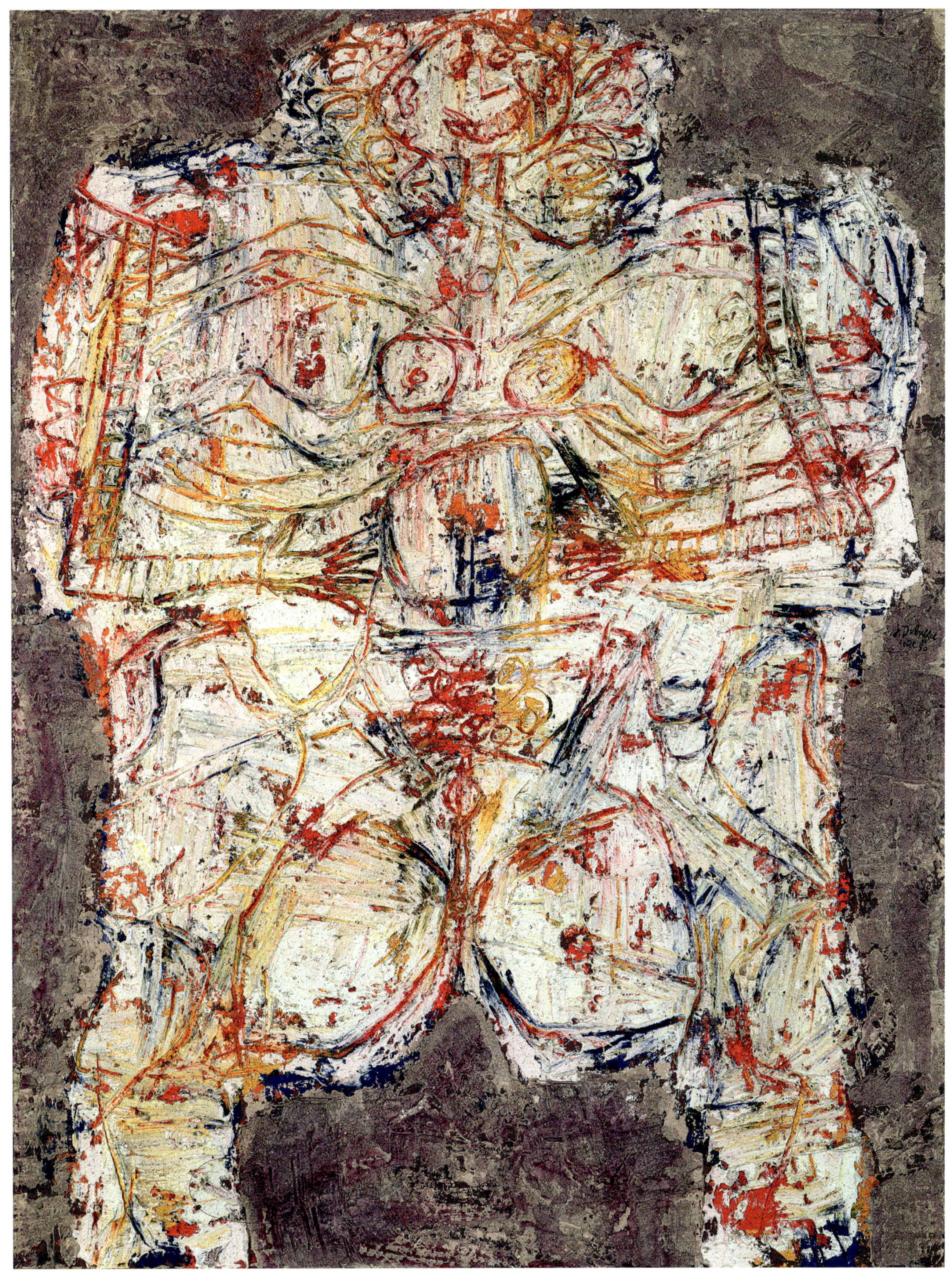

Introduction

Over 30 years ago, my life changed forever when I began working as a volunteer at a day centre for adults with learning disabilities. I remember the old Victorian church where the centre was based, and the noise and chaos of over 80 people in the space; it was like bedlam. The day centre manager, knowing I was an artist, offered me the opportunity to work with a small group of people to deliver an art project. We were eight adults sat around a table, with the cheapest of materials at our disposal – sugar paper, pencils, felt pens and poster paint. As soon as they started to work, I realised I was witnessing something extraordinary. With no regard to me or my intentions for the project, each of them started working on their own, with a distinctive voice and style, beautiful and exceptional. I recalled that I had experienced a similar sense of wonder when I visited *Outsiders* at the Hayward Gallery in 1979 as a young art student.

Inspired by their work, I organised an exhibition at the local library. On completing the project and returning to collect the art to frame, I was informed by the day centre staff that the work was no longer available as it had been pulped to make papier mâché for the artists to model. I can still remember my shock and outrage. The staff were blind to the value and talents of the artists they were working with, their art-making seen as nothing more than a containment activity. The final indignity was watching the artists repurpose their work into cups and bowls which inevitably ended up in the bin – a grim cycle of creativity and destruction, which nonetheless did not crush the spirit and creativity of those involved. From this experience, I asked myself, 'How do I enable those overlooked and misunderstood artists to get their work into settings where its true value will be recognised?', and 'How do I enable audiences (such as the day centre staff) to understand and appreciate the talent of artists who do not conform to their expectations of who can be an artist?' My first experiences of working with that group of artists, in one way or another, shaped my career and led to the creation of Outside In at Pallant House Gallery[1] in 2006.

Outside In enables the artists it works with to present themselves as artists in their own right, outside of any label that might be attached to them, whether that is medical or societal. Artists choose what they wish to say about themselves in their artist statement and only if they wish to.

A question we often get asked is how we find our artists. Artists with the means and capacity find us themselves, often through the website, completing a confidential signing-up process evidencing their need of our help, and can upload their work to create an online gallery. Harder to reach artists are found through our programme of artist support days. The increasing digital divide in our society means that many people lack access to technology or the knowledge to use it. By using networks and contacts in health and social care, and other support organisations, we reach out and identify artists that need our support. The artists have an hour's session with a member of the Outside In team to create their online gallery, often the first time that they have shared their work, and a small hand-held step is taken into the art world.

The main vehicle for presenting the work of artists supported by Outside In is our National Exhibition, which has been held five times since 2007 at Pallant House Gallery and at other venues across the UK. In 2012, the exhibition was held alongside *Jean Dubuffet: Transitions* at Pallant House Gallery, a contextual exhibition of the work of Jean Dubuffet (1901–1985), the French artist who coined the term Art Brut and is considered by many to be the father figure of outsider art. The exhibition attracted 2310 submissions from 1958 artists, resulting in an exhibition of 80 artworks that also toured across the UK. Jonathan Jones of *The Guardian* described the exhibition as offering a 'radical perspective on Britain today'.

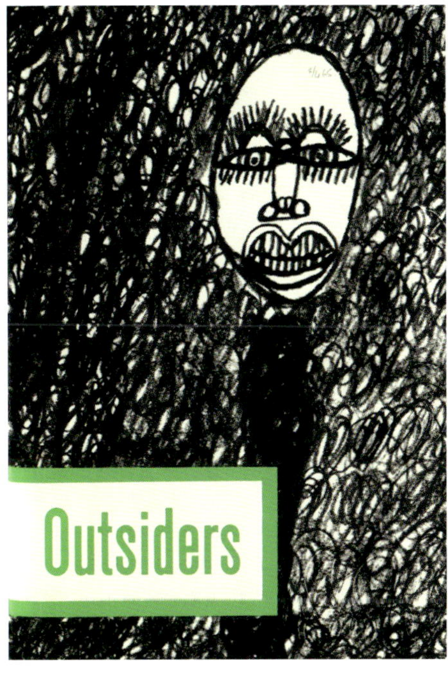

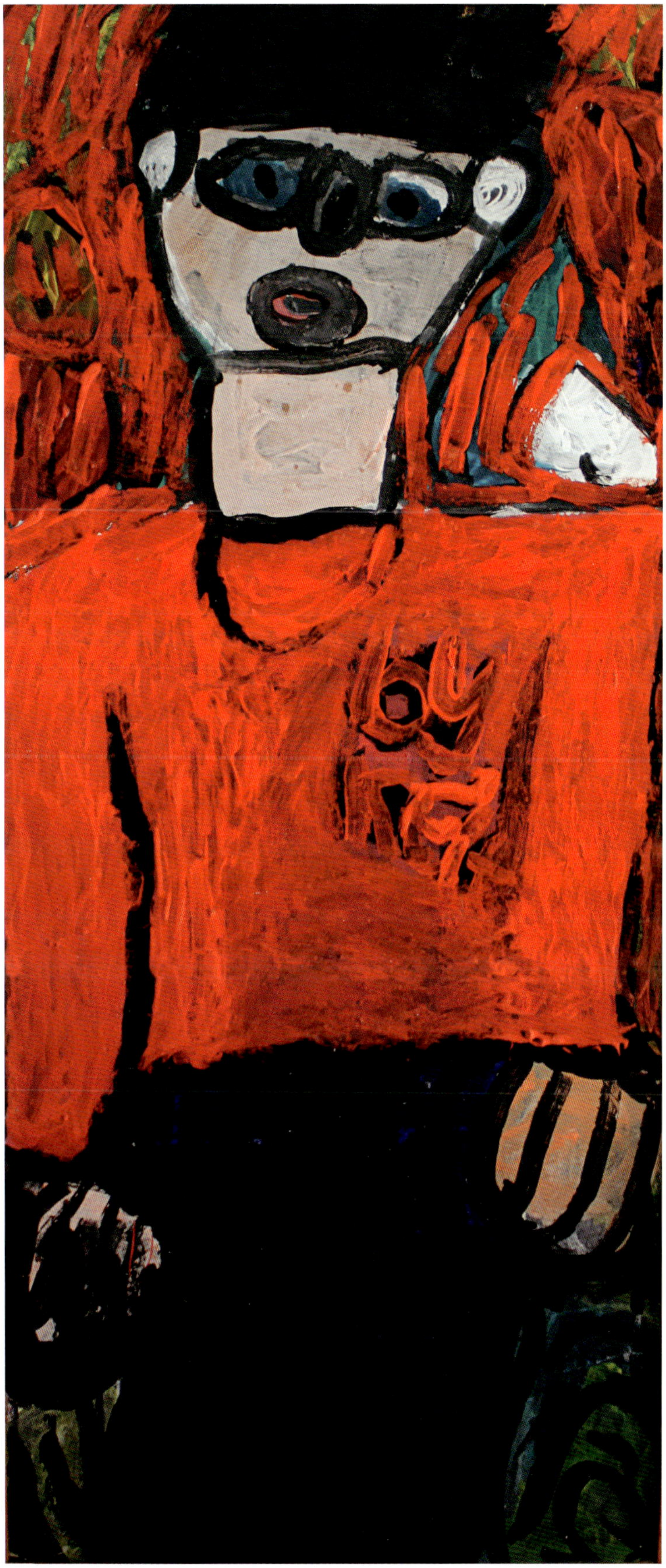

Johann Hauser (1926–1996)
Outsiders: An Art Without Precedent or Tradition', 1979, Hayward Gallery catalogue

Keith Purcell
Portrait of Marc Steene
c.1999
Acrylic on board
54 × 38 cm

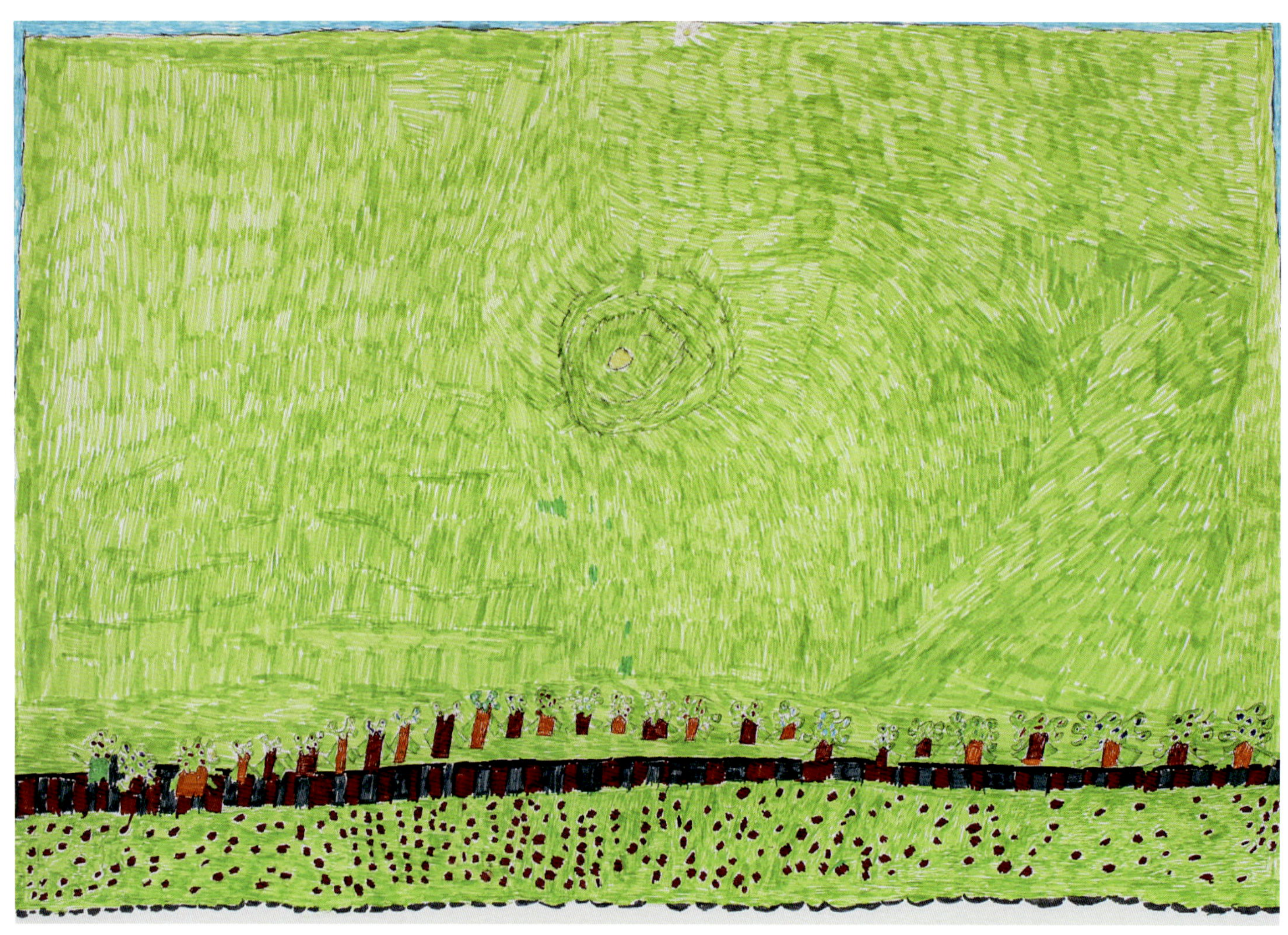

Alan Payler
The Garden
2019
Felt pen on paper
84 × 59 cm

Our 2019 National Exhibition, titled *Environments*, took place at Kings Place in London. It received 900 submissions and 80 works were selected for display. A panel of judges – including the artists Grayson Perry and Cathie Pilkington, and the gallerist Robert Travers – selected artist Alan Payler's *The Garden* as the award-winning piece, bringing with it the opportunity to hold a solo show of his work.

The charity has held over 60 exhibitions at established arts venues, museums and galleries across the country and many artists have received vital exposure, transforming themselves and the art world in the process. Through the support of Outside In, its artists have sold their work, some to major national and international collections, and gone on to establish careers and achieve success.

Outside In recognises that in addition to the importance of exhibiting the work of excluded artists in galleries and museums, opportunity also lies in the many roles available in the art world. The Step Up training programme covers a range of arts sector skills such as curating exhibitions, leading workshops and researching collections. As well as helping to provide the means for the people we work with to make a living, there is a wider aim to change perceptions. Diversifying traditional roles is vital in humanising the art establishment, enabling an appreciation that a lived experience can be as important as expertise derived from academic training.

The charity now supports over 3500 artists with online galleries, works with an average of 600 artists annually, has 100 volunteer artist ambassadors, and has trained over 300 artists to gain arts sector skills and seek employment. Alongside our base in the south, we have established hubs in the Midlands and the North West, working in partnership with arts venues and local arts organisations. During the 2020 lockdown, we developed a programme of digital activity to support our artists, which included workshops, talks and exhibitions. We discovered a new audience of artists who did not visit venues or meet other artists socially, due in large part to their disability and mental health issues.

Partnerships are vital to the work of Outside In and its work would not be possible without the support and skills they bring. As a peripatetic organisation, we depend on our partners for delivery of our physical programming which enables many of our artists to engage directly with us. As well as our long-standing relationship with Pallant House Gallery, we have established significant partnerships with the Whitworth in Manchester, Fabrica in Brighton, the New Art Gallery in Walsall, and numerous others.

Structuring this book and working out how best to celebrate the diversity of the art and artists presented here has been a challenge. I have chosen to revisit the structure I used to curate the 2012 National Exhibition at Pallant House Gallery in which the work was displayed in three rooms, each given a different title: Intuition, Introspection and Insight. I used these themes to help audiences explore the different approaches that some non-traditional artists use in their techniques and subject matter. These themes are not intended to be definitive when it comes to the artists and their work. There is a lot of crossover and many artists could fit into one or more of the themes.

The first chapter is titled 'Intuition' and focuses on artists who work spontaneously and often circumvent traditional art processes. The second chapter, 'Introspection', focuses on artists whose work is informed by imagination and the inner workings of the human mind. The final chapter, 'Insight', explores how artists with experience of being disabled, or of facing a life-changing event, create art to share and develop understanding.

In 2017, Outside In established itself as a charity and moved out of Pallant House Gallery, retaining a strong connection to its home through a biennial co-commission. In 2018, it became an Arts Council England National Portfolio Organisation, one of 829 and considered 'leaders in their areas, with a collective responsibility to protect and develop our national arts and cultural ecology'.[2]

Outside In has won a number of awards, including the Charity Award for Arts, Culture and Heritage in 2013, and the Queen's Award for Voluntary Service in 2022. We are an established and respected charity that embraces diversity and champions the under-represented. I hope this book will pose some questions about how we define what art is, and who is an artist, and how we can best support artists to make their work and be supported in the wider art world. It celebrates the achievements to date and anticipates an exciting future.

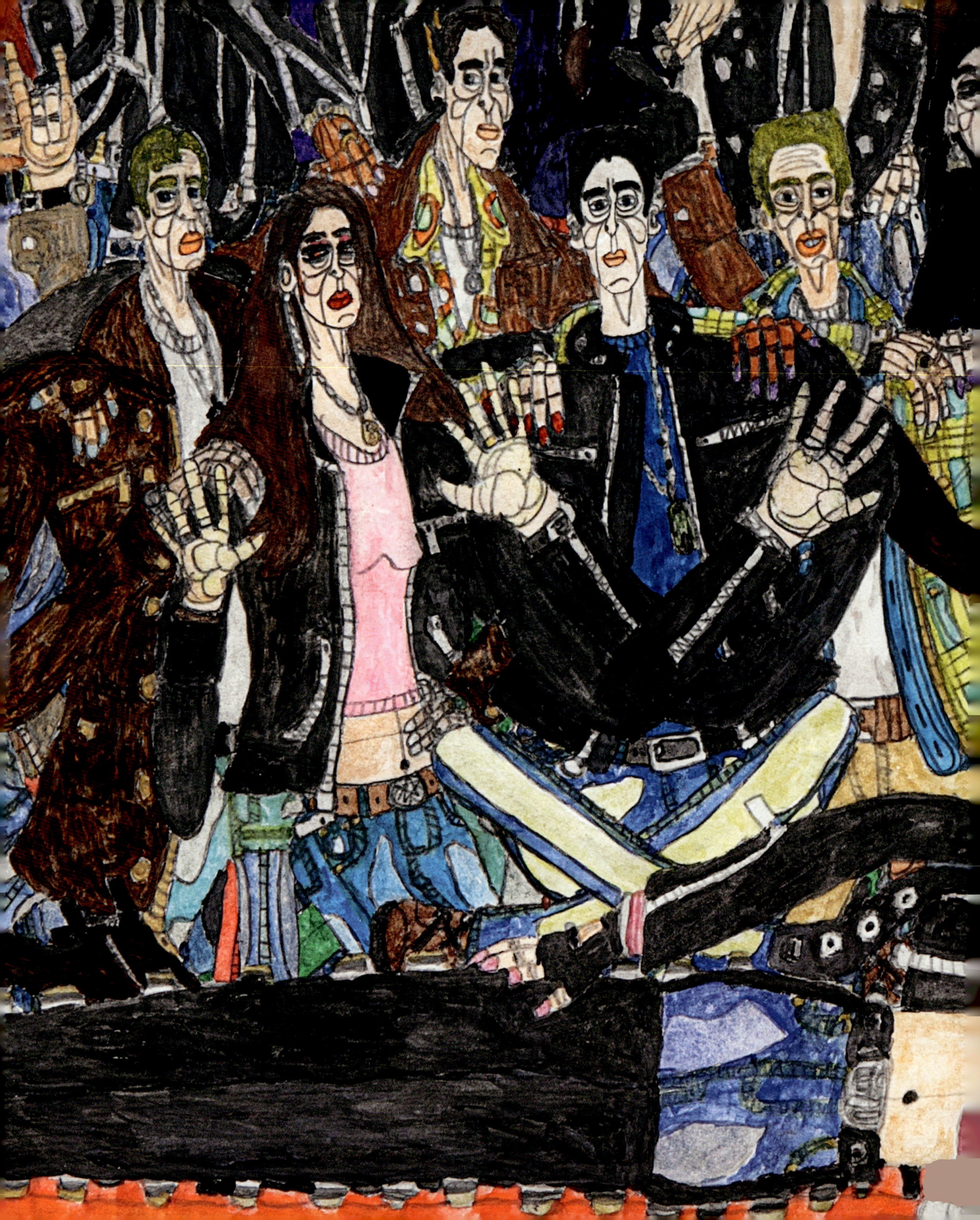

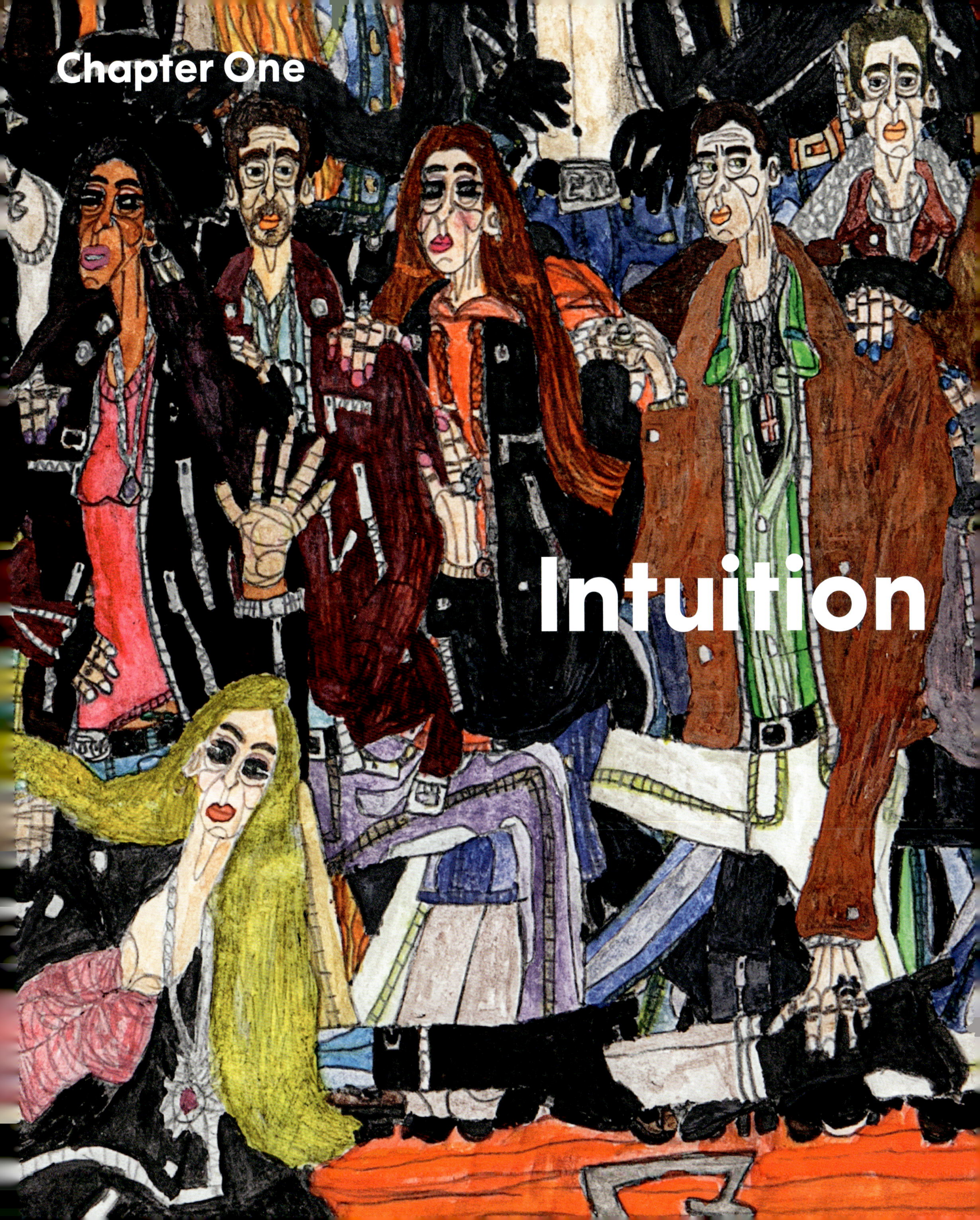

Chapter One

Intuition

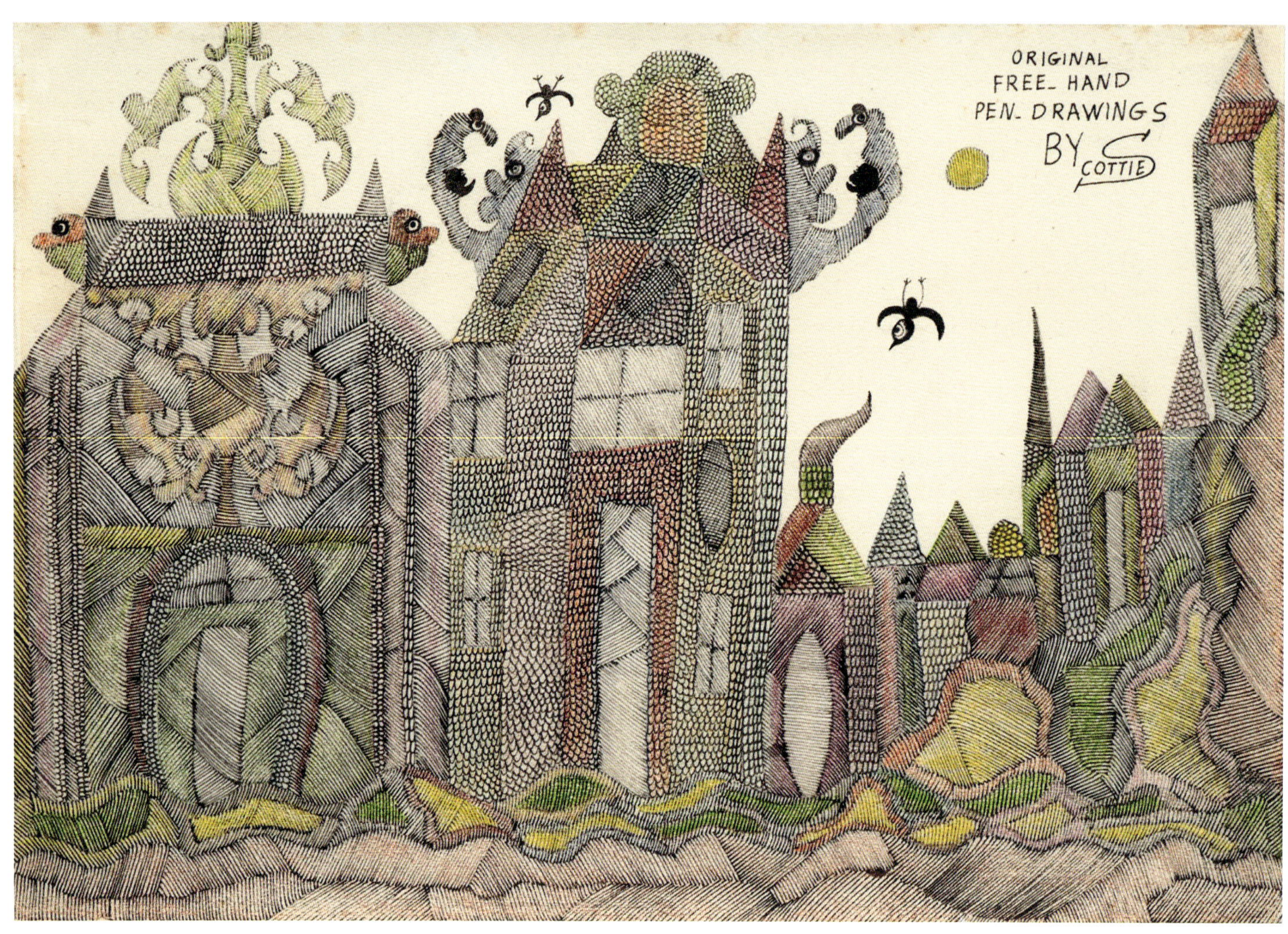

previous
Rakibul Chowdhury
In Vue (detail)
unkown date
Pen and paint
on paper
60 × 40 cm

Scottie Wilson
Capture d'eĕcran'
c.1945
Coloured pencils
on paper
27.5 × 37.5 cm

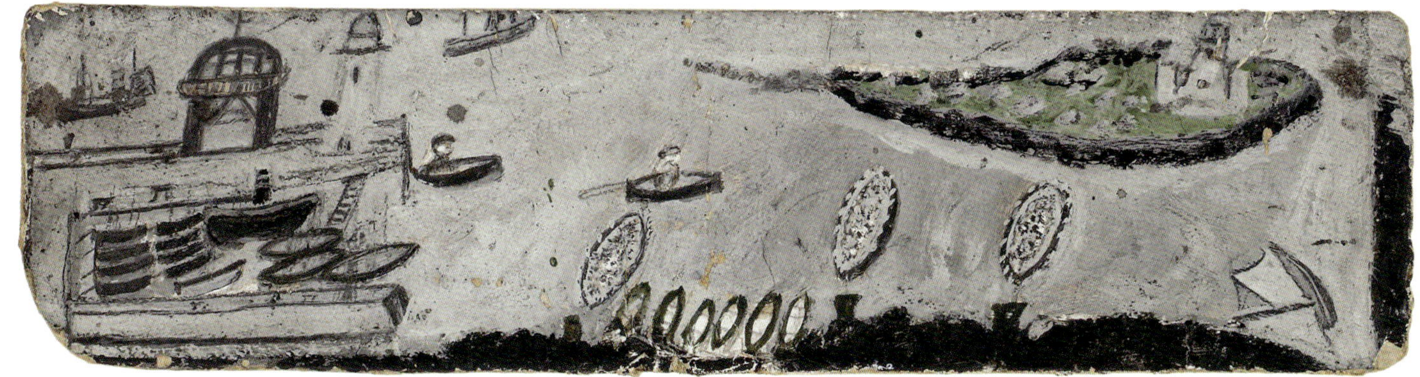

Creativity and mark making are primary tools of expression and communication, innate within us all. As children we are all able to pick up a pen or pencil and make a drawing without worrying about whether it is considered art. Children discover drawing and mark making in a completely natural way with no formal understanding of technique or composition, especially before the confines of art education come into play. But their work has a charm and completeness. There is no interruption between the mind and pen. The marks are without hesitation and have a quality most artists would strive to achieve. Picasso famously said when visiting a children's art exhibition in 1956, 'It took me four years to paint like Raphael, but a lifetime to paint like a child.'[1]

Being intuitive is a rare skill and not all can access it, though many try. It is difficult to bypass the conscious and verbal self to find the point where you are no longer thinking but doing.

There is an appreciation and valuing attached to work that strives to be intuitive. It can have significant cultural and financial value, especially if the artist is articulate and able to explain their rationale and reasons for creating the work. The same is not true for artists who work intuitively but have developed their work outside of formal art training or without a contextual awareness of the art world. Such overlooked but truly insightful and intuitive artists will often be neurodivergent or may have a disability. This difference in attitude towards the value of their work could be seen as an inherent prejudice towards people who are disabled or behave differently. Their works are often seen as childish and uninformed. If we do not grasp the nettle of prejudice and stigma, we are doing an injustice to countless artists, alive and dead, who have not been accorded the common decency of being seen to have the right to create or whose work is perceived as being without value. Hester Parr, professor of social and cultural geography, commented on the position excluded artists often find themselves in:

> For the majority of studio artists whose work encompasses a variety of versions of fine art, a distinction is made between them and other professional artists. Their work is not deemed good enough to be completely inside the cultural project ... Their curious in-betweenness, as full-time artists ... who do not occupy fully insider positions through – ironically – not being categorised as sufficiently 'outsider', but nor being 'good-enough', trained or time-served professional artists, means that their senses of artistic belongings are often ambivalent and tenuous.[2]

A few artists – the truly intuitive – have crossed this divide, such as Judith Scott (1943–2005), Alfred Wallis (1855–1942), Scottie Wilson (1891–1972), or Hilma af Klimt (1862–1944), but these are the exceptions. Far too many artists labelled as 'naive' or 'primitive' have been lost from our history, collections and culture. If an artist has made the transition from the margins of culture, this has often been a matter of good luck or through a respected member of the art elite recognising the value of their work. This was the case with Alfred Wallis, famously 'found' by Ben Nicholson (1894–1982) and Christopher Wood (1901–1930), but also with Scottie Wilson, who was championed by Picasso and others.

Alfred Wallis
St. Ives Bay.
Unknown date
Pencil and oil on board
7.5 × 30.1 cm

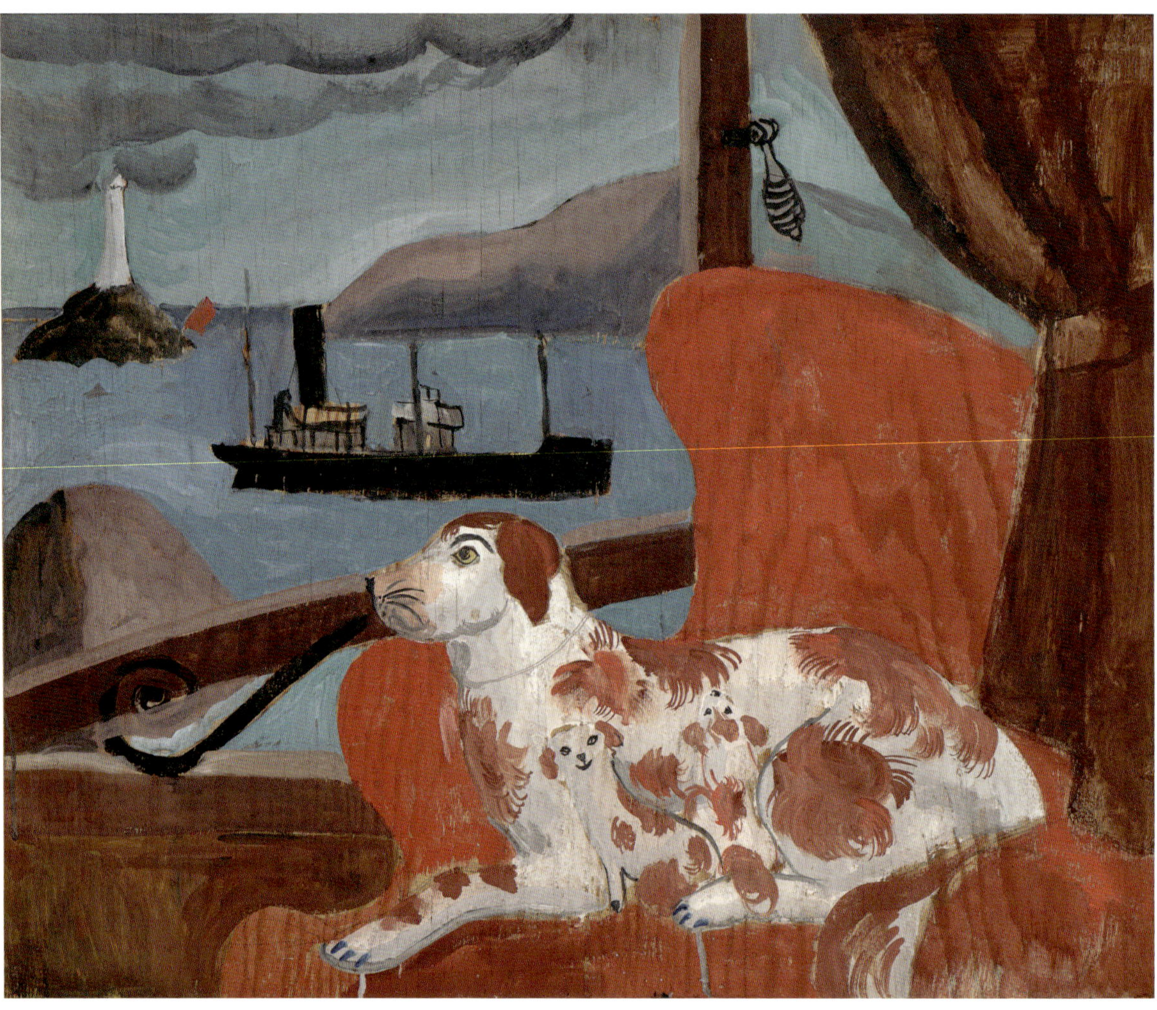

Christopher Wood
China Dogs in a St Ives Window
1926
Gouache on panel
63.5 × 76.8 cm

For Ben Nicholson and Christopher Wood, Wallis provided the validation of the simplicity of style that they were seeking in their work. It gave them a model and a means to arrive at a new way of working, but it is clear that both paraphrased Alfred Wallis's work in theirs, including his use of perspective, handling of paint and most tellingly the boats that seemed to have sailed from one artist to each of the others.

It is interesting to reflect on what these endorsements represent – in essence the gateway to acceptance, the invisible threshold that so many artists have found impossible to cross. The people with the power in these instances are well-respected artists who the art establishment has bought into, both financially and intellectually, enabling them to forego their prejudice.

When working with artists on the periphery of the art world, it is noticeable how some of them have maintained an innate way of creating and expressing themselves. It may be that by circumstance, which some might even consider fortuitous, they have bypassed the conventional approach to making art drilled into all of us at an early age. Often left to develop their own techniques, styles and subject matter, they produce art that seems to have a more direct relationship to them and their lives. Many learning-disabled and neurodivergent artists are nurtured in supported studios. The best of these, such as Creative Growth in America and ActionSpace in England, have evolved ways of working that are tailored to the individual.

Supported studios often developed out of the closure of day services in the UK and frequently employ or are led by practising artists, such as the Community Art Project in Darlington and Project Art Works in Hastings. Supported studios could be seen as anachronistic survivors of the day centre model, a separation of people with

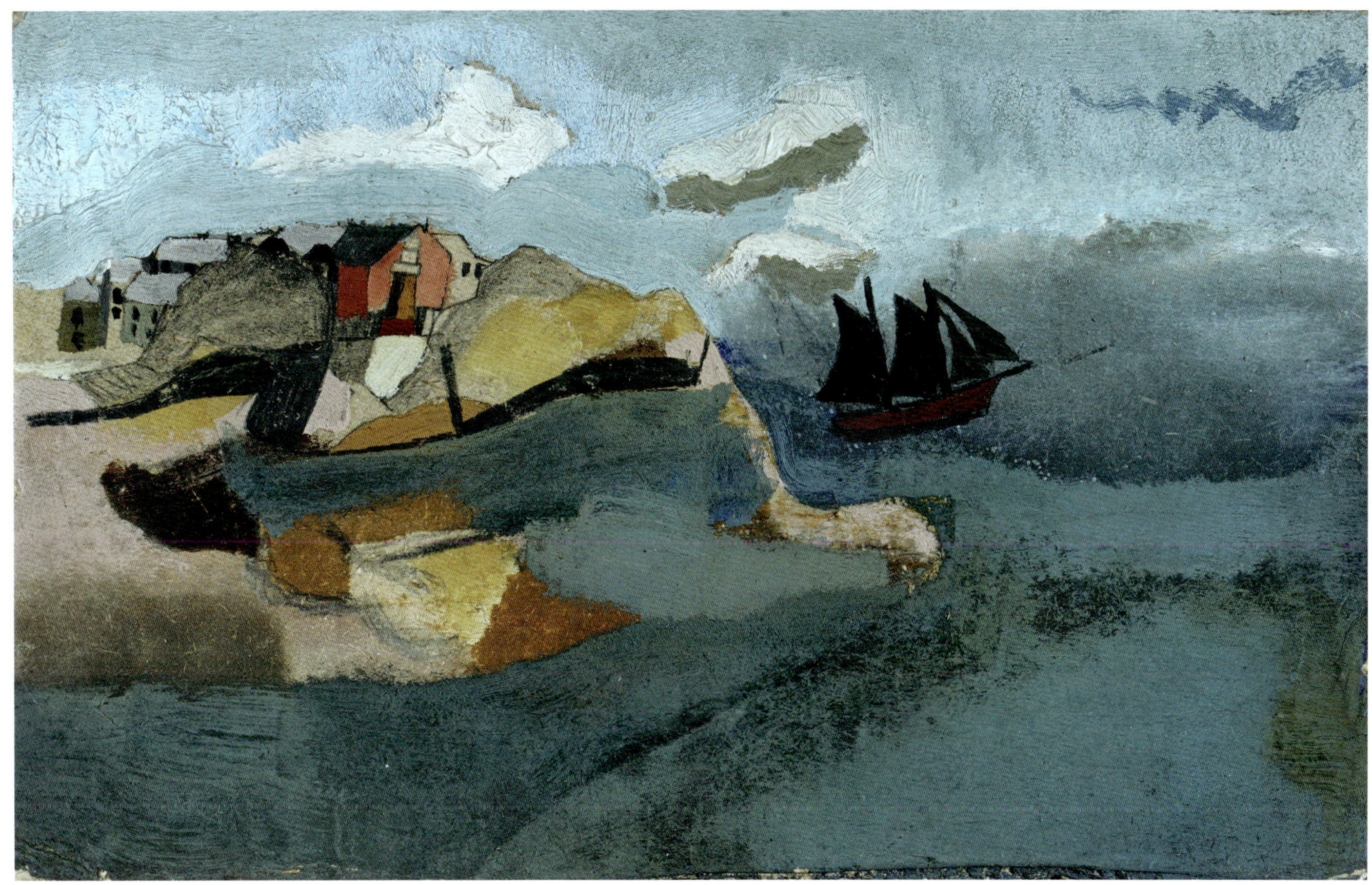

disabilities from wider society. The collectivisation of disabled artists can feel uncomfortable and there is still progress to be made to reach the point where all artists are understood and supported as individuals, and the art world has made the effort to truly accommodate them.

This model has created an alternative to art schools and other forms of art education. The best of these organisations enable their artists to stand as individual creators. The patience and care needed to prevent decisions being made on the artists' behalf are paramount. It is easy to default to the expected art materials and techniques, and far braver to stand back and allow the artists to decide for themselves. This is especially the case with people who are lacking in confidence and have had decisions made on their behalf for much of their lives.

Ben Nicholson
1928 (Cornish port)
1928
Oil on card
21.5 × 35 cm

Equivalence

Manuel Bonifacio (b.1947) epitomises the intuitive self-taught artist who has developed his own innate style and technique. He was born in 1947 in the Portuguese town of Faro and moved to England with his sister in 2001. He pursued his interest in drawing and pottery after dropping out of school at the age of eight. He is supported by Artventure in Guildford, a creative day centre for adults with learning difficulties and was first brought to the attention of the wider art world through his drawing *Mermaid*, which won him an award at the Outside In National Exhibition in 2012 at Pallant House Gallery. His work often reflects his childhood ambition to join the army, depicting helicopters, aeroplanes and boats.

In their article on Manuel and his work, art historians Roger Cardinal and Kate Davey said the following about *Mermaid*:

> Bonifacio's iconic heroine is clearly a receptacle of symbolic meaning. She dresses in a fluent costume of many colours and wears her heart on her right side. Ignoring the stock attribute of the mermaid's tail, the artist provides lace-up boots for her feet, as proof of her robust physique. Such

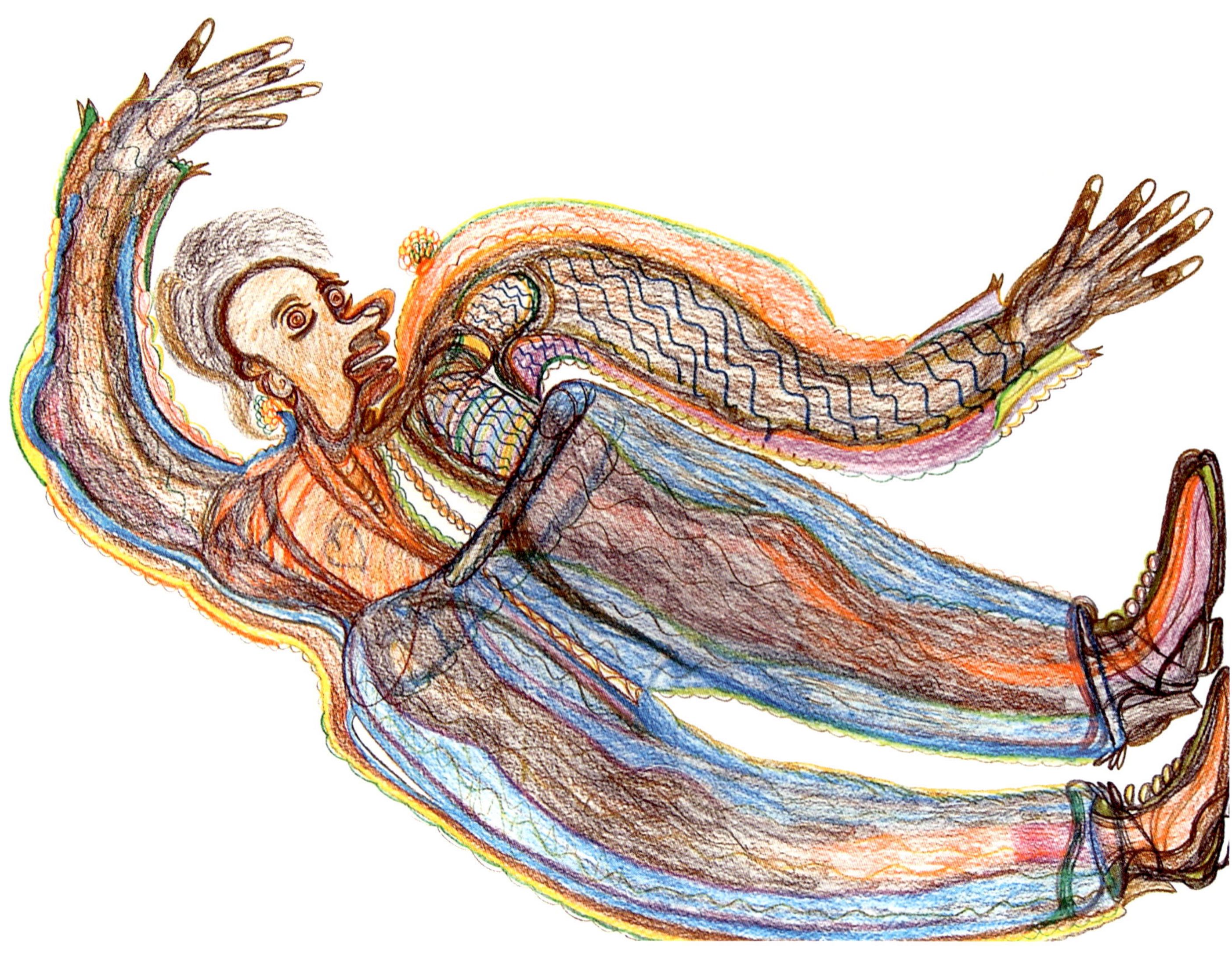

a creation seems to be a perfect reality for him. Her arms and elongated fingers could be seen as enacting the motions of swimming, although the versatile creature could also be flying. One may assume she is capable of traversing earth, sea and air, and thereby becomes an emblem of the artist's unfettered imagination.[3]

What is striking about Manuel's work is its infusion of a Portuguese folk style into his visual language. The characters, animals and beasts are all redolent of folk tales in their appearance, style and clothes. There is humour in the work and his cast of characters is seemingly involved in various narratives. He also has that wonderful quality of making everything his own, arriving at a reimagining of what he is seeking to represent. The importance of equivalence in art can be seen in the work of Matisse and Picasso. This was an important step in the development of modernism: the realisation that one can create an equivalent truth which is not a reflection of what the artist sees but something recreated through using new and other forms. This development meant that artists were able to use a range of forms to reimagine their practice, drawing from other cultures, their imagination or nature. In his revolutionary painting *Les Demoiselles d'Avignon* created in 1907, Picasso used African and Iberian masks, borrowing from cultures that were not his own, to arrive at a form of 'primitivism' and to break from the literal.

Manuel Bonifacio
Mermaid in the Sea
c.2012
Coloured pencils
on paper
21.0 × 29.7 cm

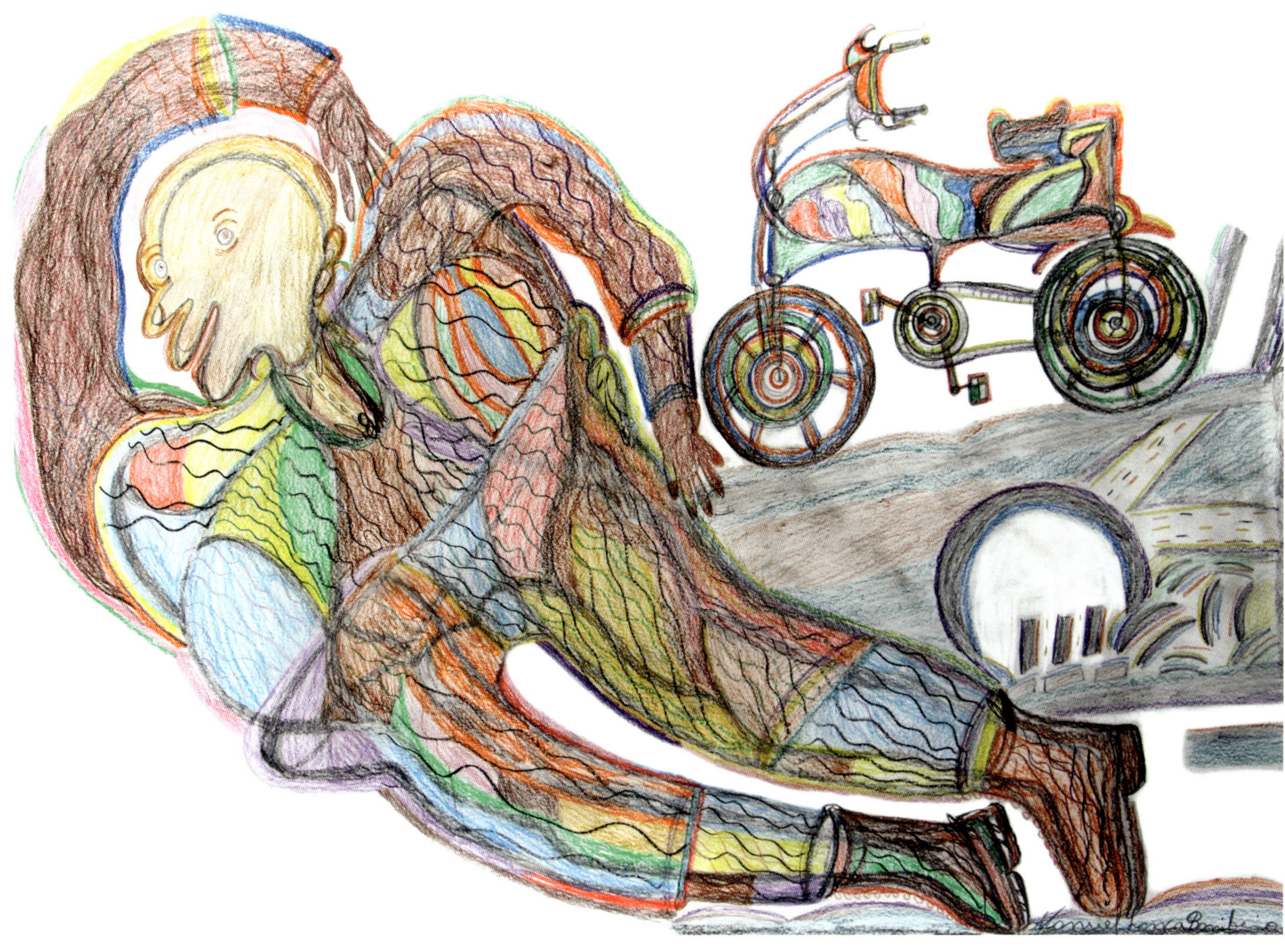

Manuel Bonifacio
Motorbike and Man
2012
Coloured pencils on paper
59.5 × 84cm

The American art historian Leo Steinberg said that 'Picasso was resolved to undo the continuities of form and field which Western art had so long taken for granted. The famous stylistic rupture at right turned out to be merely a consummation. Overnight, the contrived coherences of representational art – the feigned unities of time and place, the stylistic consistencies – all were declared to be fictional.'[4]

The capacity for equivalence can be seen in all Manuel's work and in his drawings of vehicles, buses, motorcycles and aeroplanes, having been reinvented through the artist's imagination. Not unlike Picasso reimagining the human form through the vernacular art of other countries. As Manuel says: 'My work comes from my heart and what I see. I love mermaids, transportation, architecture, and anything I see on the news like politics'.

Rakibul Chowdhury (b.1987) is an artist of Bangladeshi descent who lives and works in Portsmouth and is supported by Art Invisible. Raki (as he is known), like Manuel, creates his own world, populated with characters and settings held in highly controlled compositions. He draws his inspiration from popular culture, as well versed in the subject of celebrity as any academic is in their area of specialism. Raki has studied countless magazines on the lives and stories associated with celebrities. It could be seen as an obsession, but what is remarkable is how Raki uses this to create complex multi-figure compositions in which he is the composer and controller of the celebrities he seems so obsessed

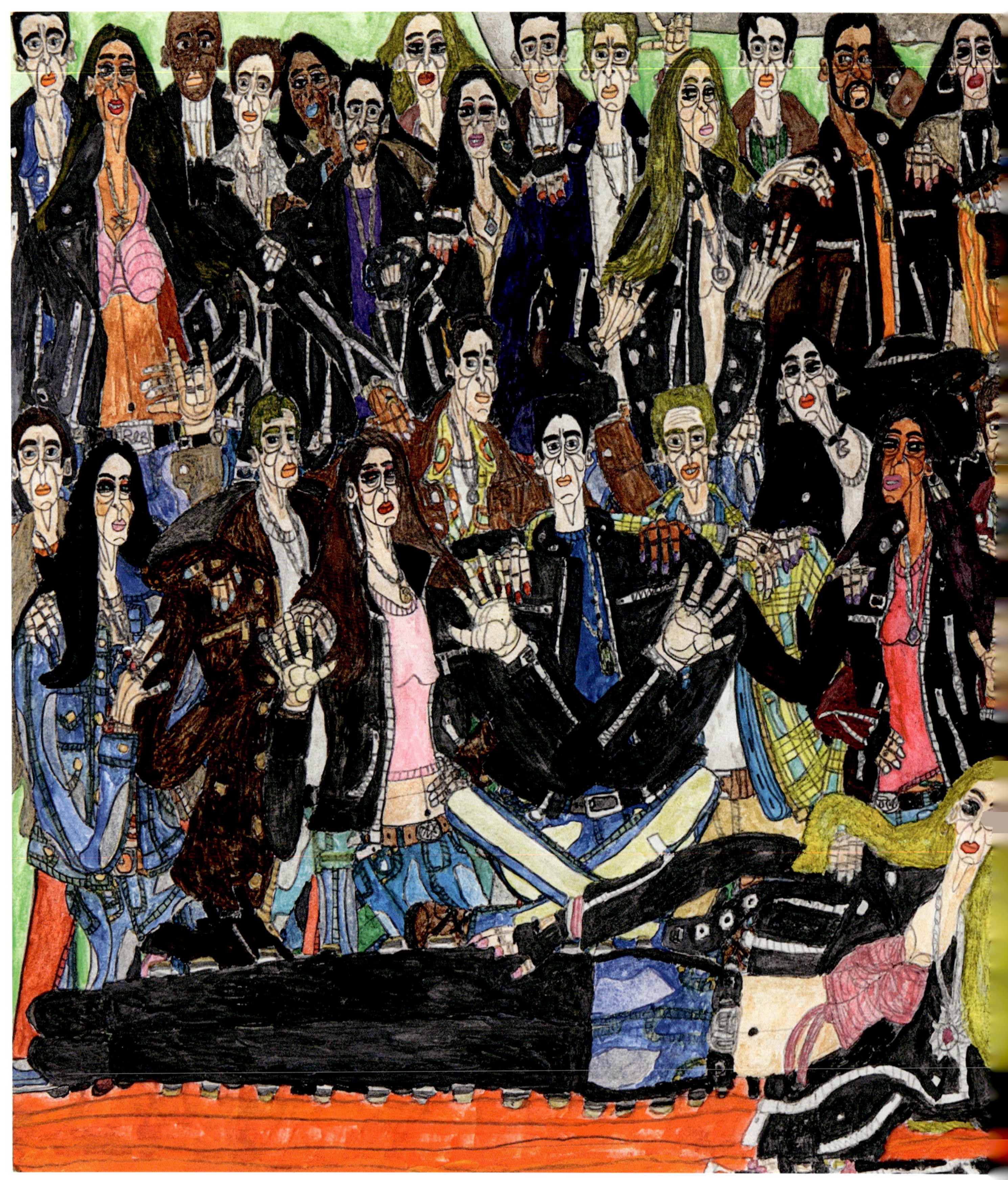

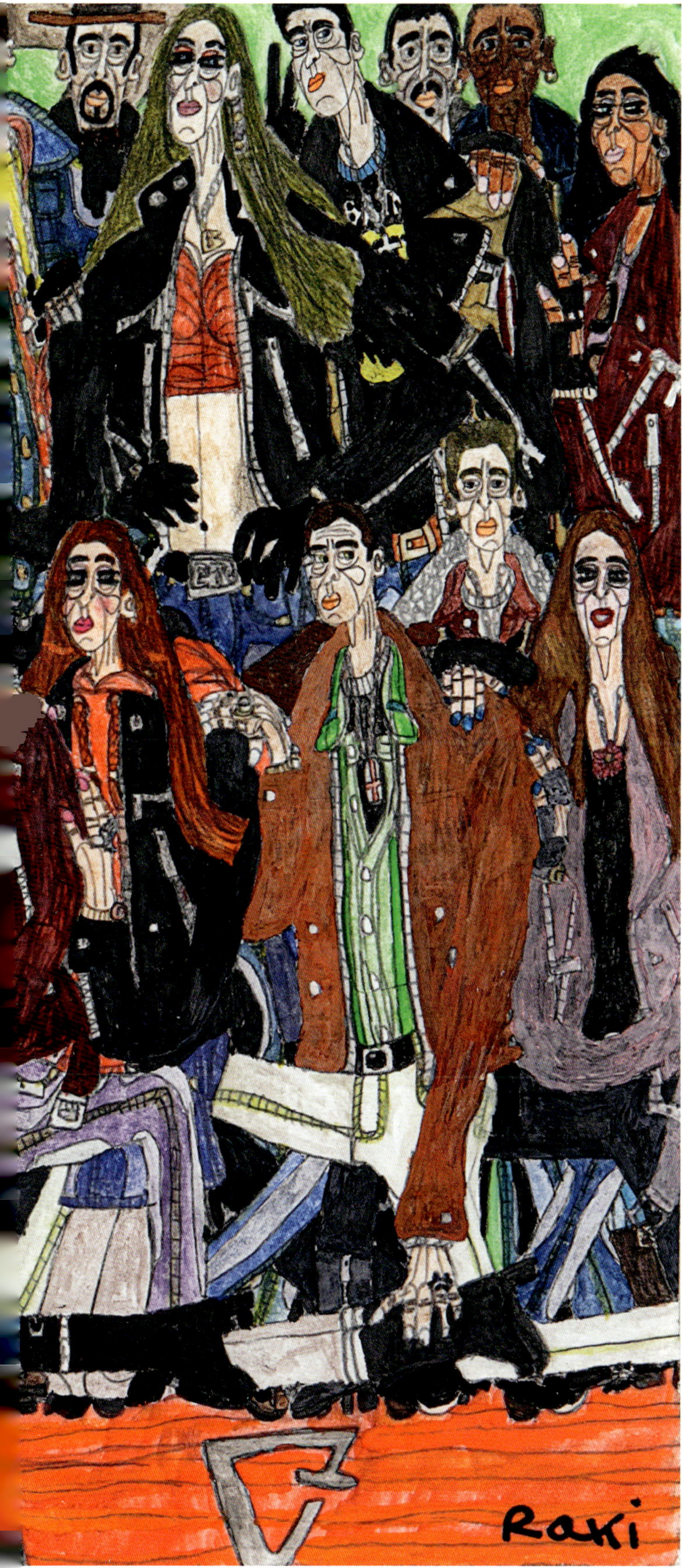

with. He sometimes creates themes for his larger group portraits, which often refer to popular culture, Disney or Batman, themes that are infused into the work and each of the characters, informing their attire and stance. Fashion plays a significant role in his work, and it is clear that Raki enjoys designing clothes for his cast. On one occasion, Raki drew himself into one of his works wearing a jacket he would buy for himself should the work sell.

There are 36 portraits in his painting *Inside Vue*, each dressed differently for the occasion. They are his favourite film stars from *vue*, a free cinema magazine, each recreated and carefully positioned. They stare without smiling, some with their hands held out. You might wonder: are they keeping you back or reaching out to pull you in? There is a rhythm to the composition, and he has carefully made the characters in the first row kneel to fit into the picture. In front of them is an elongated woman stretched out on the floor and seemingly wearing leather chaps.

'Art is my favourite activity. Deepika Radukone is my favourite Indian actress. Outside In sold my pictures. With the money I am going to buy a black leather jacket, TV films ... I am going to buy *Wonder Woman* DVD and a waistcoat. I want to keep painting my pictures. I want to sell my work. I want to go shopping.'

Raki's father and family have undertaken a journey alongside his, as described below by a member of the team that supports him:

> Raki had spent most of his life using aggressive behaviour to convey his mood and frustrations. Through art he flourished. He saw how people loved and respected his work. He enjoyed being liked and respected and not feared. Whilst Raki drew at home, his parents and siblings were unaware of just how talented he was. Raki's father readily admits that he chose not to attend gallery viewings etc. with Raki as he was uncertain of how he might behave. Raki started communicating at home and his negative behaviour lessened, he started attending family events and his father now describes Raki as his best friend.

Families often recognise the talent and creativity of their family member, many actively encouraging it. Others may feel uncomfortable or challenged by the work they produce. This

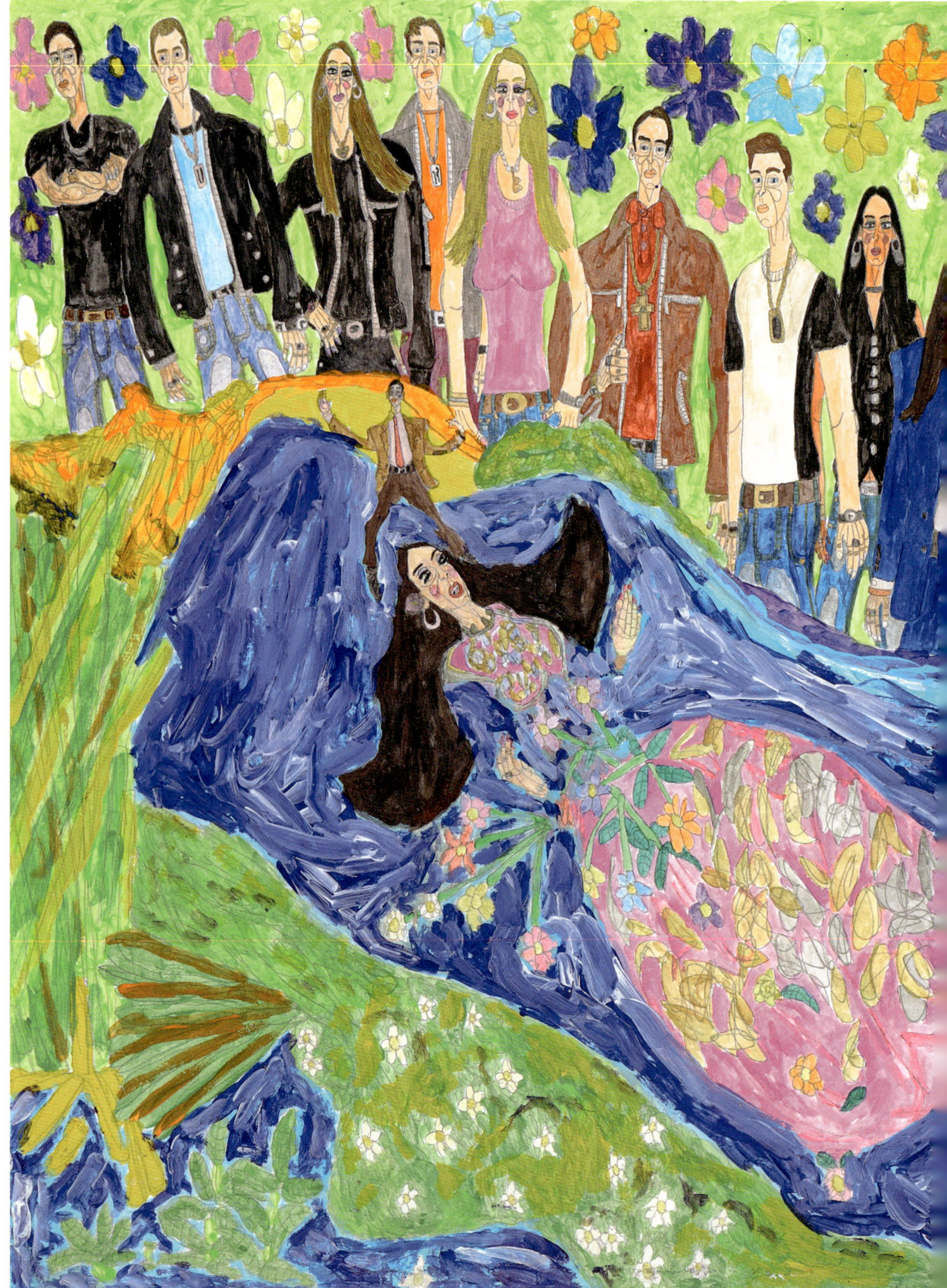

previous
Rakibul Chowdhury
In Vue
unkown date
Pen and paint
on paper
60 × 40 cm

Rakibul Chowdhury
Ophelia after a painting by Millais
2017
Acrylic and watercolour
on paper
60 × 40 cm

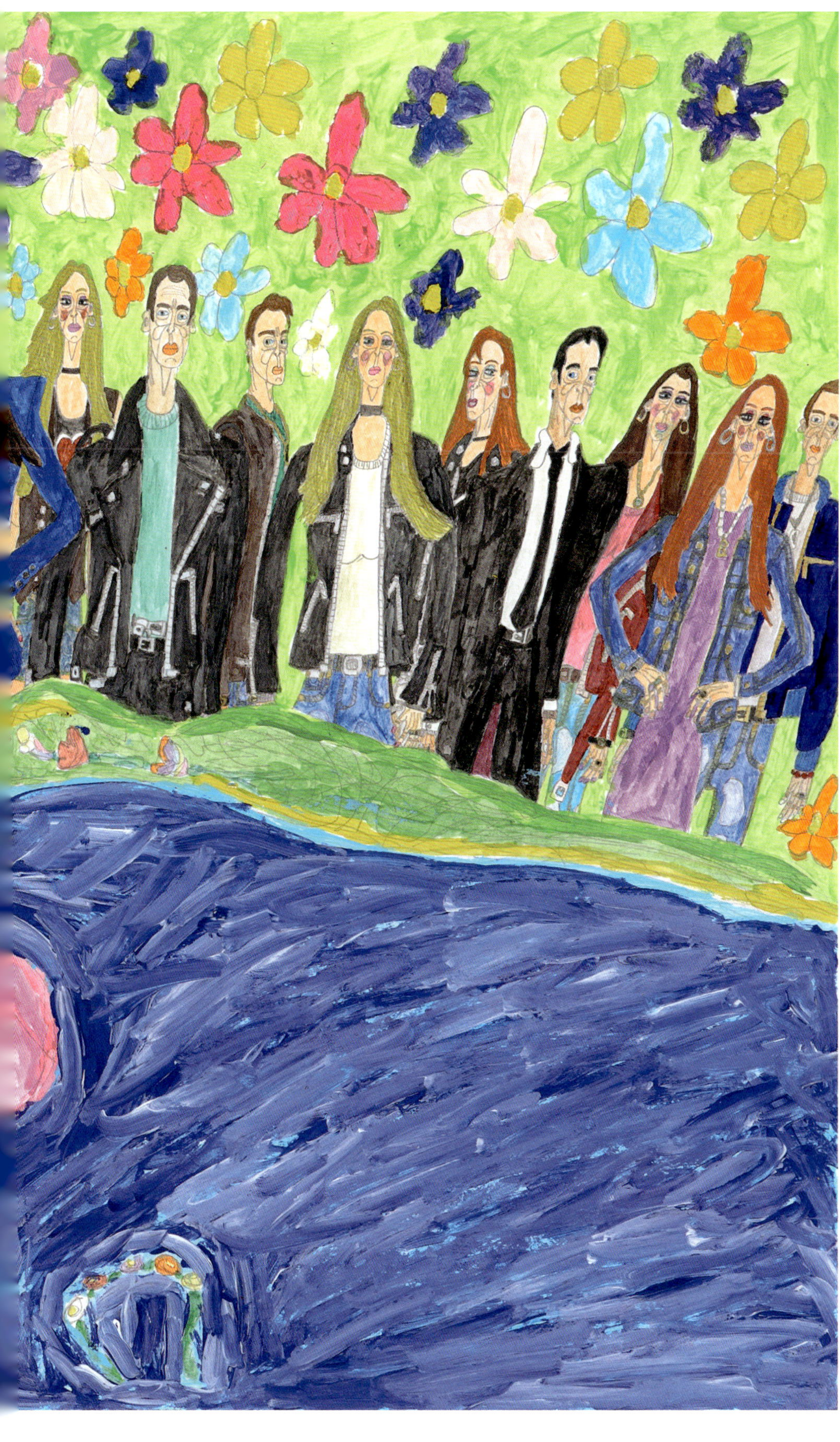

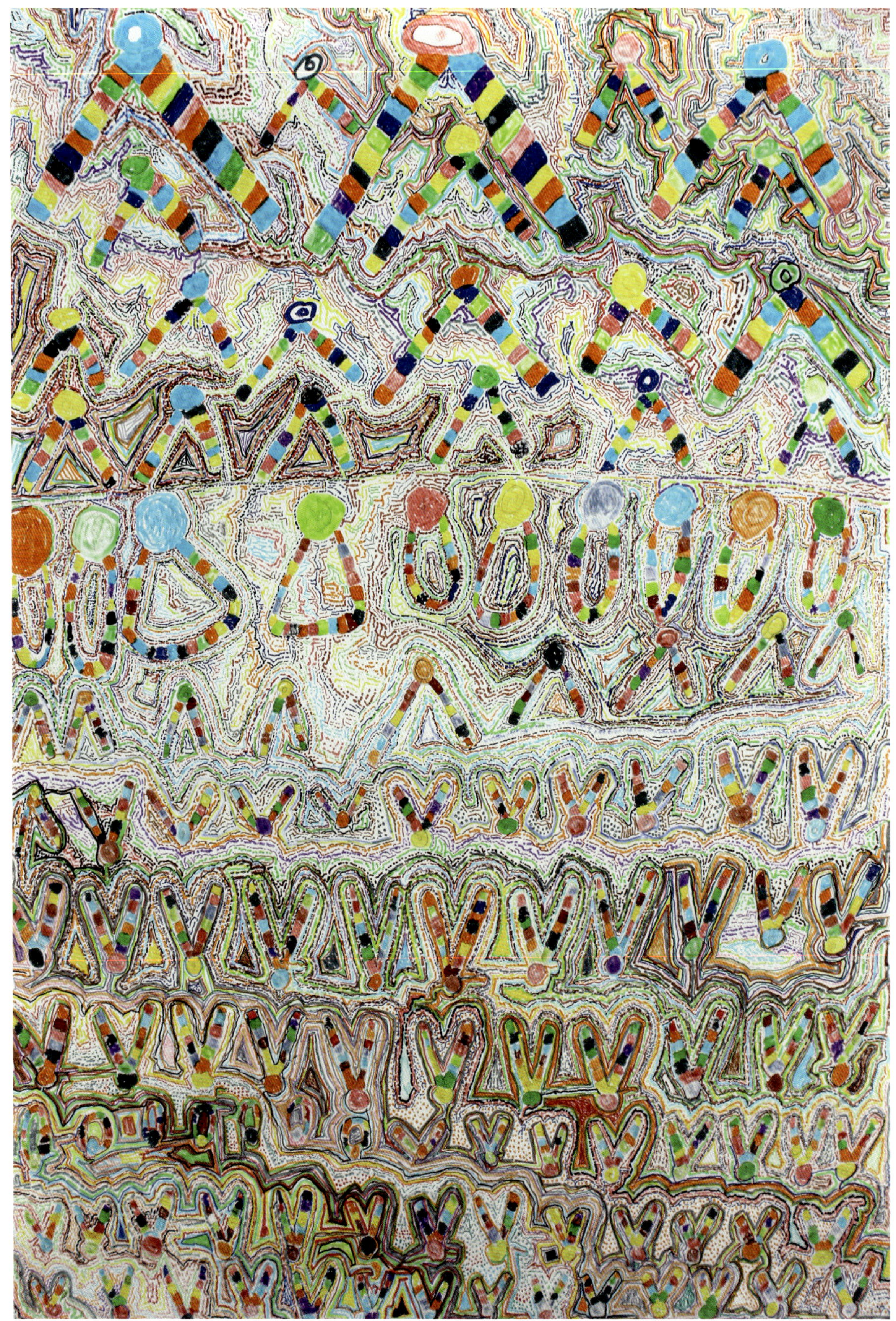

Victoria Bowman
The Coloured Mix
2021
Pen on paper
84 × 59 cm

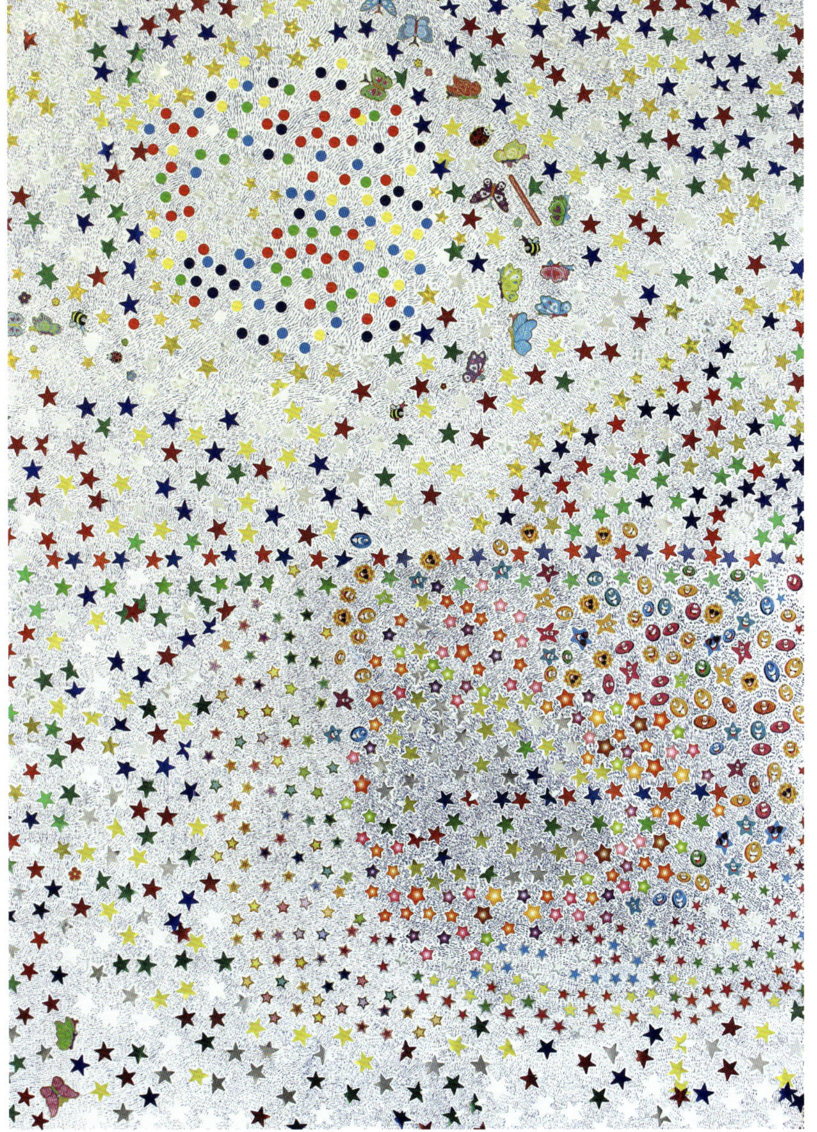

Victoria Bowman
Stars
2019
Stickers, pencil and pen on paper
84 x 59 cm

could be for aesthetic reasons or because the work doesn't accord with what they consider 'art'. Despite this lack of acceptance or achievement in the wider art world, once the talent and worth of their family member is recognised, through an exhibition or their work being put online and shared, a profound change can happen to the artist and those associated with them. There are many affirmative steps that the art world can provide, but this one, the one of recognition, is often the most powerful and moving.

Manuel and Raki's works are informed by their interests, which act as the inspiration for them to create. Some other artists in this book produce work in a more directly intuitive way. They seem to form a connection with their imagination and subconscious through the process of repeated mark making. The ability to arrive at an image through intuitive pattern making is something often accomplished through practice and an innate ability to compose. Victoria Bowman (b.1984) reflects this experimental and intuitive way of making art. She generally does not use source material as inspiration but creates designs from her own imagination, often working for weeks and months to produce her intricate images using pens and paint. Through her considered working, Victoria arrives at complex patterns that have a delicacy and beauty uniquely their own. They can seem like a fantastic patchwork, sometimes with repeated motifs or glyphs. There is an innate pattern making in her work, a gradual arrival at a harmonious whole.

Materials

Materiality and the use of different materials to make art plays a significant role for some of the artists included in this book, frequently arrived at by a combination of intuition, circumstance and chance. Often it can be a case of using what is at hand or using traditional or taught skills which are then adapted to new ways of making, such as the use of gum nuts in the Gum Nut Folk created by Joanna Simpson (b.1959) or the use of recycled materials in the bedroom ceiling decorations by Gary Williams (b.1957). American artist Judith Scott (1943–2005), whose large and powerful wool sculptures have found critical acclaim, is a good example of an artist who evolved her own intuitive way of working, and is now collected and on display in major galleries around the world. Her work consists of large bound wool objects,

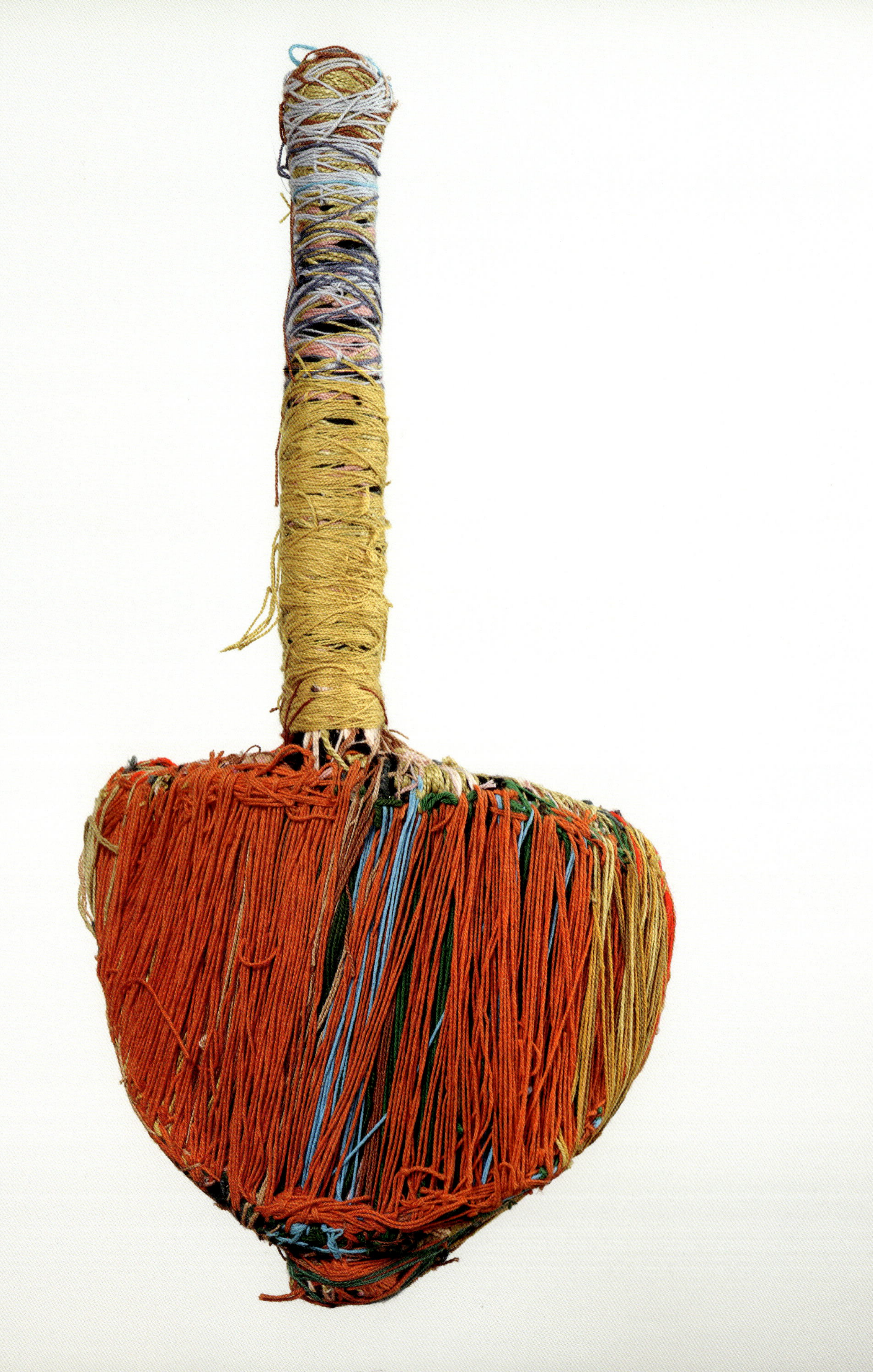

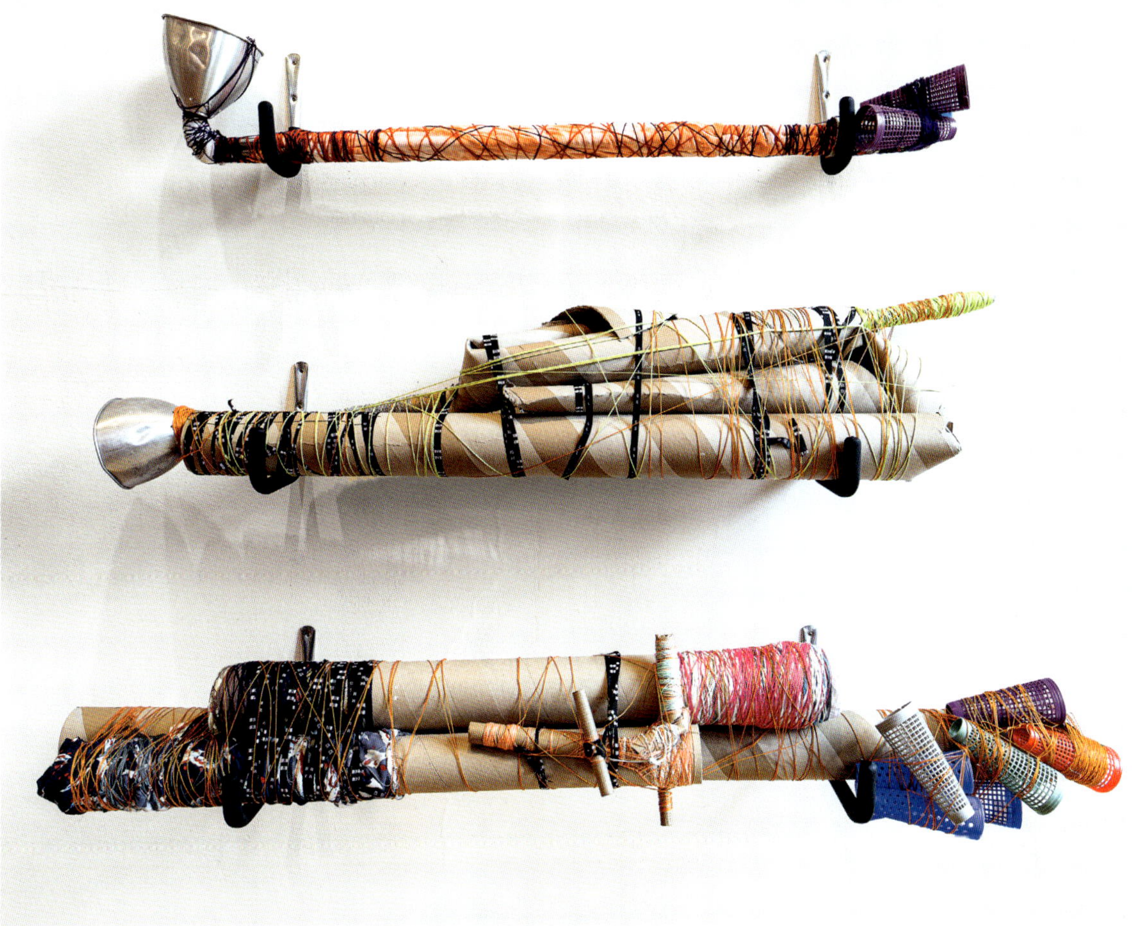

Judith Scott
Untitled
1990
Acrylic and watercolour on paper
60 × 40 cm

Andrew Omoding
Collection of musical objects for the parade from 'It's my work, come see, come see'. Artist Residency at Camden Arts Centre, London
2019
Mixed media
150 × 40 cm, 175 × 75 cm, 200 × 75 cm

next page
Nnena Khalu
Wrapping
Found objects and ceramic
2019
Mixed media
approx. 250 × 250 cm

often with things hidden inside. Some British artists have produced work redolent of Judith Scott's such as Nnena Kalu (b.1966) and Andrew Omoding (b.1987). There is an excitement when seeing work that has been produced using non-traditional materials and techniques, and this ability to explore and experiment intuitively is something often found in artists who have developed their own way of working outside of a formal art education.

Nnena Kalu and Andrew Omoding are two exceptional artists supported by ActionSpace in London. Both have developed their practice over time with the careful guiding hand of the charity and its staff, and have now established significant profiles in the art world. Nnena works in both two and three dimensions. Her sculptural work consists of wrapped and bound objects, often site-specific and ephemeral in nature. Her use of non-traditional materials such as plastic and wool renders her work accessible and liberating to art audiences unfamiliar with instinctive and intuitive making. Andrew Omoding's sculptural work shares some familiarities with Nnena's in its use of wrapping and material, but Andrew also creates costumes and performances to go alongside his work. He is first and foremost a storyteller, and in the creating of his art Andrew will often sing and tell stories. It is as if he lives and breathes his art, seemingly intrinsic to his nature and personal history and life journey.

Unlike with Nnena Kalu and Andrew Omoding's spontaneous practice, James Gladwell (b.1952) continues a craft handed down to him from his Romany grandmother following a tradition his family has used for generations. His wonderfully decorative stitchwork pieces have a folk-art quality, often containing subjects reminiscent of a lost history of farms, animals and places. He is inspired to create by his dreams, visions and the world around him. Some of his other subjects

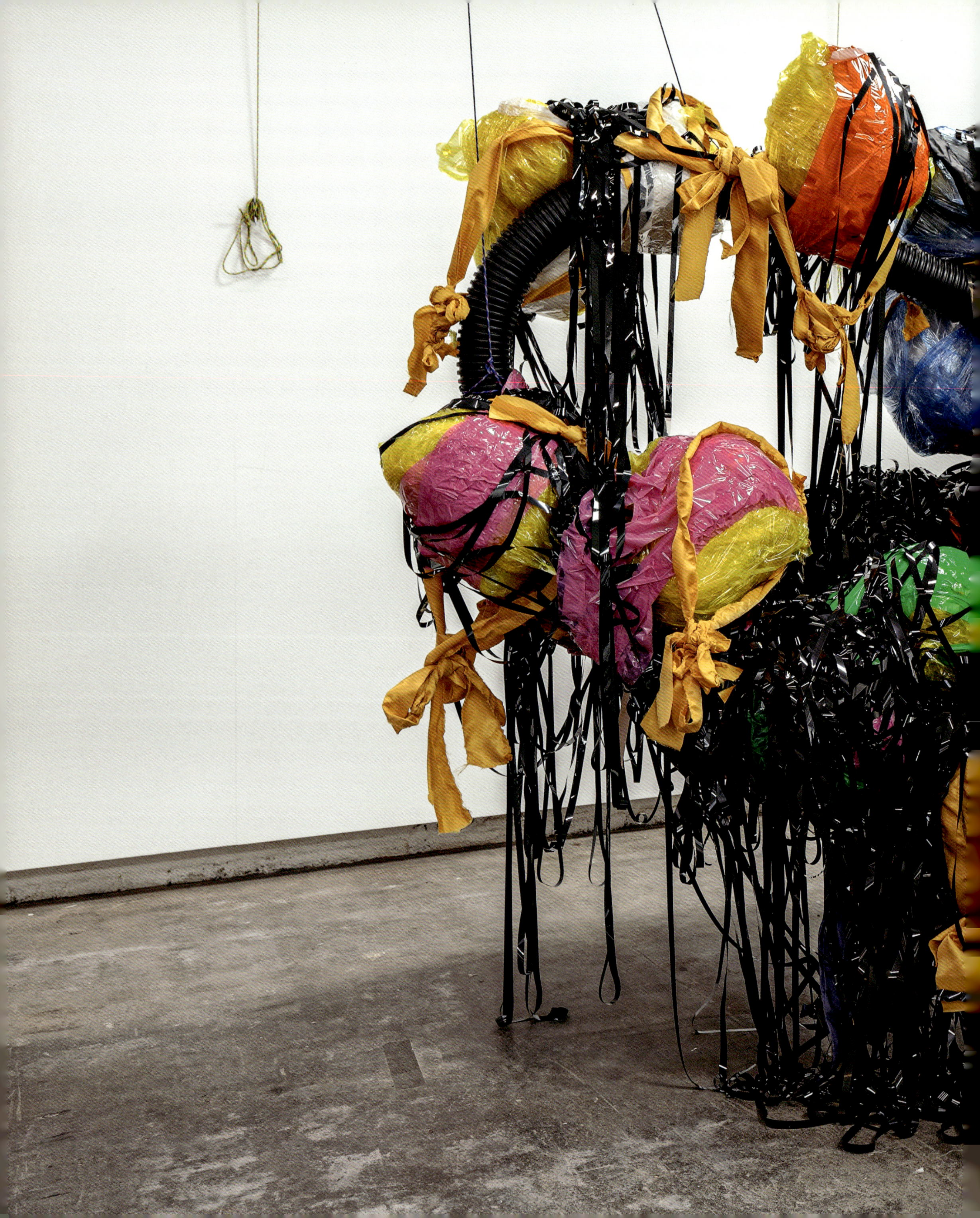

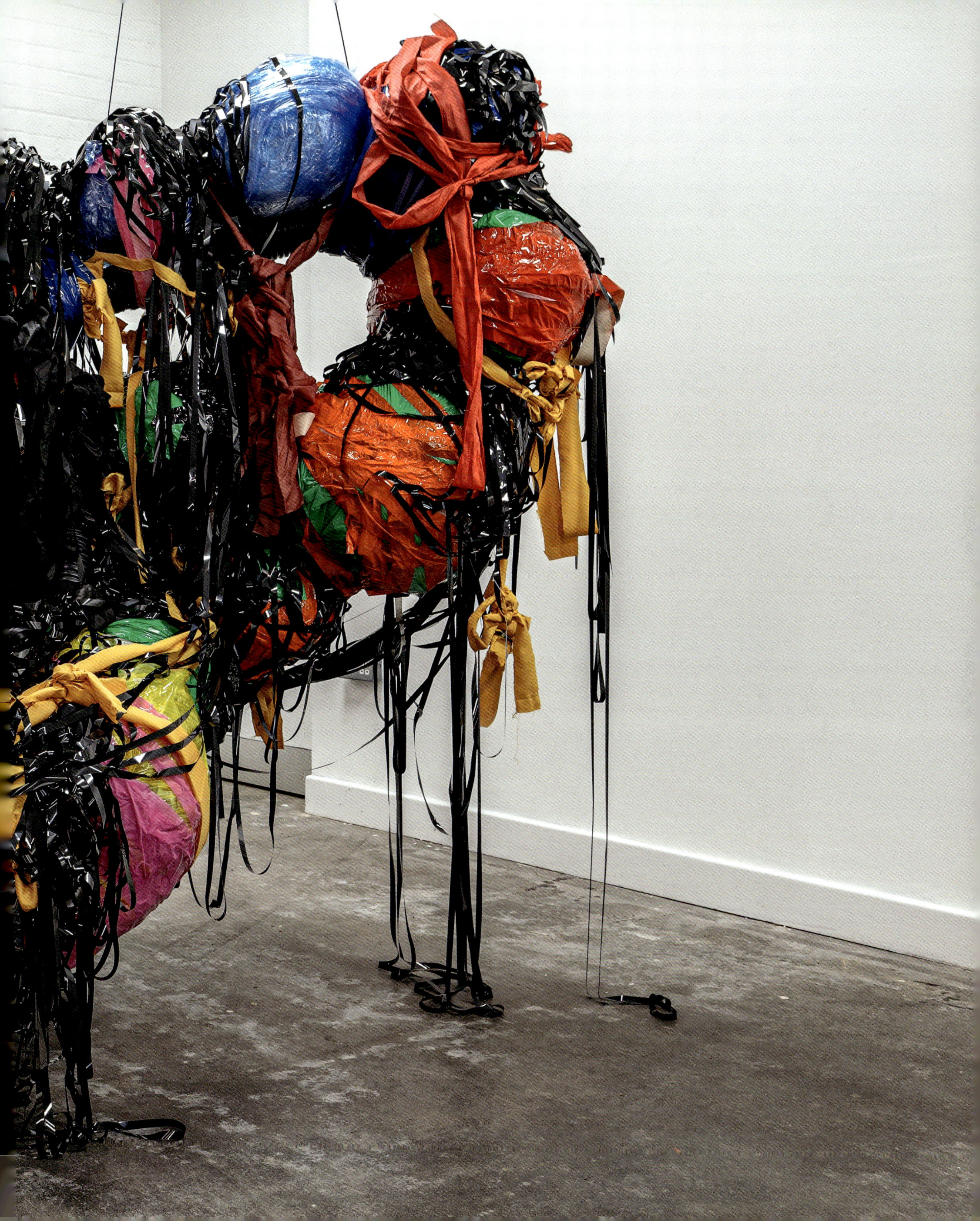

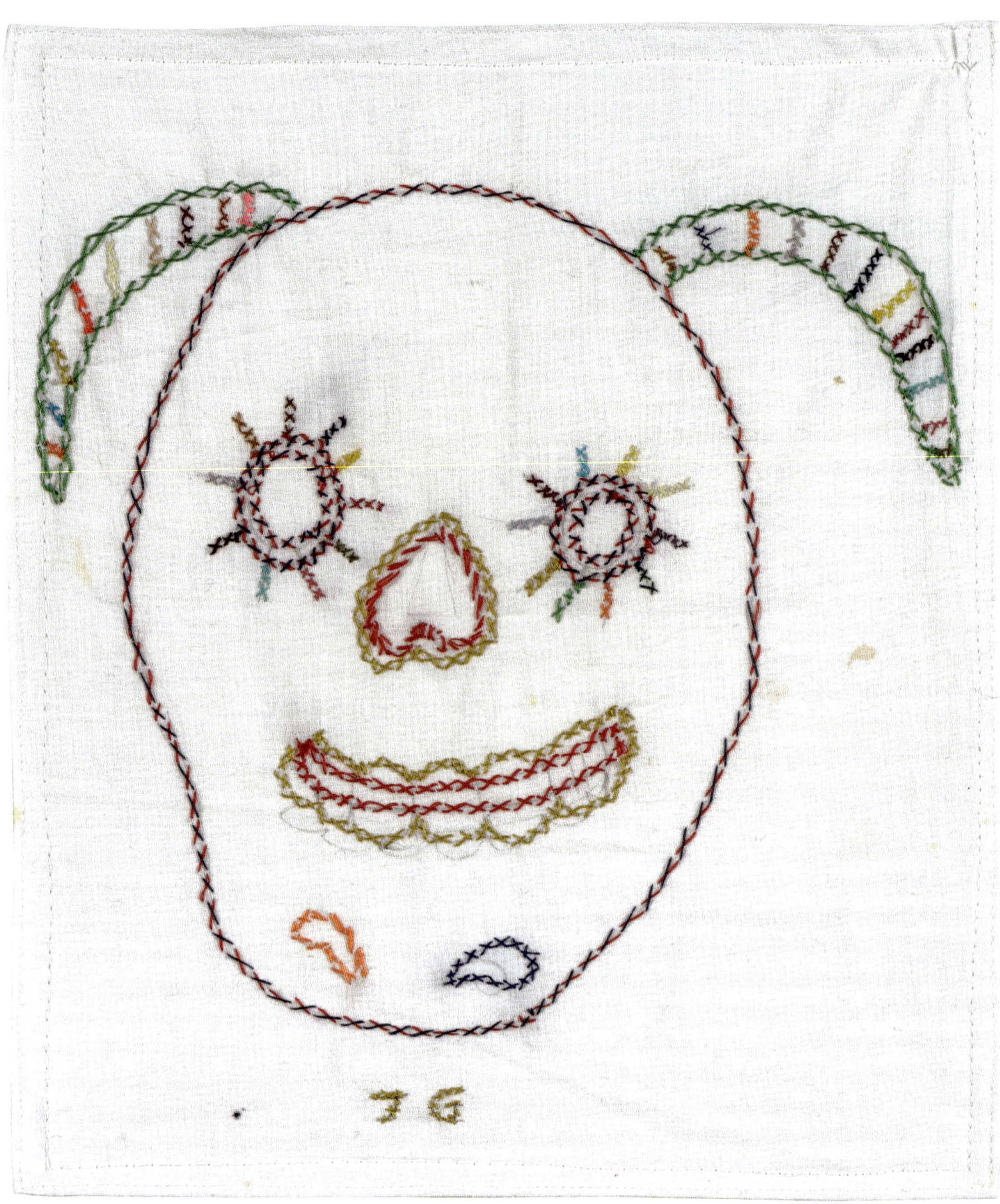

James Gladwell
The Horns and the Face
c.2016
Hand stitch on cloth
40 × 40 cm

James Gladwell
The Farm
c.2016
Hand stitch on cloth
146 × 130 cm

include Elvis, horned heads and motorbikes. There is something disarming about a man making stitchwork pieces, traditionally a female pursuit, that adds to the impact and charm of his work. 'My family were Romany gypsies and I started doing needlework when I was seven,' says James Gladwell. 'My Grandma taught me how to stitch. I have been on the road since I was nine around Essex and London. I do drawings and needlework inspired by my dreams.'

Joanna Simpson lives in North Wales and had previously lived in Australia for four years, where she collected the fruit of the eucalyptus tree, gum nuts. Her use and repurposing of found materials is shared with other artists in this book such as Friedrich Nagler (1920–2009). Joanna uses the gum nuts in an instinctive way to create a series of characters, each individually crafted with the addition of clay heads and caps, and standing on a one-penny coin. Joanna can make up to

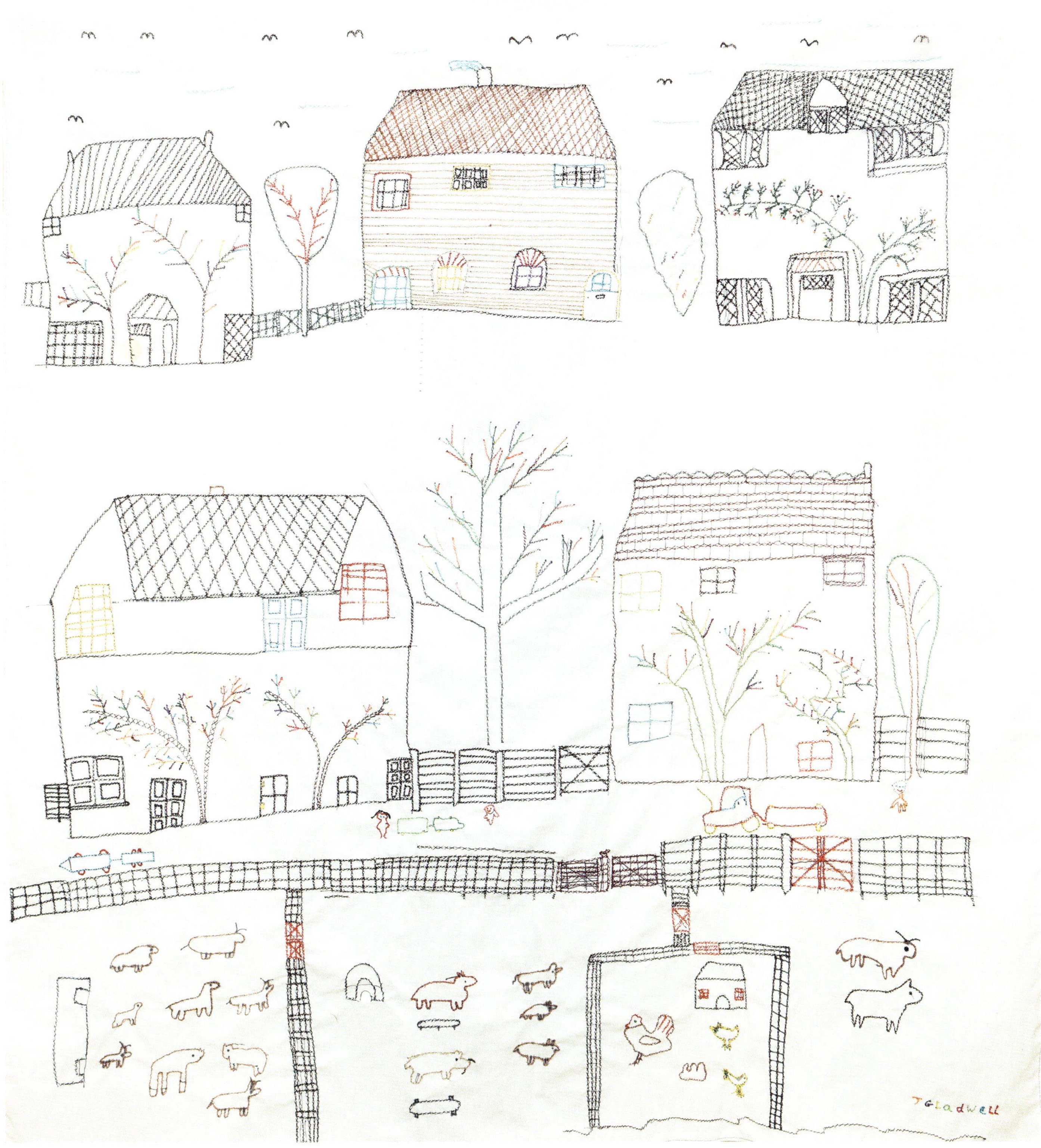

J GLADWELL

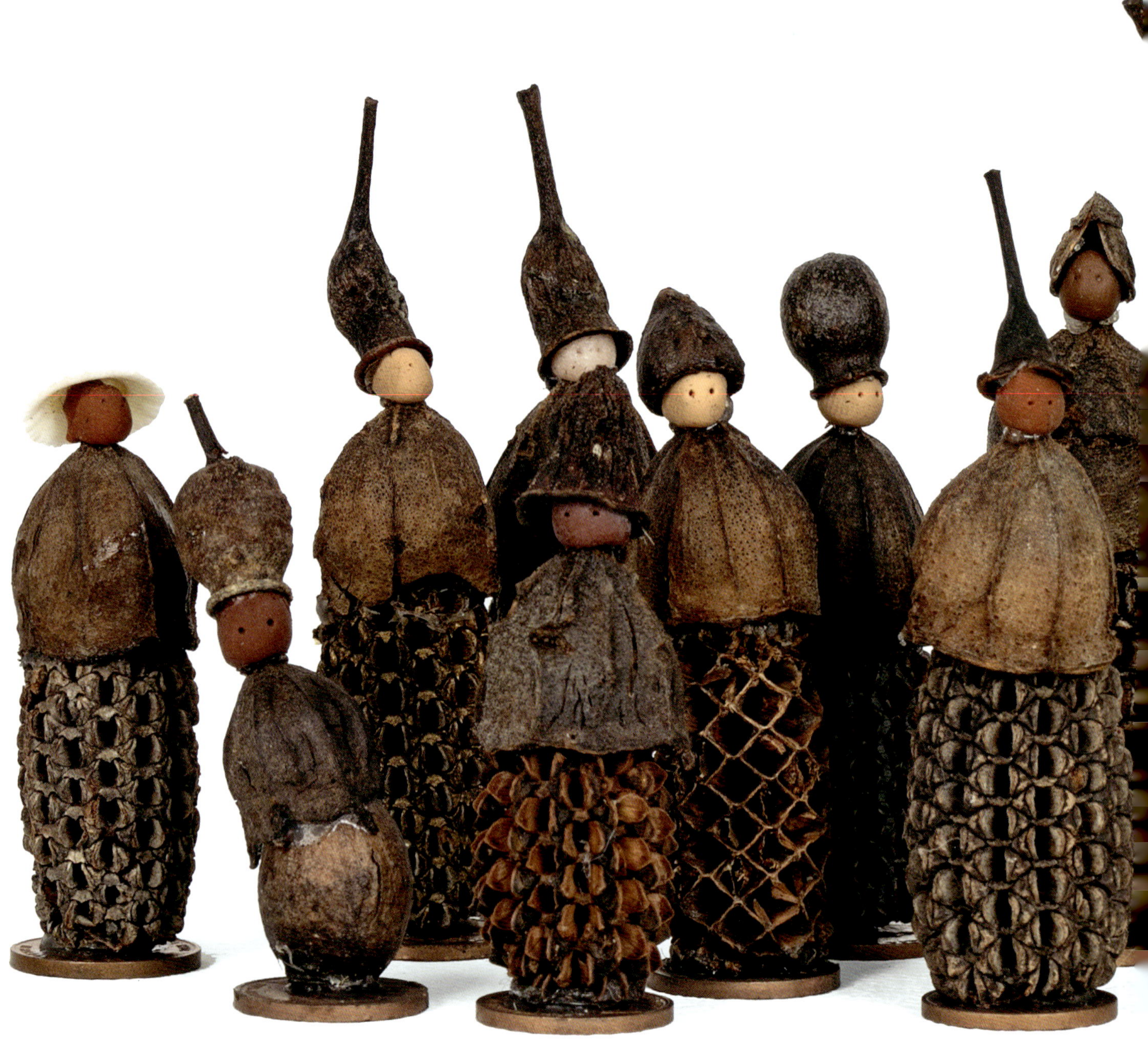

Joanna Simpson
Gum Nut Folk
unknown date
Found objects
and ceramic
Approx 2 × 1 cm to 5 cm

200 characters a day and she has thousands of gum-nut people, all carefully packed and stored. The Gum Nut Folk represent lost children, her own and others, and when making them she is sometimes brought to tears. Each has a distinct personality and as she says they 'explore ideas about autonomy, inclusion and exclusion'. Joanna assembles her folk into families and communities in which they strike relationships and connections with each other, each with its own personality shining clearly. 'I am inspired by materials that are readily available to me and my work is always created in response to the environment, my love for my own four children and my compassion for the "lost" children of the Stolen Generations,' says Joanna.

Gary Williams attended a day centre for many years. He spent a lot of his time colouring

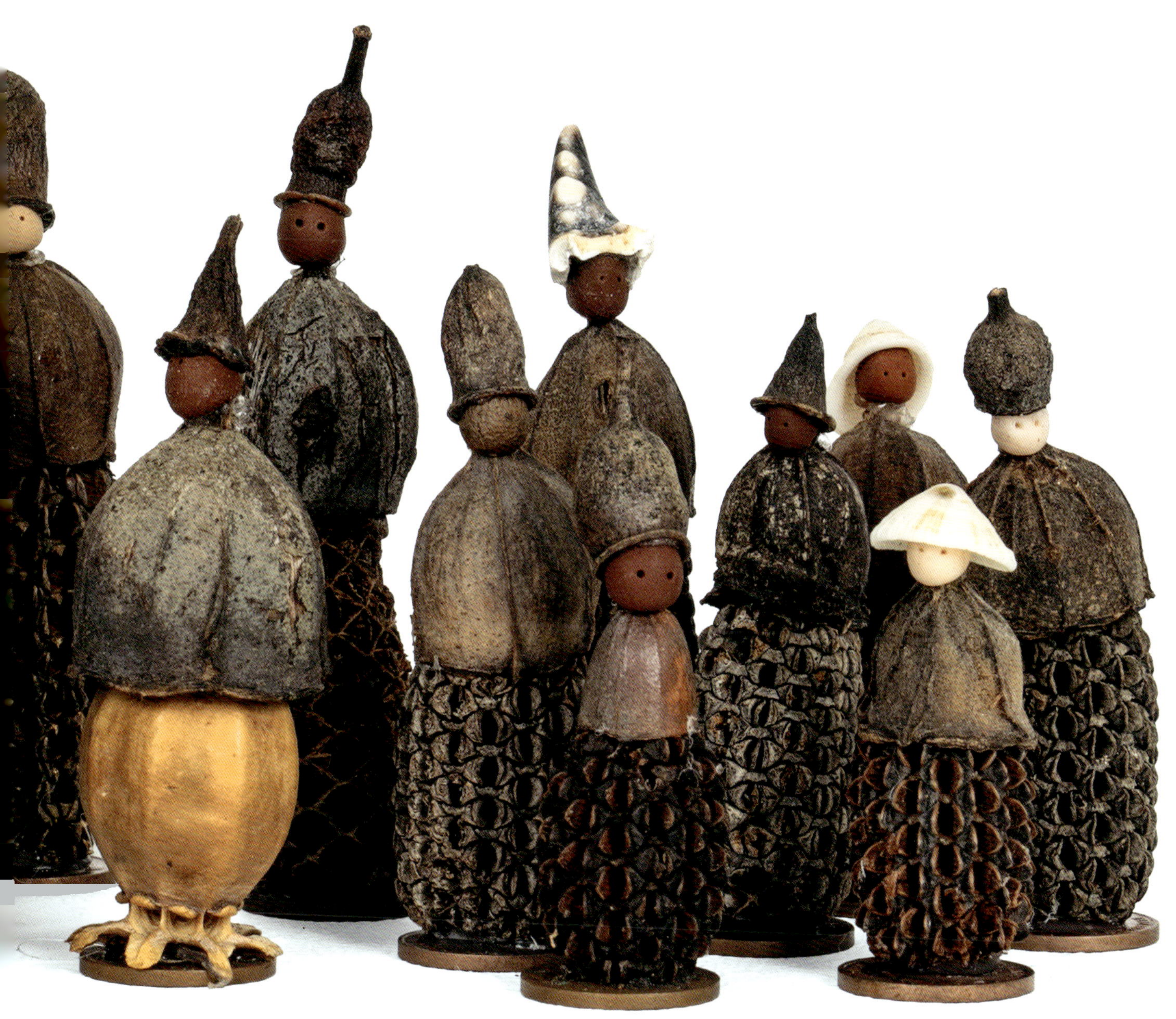

in children's colouring books with felt pens. Gary carried with him a box of photographs which he regularly shared with visitors. The remarkable photographs documented Gary's various ways of decorating his bedroom ceiling over an extended period of time, and it was clear that he was an artist with a distinctive and original practice. His father had documented Gary's series of installations, clearly impressed by his son's endeavours, a remarkable archive in their own right, but apart from his family no one else had really appreciated his unique vision. Without guidance or external support, Gary's innate creativity allowed him to see the opportunity that his bedroom ceiling offered. He realised his various geometric designs using recycled materials that he collected such as old CDs and plastic containers.

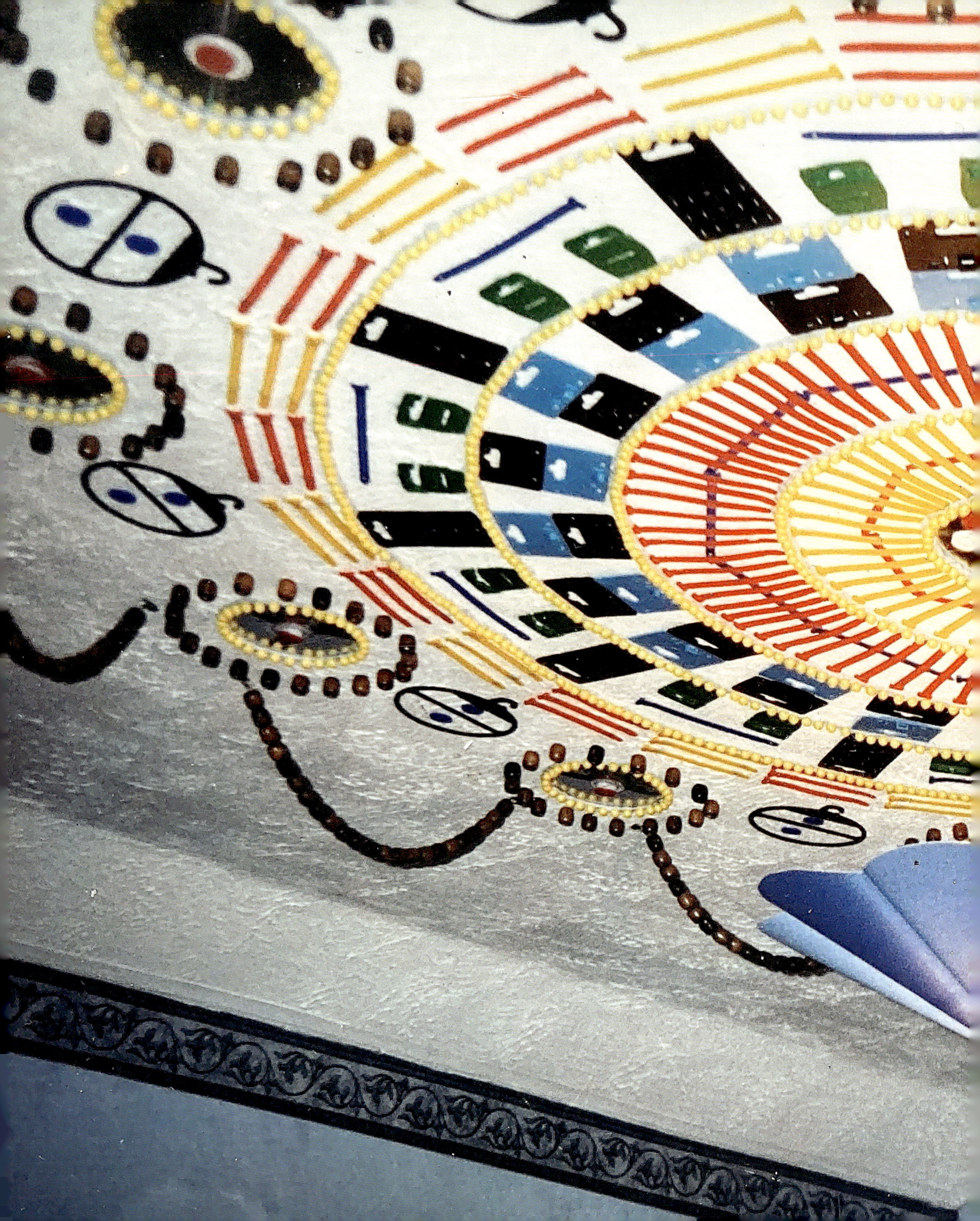

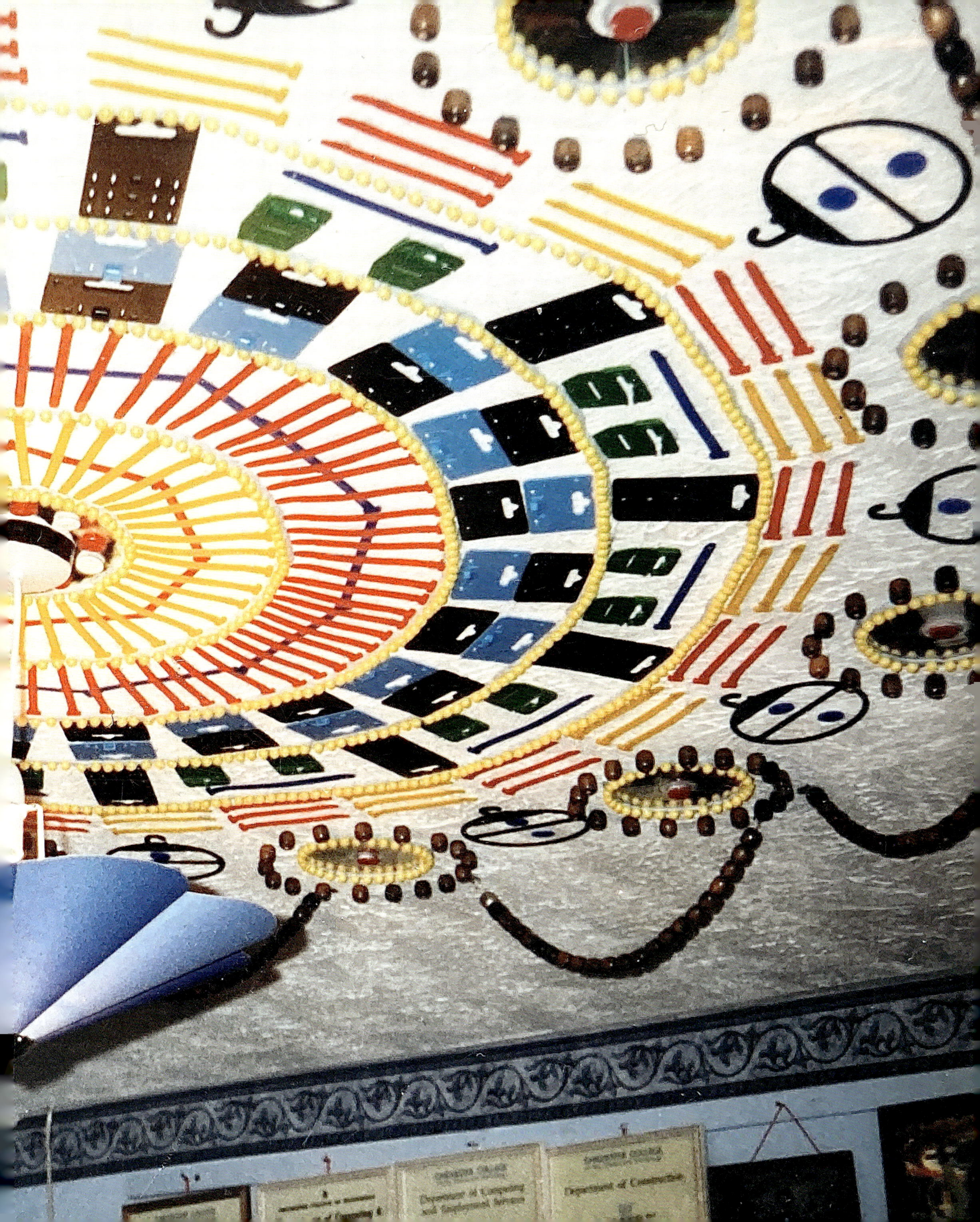

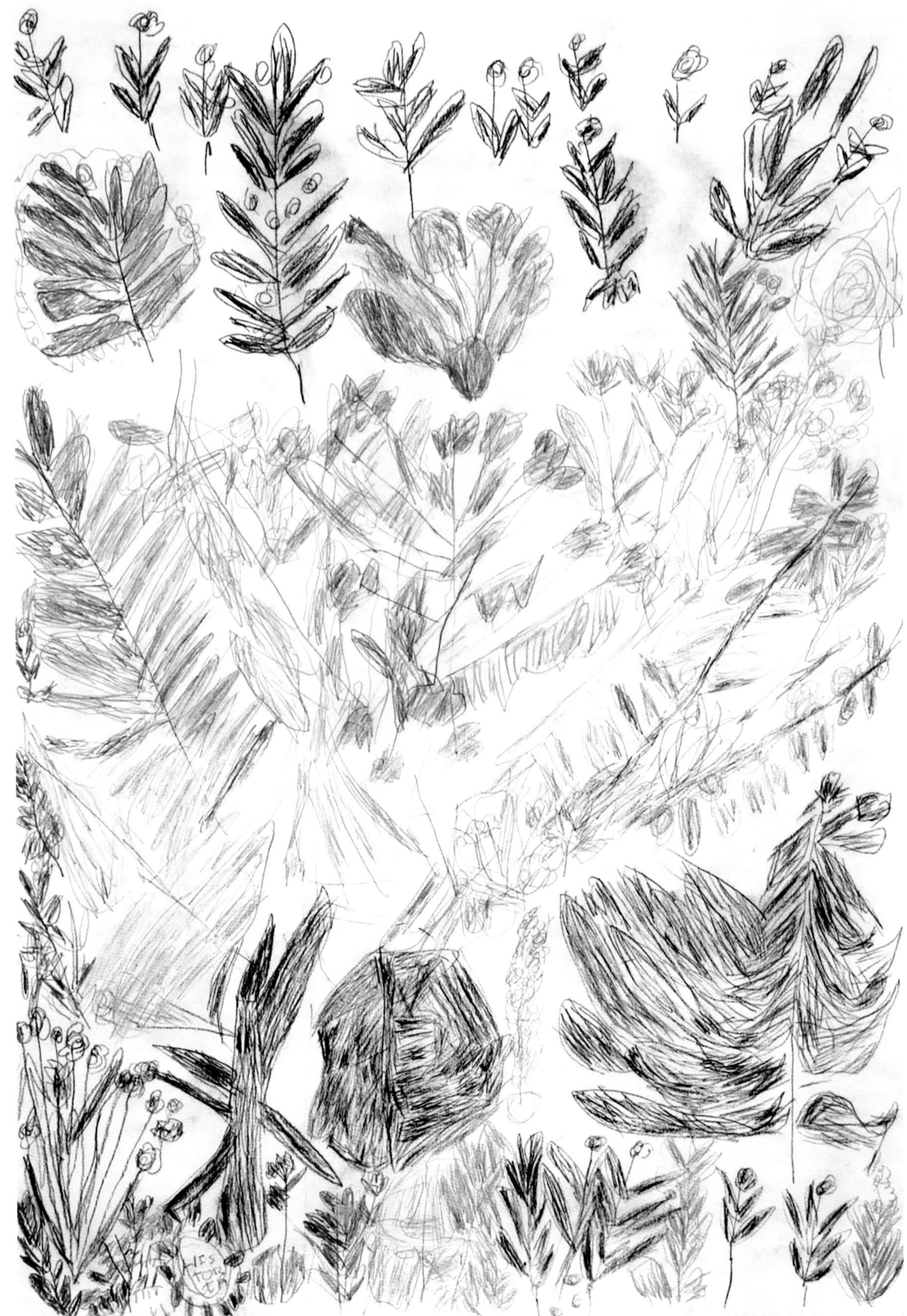

previous
Gary Williams
Untitled
unknown date
Mixed media,
bedroom ceiling

Joan Wilkinson
Flora
2011
Pencil on paper
59 × 42 cm

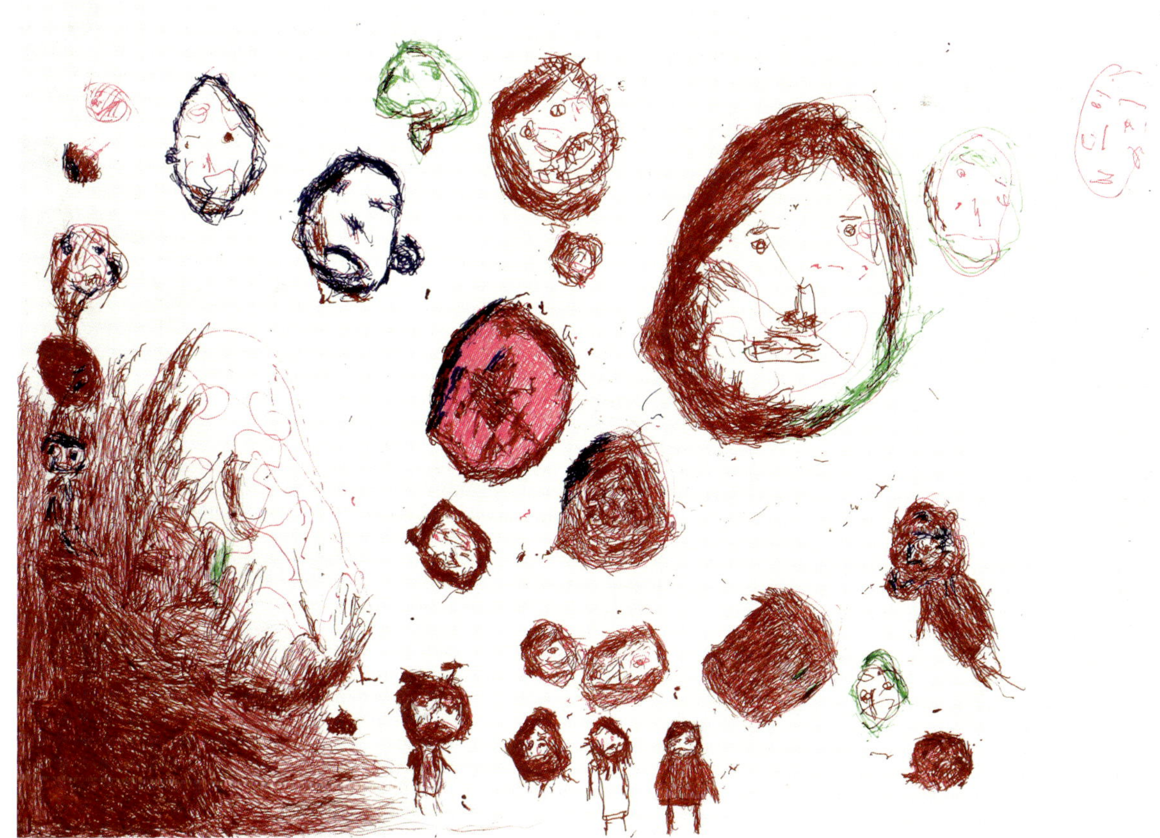

The need to convey and communicate feelings and emotions is shared by all art and artists, but there is much to learn from the approach of artists whose main purpose is to express themselves regardless of audience or commercial value. Their work comes from a connection with their innate selves, a desire to communicate at a deeper intuitive level, a natural connection to creativity too easily lost in our schooled approach to making and appreciating art. There is something to be learnt about keeping one's creativity for the purposes best suited to oneself and not trying to be something you are not. Creating art is more than learning a skill or technique, or trying to become an artist by learning the language and history of art. Believing that your art can heal and be a gift, and can convey the love you feel, is something that lifts creativity to another realm and purpose.

Joan Wilkinson
Faces
2012
Pencil on paper
42 × 29 cm

Love

As well as the other artists in this chapter, Joan Wilkinson (1946–2020), Chaz Waldren (b.1950) and Nigel Kingsbury (1949–2016) show this connection to their innate need to express themselves outside of a traditional art convention. Joan is another artist who, like Victoria Bowman, was supported by the Community Arts Project in Darlington. Her work has a distinctive quality, especially in the marks she makes using pencil, which create often complex and highly sensitive works. Her personality shows clearly, and her love of nature and life is apparent in all her work. Joan had an amazing memory, especially of her immediate and extended family, and in her drawings of people and heads you have a sense of each individual and their character. This is shown in the way they are drawn, and the forms used, shifting in scale and importance, seemingly arriving from her subconscious without intervention. They gather together, staring at the viewer, often smiling in a disconcerting way. One drawing, mostly done in brown ink, builds from an area of intense mark making in the bottom left-hand corner, covering up some heads and figures, and is then released into a series of heads, like soap bubbles, floating away. It is mysterious and beautiful.

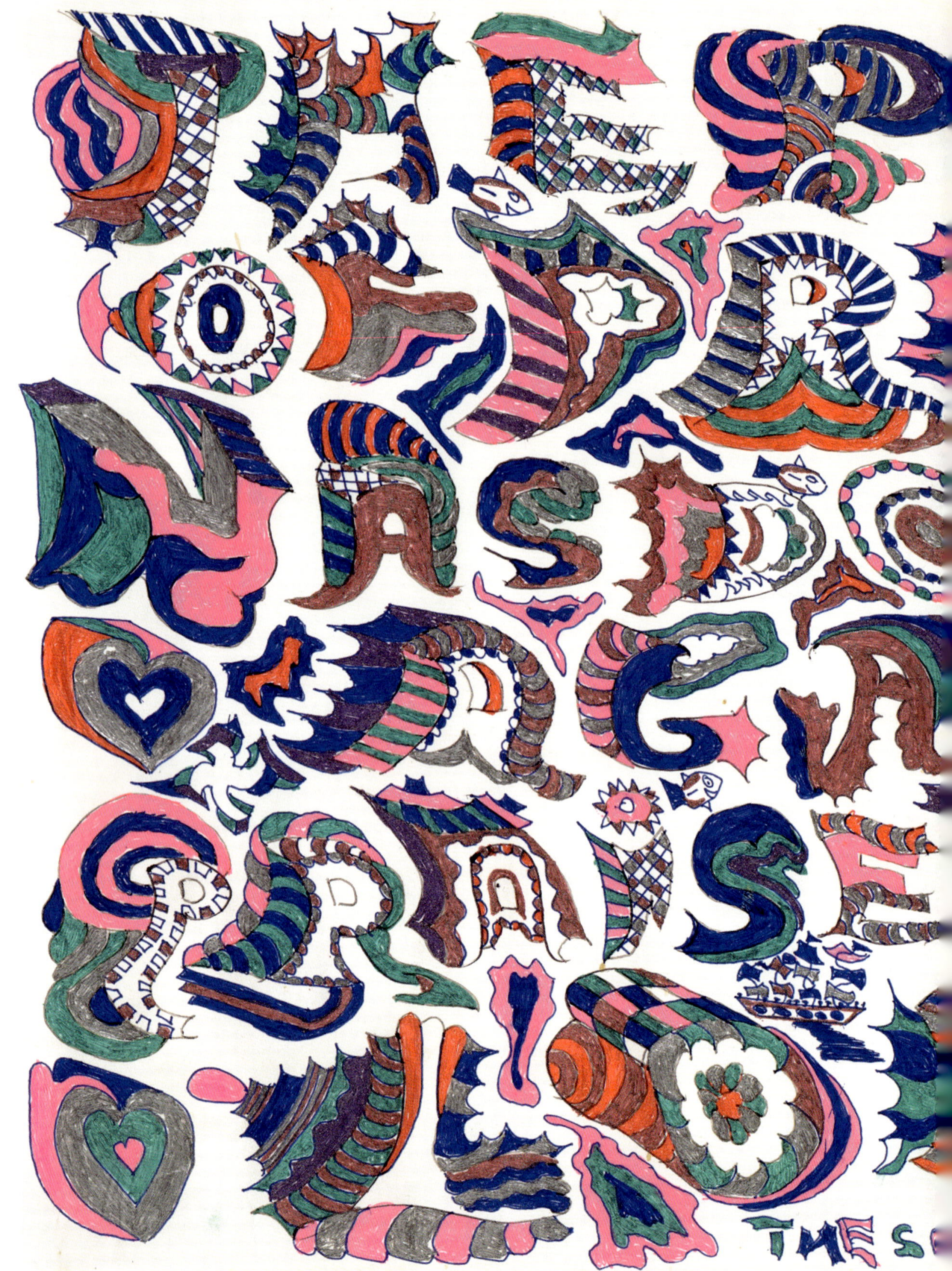

Chaz Waldren
Prayer
2009
Pen on paper
30 × 40 cm

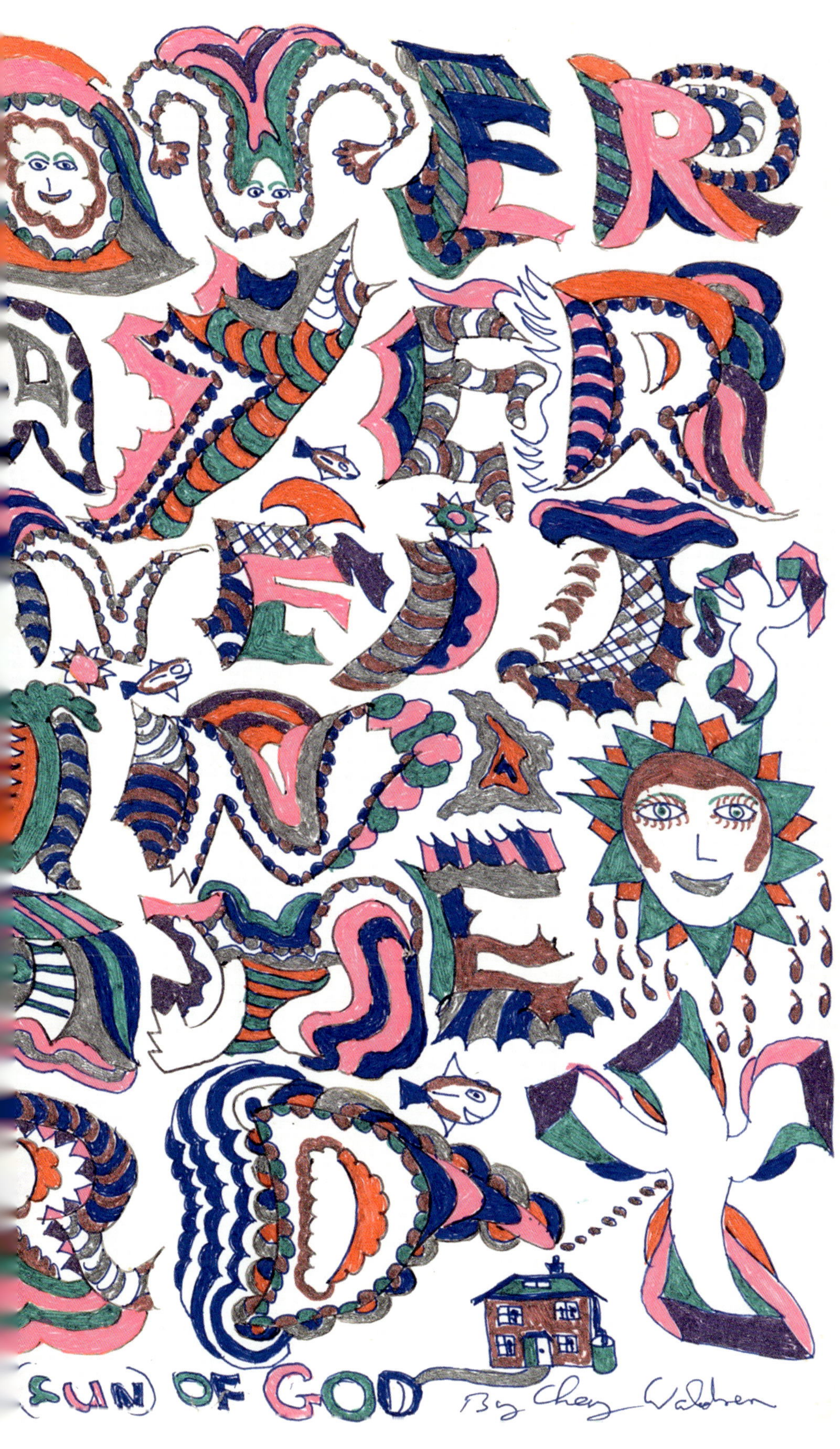
(SUN) OF GOD

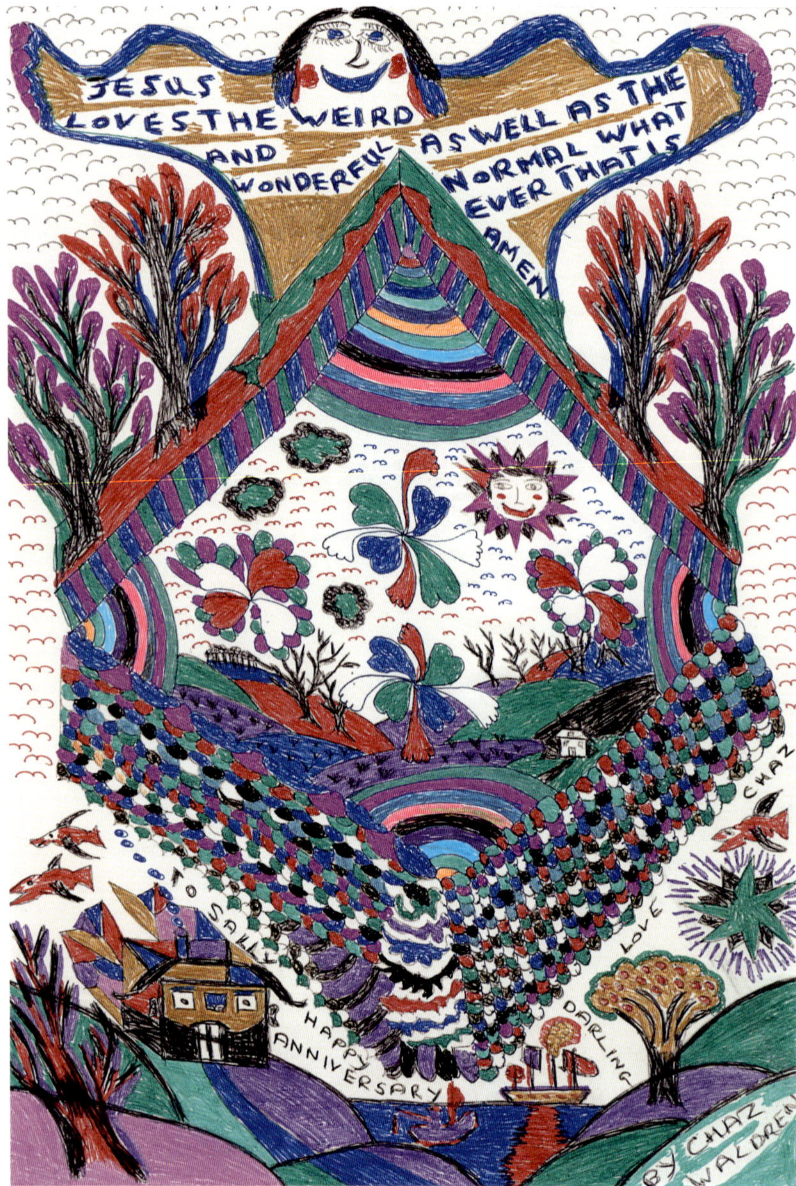

Chaz Waldren
Jesus loves the weird and wonderful
2008
Pen on paper
29.7 × 21 cm

The work of Chaz Waldren is infused with love. He has created a world full of the affection he feels for his twin passions: his wife and religion. A picture by Chaz titled *Jesus Loves the Weird and Wonderful* was exhibited as part of a group show at Pallant House Gallery. It stood out from the rest because of its distinctive drawing style and message. Created using gel pens and biro, it feels as if it comes from another era with its religious message and folk-art style. It consists of an image of Jesus holding a prayer, 'Jesus Loves the Weird and Wonderful as well as the Normal whatever that means, Amen', standing above an idealised floating landscape below which lies a second landscape featuring the Sussex coastline.
Its message reveals a life that has had its challenges. Over the years, Chaz has spent time in various institutions. What strikes the viewer when looking at Chaz's work is its authenticity and honesty of intent. It comes from his feelings. The work was produced for his wife Sally as an anniversary present, a token of his affection for her, created for its own purpose – a gift and token of his love.

Nigel Kingsbury was fascinated by women and used his drawings to convey his feelings. Like the Viennese artist Gustav Klimt,[5] he often started with the naked form and then proceeded to dress his women, often clothing them in fantastic ball gowns. They seem to come from another era, as if from a *fin de siècle* ballroom, full of perfume and romance. Nigel codifies and marks his drawings with hearts and kisses, which increase in number depending on the level of affection he feels towards them. Of all the work in this section, Nigel's most clearly shows the capacity for creativity to be the means to articulate and share emotions. His drawings are charged with love, records of a passion strongly felt.

Intuition is a powerful force: it enables the individual to make decisions purely on instinct, trusting themselves completely. Bypassing the controlling, verbalising conscious mind, the artists in this chapter have all developed their work instinctively, responding to their inspiration and realising their feelings through art. It is, of course, true that you can only ever be yourself, that each person has their own innate way of being in and seeing the world. With this in mind, it should be obvious that

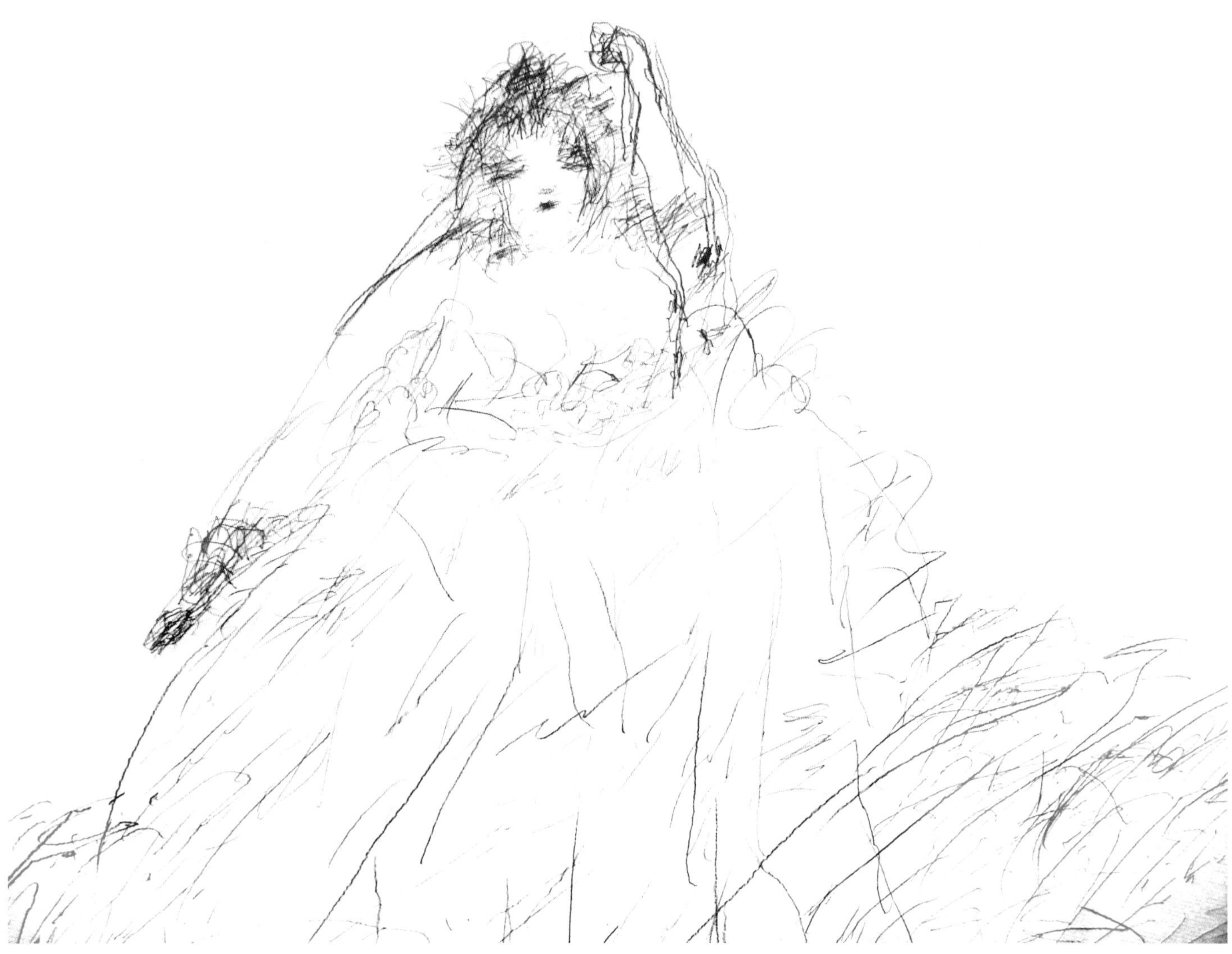

Nigel Kingsbury
Woman
2011
Pencil on paper
155 × 90 cm

one solution does not fit all when it comes to expressing one's feelings, yet we are mostly schooled into creative conformity.

Many artists have discovered this through their practice, as did Picasso and Matisse. Their strength of personality gave them the confidence to find their intuitive and distinct voices. Most of the artists in this chapter could be described as self-taught. Mostly through circumstance and their life situations, all will have received little if any conventional art education. There is a wider lesson to be learnt here about how each of us finds our own way of being and expression, and the value and importance this has. It also shows the vital importance of bringing these artists and their works into view. Many of these artists lack the capacity to navigate the art world. Without the support provided, one might worry that they would remain invisible, and it would be as if they and their work never existed – to the detriment of us all.

> A new picture must be a unique thing… The artist must summon all his energy, his sincerity, and the greatest modesty, to shatter the old clichés that come so easily to hand while working.[6] *Henri Matisse*

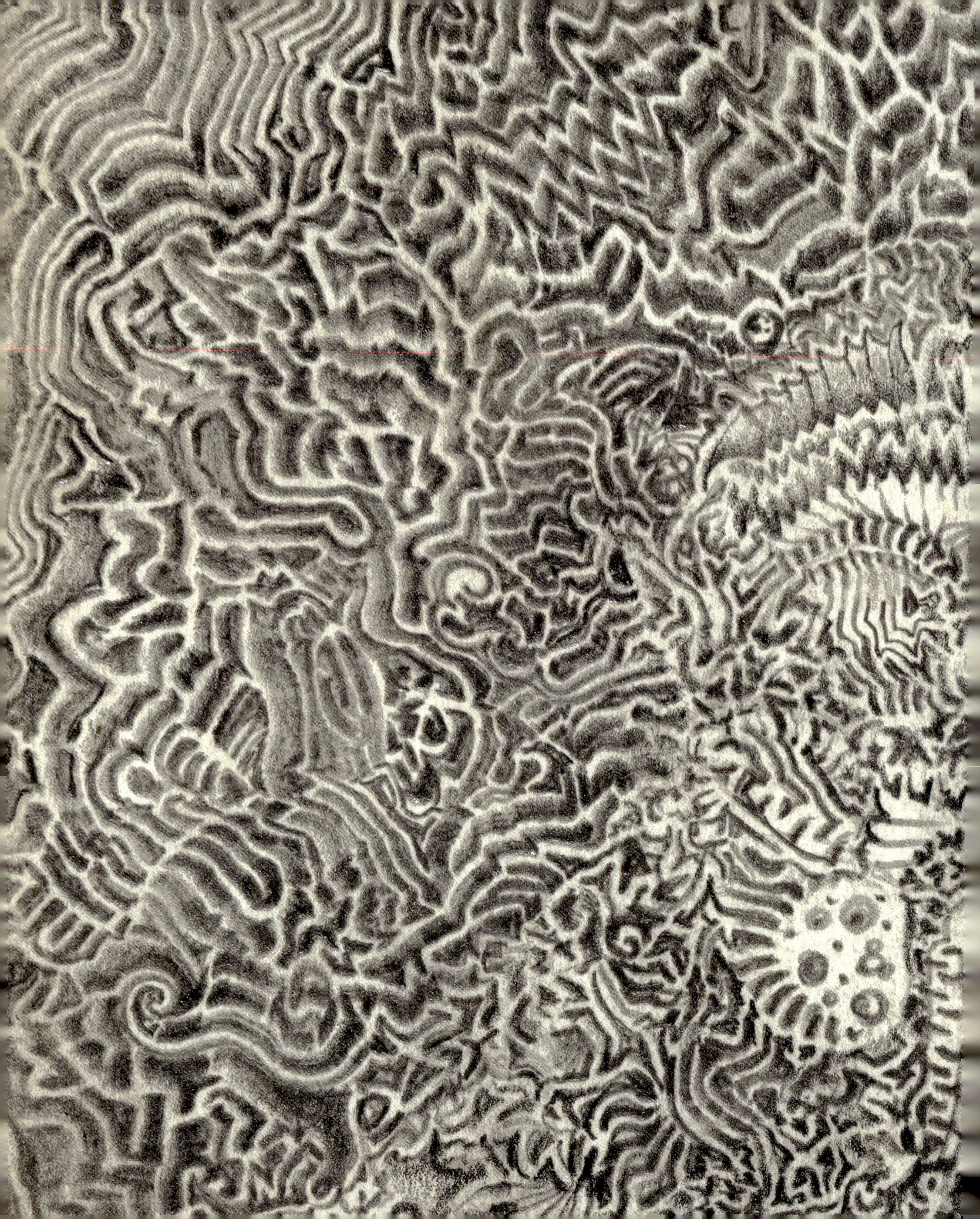

Chapter Two

Introspection

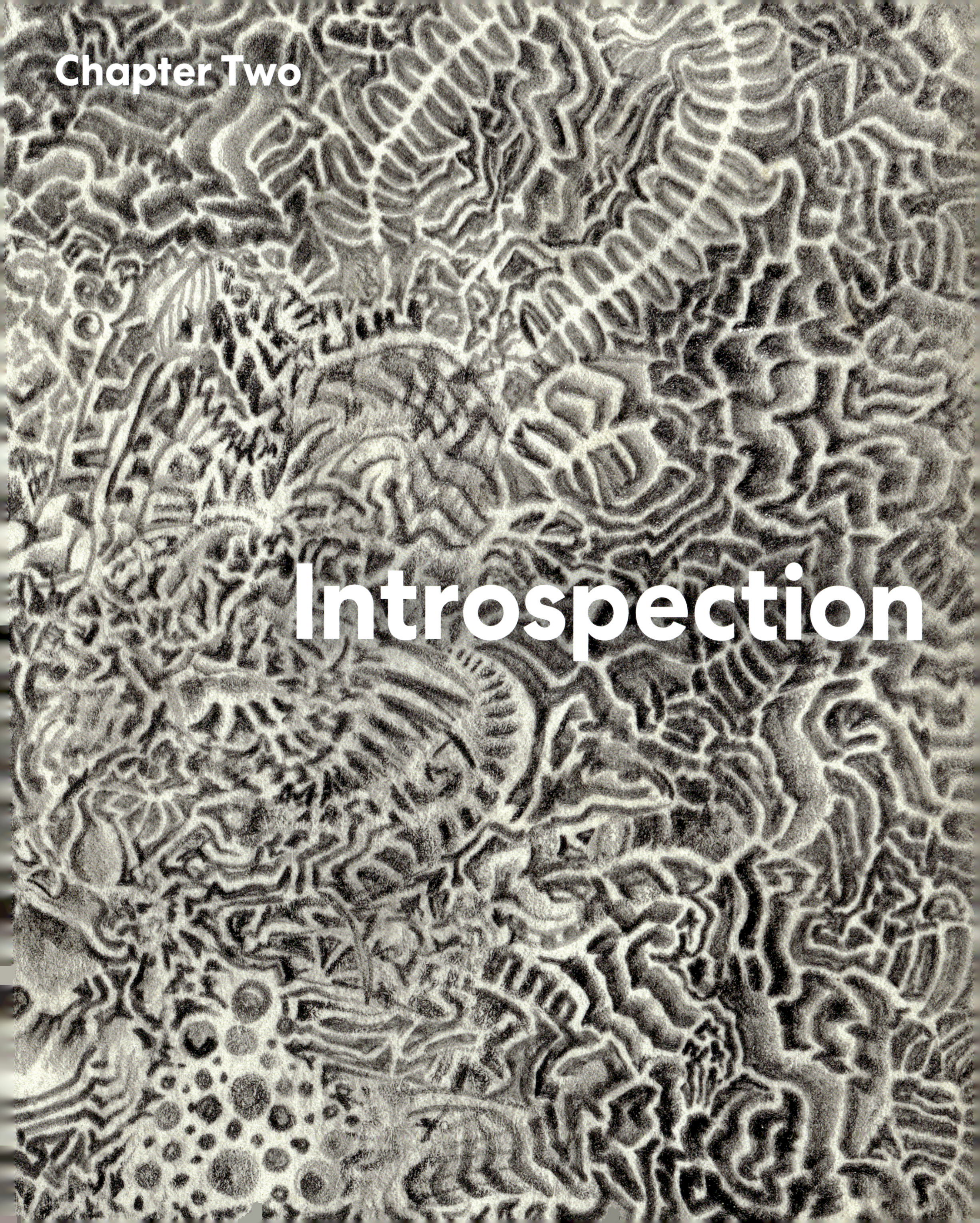

> The creation of something new is not accomplished by the intellect but by the play instinct acting from inner necessity. The creative mind plays with the objects it loves. *Carl Jung*

To be introspective is to contemplate the self – an internal process, searching the soul to find answers or to confront the demons or angels you might find there. It can lead to self-awareness or obsession; the *Oxford English Dictionary* defines introspection as 'the examination or observation of one's own mental and emotional processes'. Through being introspective the unconscious can be revealed, and we can sense the deeper impulses that drive us and play an important role in all our lives, more than we can ever fathom. We can find ourselves contemplating the bottomless pool of desires and fears, a place where the everyday is transformed and accorded new meanings and purposes. The workings of the mind can be dark, complex and intricate. It can have its own logic, language and secrets, sometimes revealed and explained, but more often not. It can be a means to make the unconscious visible, a way to enable a visualisation of our emotions, whether through structured interventions, such as counselling or art therapy, or through a self-led journey to render the inner self visible. As the psychoanalyst Bruno Bettelheim (1904–1990) said: 'The unconscious speaks to us in images rather than words and it is simple when compared with the productions of the intellect ... it is viewed as the lowliest aspect of our mind ... but when well used it is the part of our personality from which we gain greatest strength'.[1]

Art produced in asylums and mental health institutions, whether independently or through structured activities, tends to take on a particular characteristic, partly because of the setting, but also because of the purposes and motivations for which it is made. As Katrin Luchsinger said in *Extra-ordinary! Unknown Works from Swiss Psychiatric Institutions around 1900*: 'They [the artworks] deal with existential issues; the choices of material more telling of their treatment, and our ideas of artistic inspiration have to be revised'.[2]

Hans Prinzhorn's landmark book *Artistry of the Mentally Ill*[3] was published in 1922 and brought the work of artists who were incarcerated and producing art in asylums into public view. Prinzhorn wrote to asylums across Germany, Austria and Switzerland asking them to share artwork being produced by patients. He recognised that the work sent to him was art and that there was much that could be learnt about creativity from studying the work – not as an outcome of a patient's psychosis with no relevance apart from as a medical record. His book became the 'Surrealists' bible' and as Charlie English describes in his book *The Gallery of Miracles and Madness*:

> Prinzhorn's achievement was to liberate the art from the psychiatric clinics and nursing institutions where it had been made and release it into the wider world. He showed it to a new generation of artists who were seeking to explore the madness they had experienced in the First World War. These painters, sculptors, and writers – Paul Klee, Max Ernst, André Breton, and Salvador Dalí among them – saw Prinzhorn's collection as a direct expression of the human interior, untainted by bourgeois education and training.[4]

previous
Martin Phillimore
Untitled
date unknown
Pencil on paper
16 × 19 cm

Adolf Wölfli (1864–1930)
St. Adolf, Great God Water Noble Snake,
1915
Pencil and coloured pencils on paper,
34 × 25.5 cm

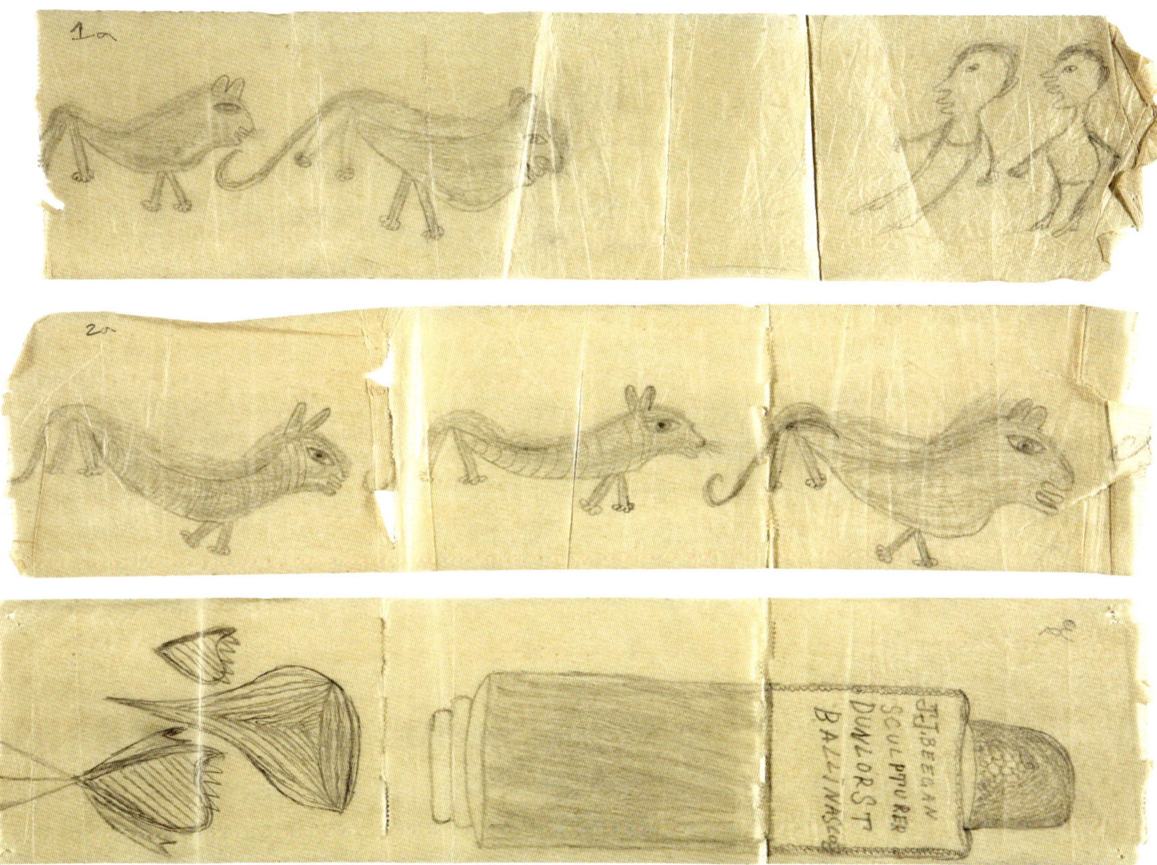

Like Ben Nicholson and Christopher Wood finding validation for their development of a more intuitive and naive style in the work of Alfred Wallis, the Surrealists realised that the artists included in Hans Prinzhorn's book showed that art can connect with, and be an innate part of, a person's psyche and enable them to tap into their subconscious. Paul Klee wrote: 'Neither childish behaviour nor madness are insulting words here, as they commonly are. All this is to be taken seriously, more seriously than all the public galleries, when it comes to reforming today's art.'[5]

Patient artwork

The artist Adrian Hill (1895–1977) coined the term 'art therapy' in 1942 after he had felt the benefit of creating art during his recuperation from tuberculosis and in 1945 published the book *Art Versus Illness*. The artist Edward Adamson (1911–1996) met Adrian Hill after the Second World War and they went on to establish art therapy sessions at the Netherne Hospital, Surrey, in 1946. Both Adrian Hill and Edward Adamson believed that art could heal and, thanks to their experience as artists, saw the benefit of creativity in its own right. Adrian Hill said in 1945: 'To be happily occupied is at all times a gift from the gods, and in a period of long convalescence, it is a positive saving grace ...'[6]

During his time working at the Netherne Hospital, Adamson formed a collection of patient artwork which is now held in the Wellcome Collection.[7] The first works acquired for the collection were some very moving drawings by the artist, J.J. Beegan (dates not known). Using the burnt end of a match on toilet paper, the only materials he had at hand, he produced a small series of beautiful drawings. Asylums and mental health hospitals have historically been built on the outskirts or fringes of communities, continuing the tradition of the leper colony in putting the dangerous and infectious outside of human contact[8], but there are lessons to be learned from the artists held there and their work, often a tool to enable their healing and share their experiences.

An early example of work produced through art therapy is that by an unknown,

JJ Beegan
Graffiti on Lavatory Paper
undated (c.1946)
Match char on Izal Medicated Toilet Tissue Paper 1–3
11.5 × 45 cm

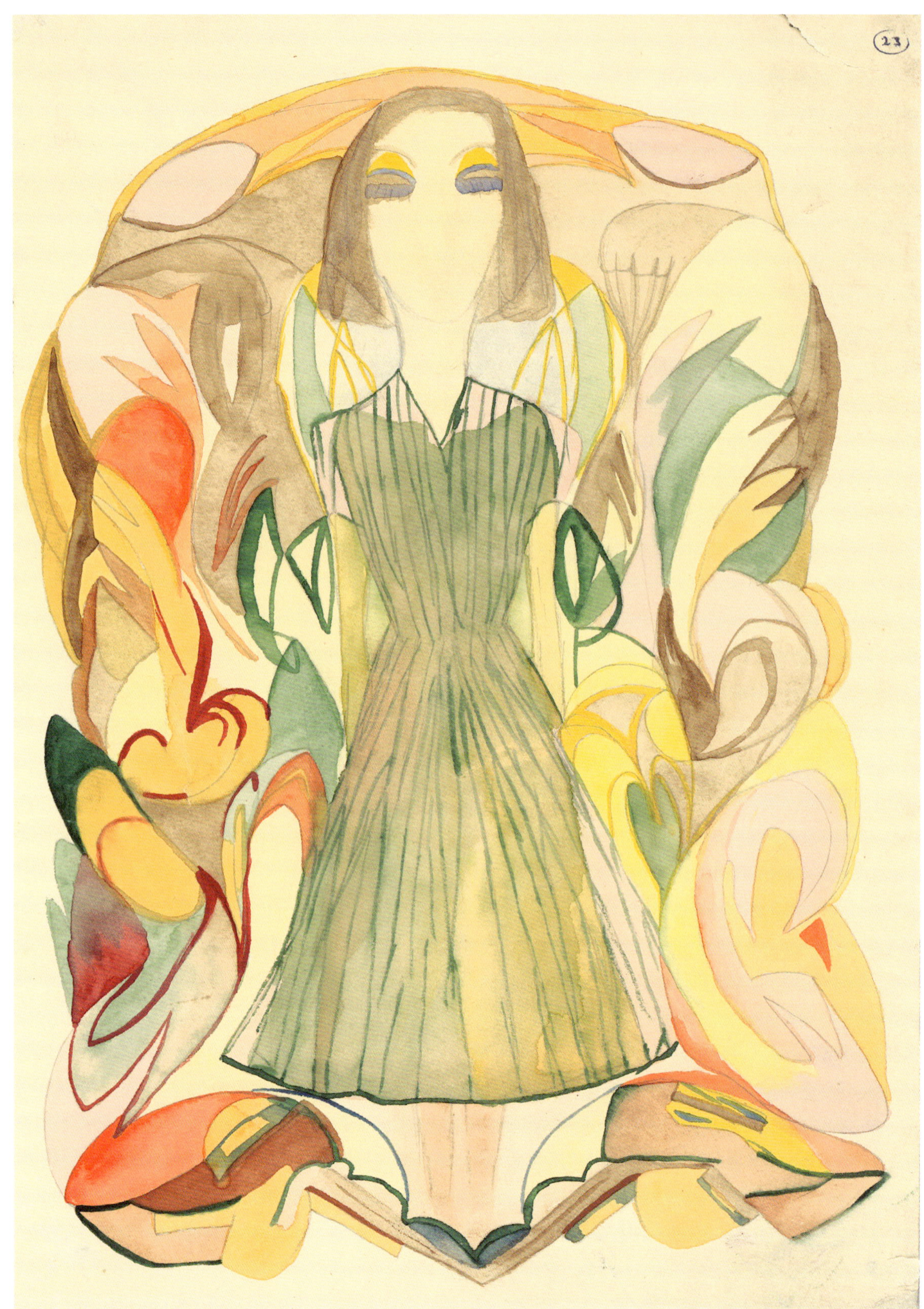

Miss B. M.
Untitled artwork [figure in green dress] by Miss B. M., referred to by Dr Brian Vawdrey as *'Case 2'*, 11 Jul 1952 (West Sussex Record Office, Vawdrey 2/23)
Watercolour and paint on paper
28 × 38 cm

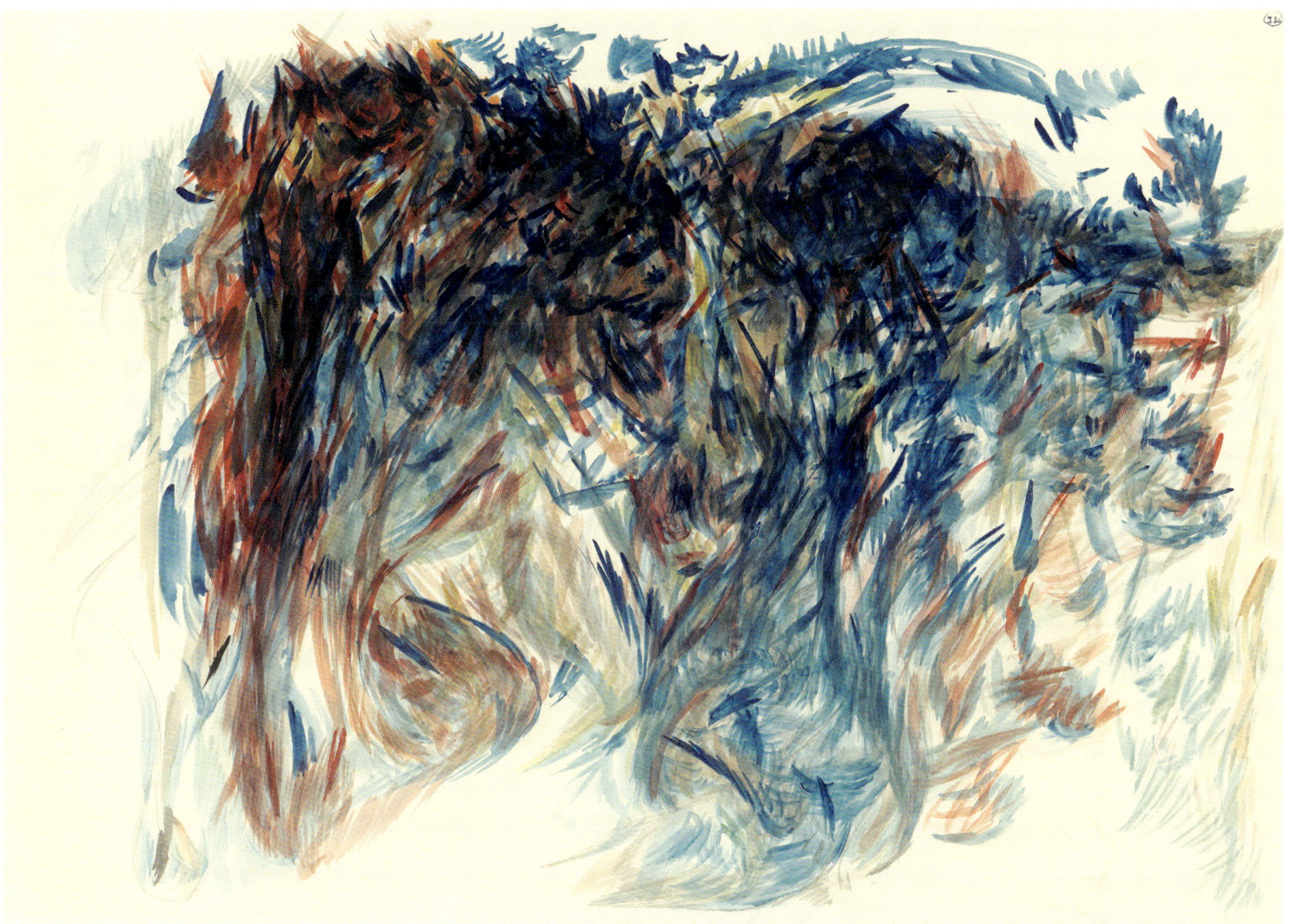

Miss B. M.
Untitled artwork [abstract in blue and brown] by Miss B.M., referred to by Dr Brian Vawdrey as 'Case 2', Mar 1953 (West Sussex Record Office, Vawdrey 2/70)
Watercolour and paint on paper
38 × 56 cm

but remarkable artist discovered during the Graylingwell Heritage Project[9] in 2014. She was referred to as Case 2 by the psychiatrist Dr Vawdrey[10] in his 1952 dissertation. He worked with her as a patient in 1951/2, engaging her in art therapy sessions.

The work came to light among many other pieces donated to the project by the psychiatrist's son, Alan Vawdrey, who had kept them after his father's death. The work had been carried in black bin bags, a lot of it badly decayed and eaten by mice, but it had survived. This overlooked work, and its fragile state, evidenced the precarious journey it had been on. One can only imagine how much of this art has been lost forever, possibly due to it being seen as a medical record and of no artistic value.

It is not known if she had produced artwork prior to her entry to the hospital and it might be wondered if the work would have been produced at all without the art therapy sessions she undertook. But it is clear that the process of creative introspection allowed her both to explore her emotions and to use her art as a means to express and then move beyond them. The work is also a visual testimony of her journey through the psychiatric system of the day. The notes in Dr Vawdrey's dissertation reveal that she was given electroconvulsive therapy (ECT) and forced to undergo insulin-induced comas as part of her treatment. On one occasion the insulin treatment went wrong, and she was left comatose for 17 hours, which was followed by a series of epileptic fits. This is how she described her amnesia: 'Now, I stand on the tip of the present like the tick of a clock, a mechanical record of what is being measured ... It is like trying to build a bridge over an unbridgeable chasm.'[11]

Her works start relatively formally, often including images of herself, sometimes wearing

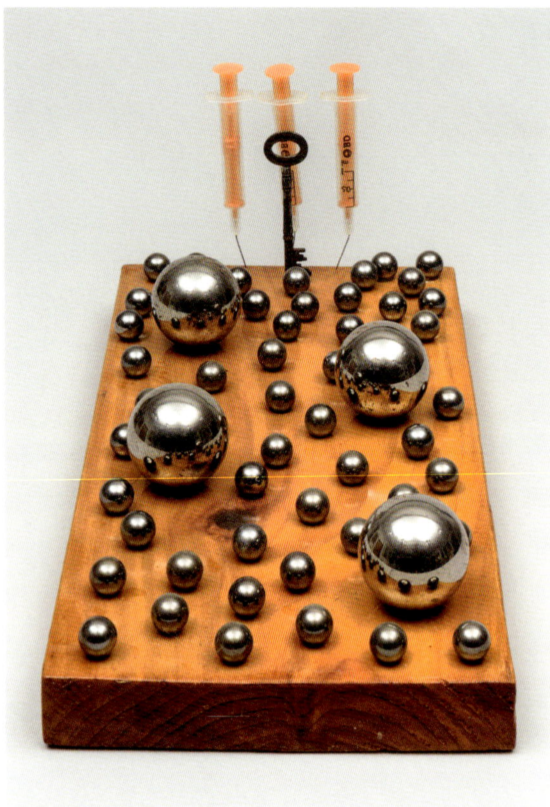

Tess Springall
I've Lost my Marbles
2011
Wood, syringes, key, ball bearings
16 × 33 × 13 cm

red ballet shoes, referencing the choreographer and ballet dancer Léonide Massine and the 1948 Michael Powell and Emeric Pressburger film *The Red Shoes*. They are colourful and carefully painted, but with a clear narrative. Some of the early works also include her own interpretations and Dr Vawdrey's notes on the back. What is remarkable is the gradual transformation of the work: moving from the early figurative work, it becomes increasingly abstract to the point where the work is just a series of marks and the colours have evolved from bright primary colours to a more sophisticated pallet of browns and blues. They are beautiful, all of them, but especially the last works: they show an artist in development, despite or because of her situation. It might be that she was seeking to hide herself in her abstractions, trying to avoid her analysis by the psychiatrist, but it feels more urgent than this, and at one point she was painting 24 paintings a week and had 'the overwhelming urge to produce'.[12] The question might be: is this art or treatment, or both? It would seem that the work is art and she an artist, working in an asylum, but finding the means to use her creativity to heal herself and communicate her innermost feelings and unconscious self. The artist Rachel Johnston, who worked on the Graylingwell Heritage Project, said of her work:

> The simple process of applying pencil and paint to paper allowed her a means of expression which went beyond words, 'what I need my hands to talk about'. This collection of artworks is a reminder of the power of making and of the way that art can allow a person to exist, for a while, in the moment.

The artist Tess Springall (b.1965) has produced work that speaks powerfully about her mental health experiences and time spent in institutions. Tess's sculpture *I've Lost My Marbles* speaks about her experiences and treatment at the Graylingwell Hospital. Despite the dark subject matter, there is a sense of humour, as shown in the title, a well-known phrase for when someone starts acting strangely or showing signs of insanity. The ball bearings symbolise her lost marbles, the syringes her treatment and the key her freedom. Her sculptures enabled Tess to tap into and express the emotions she felt during her periods of mental illness. The production of these sculptures was a cathartic process, a physical manifestation of her journey through the mental health system.

Tess was one of three Outside In artists to be involved with the Graylingwell Heritage Project. She underwent training to become a workshop facilitator and as part of the project she led workshops with patients and staff in the secure unit on the hospital site. 'We went onto the wards of locked-up units and led various workshops where the patients created artworks. This was a strange experience for me because the last time I had been to Graylingwell I had been locked in. Now I had the key!' Tess's journey is remarkable, as is her bravery in returning to the place of her treatment helping to challenge the stigma associated with mental health issues. 'The process of making art and being creative is crucial to me. It helps me with my mental health,' she says.

Buildings

The institutions and asylums that have housed the mentally ill feature either directly or indirectly in the work of Nick Blinko (b.1961) and Albert Rackett (b.1962). Many artists have found themselves patients, living in the alternative world of the

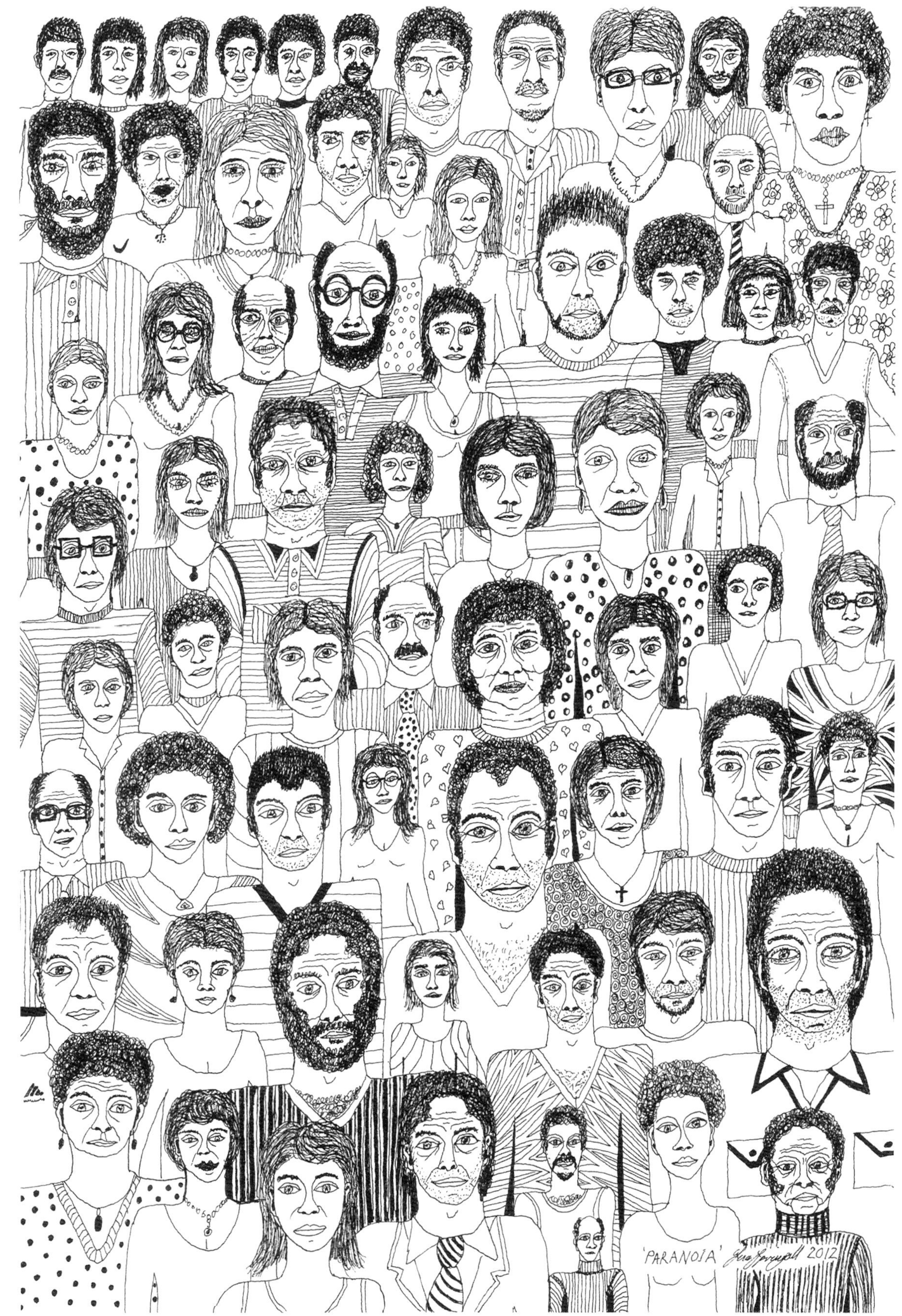

Tess Springall
Paranoia
2012
Pen on Paper
44.5 × 36.5 cm

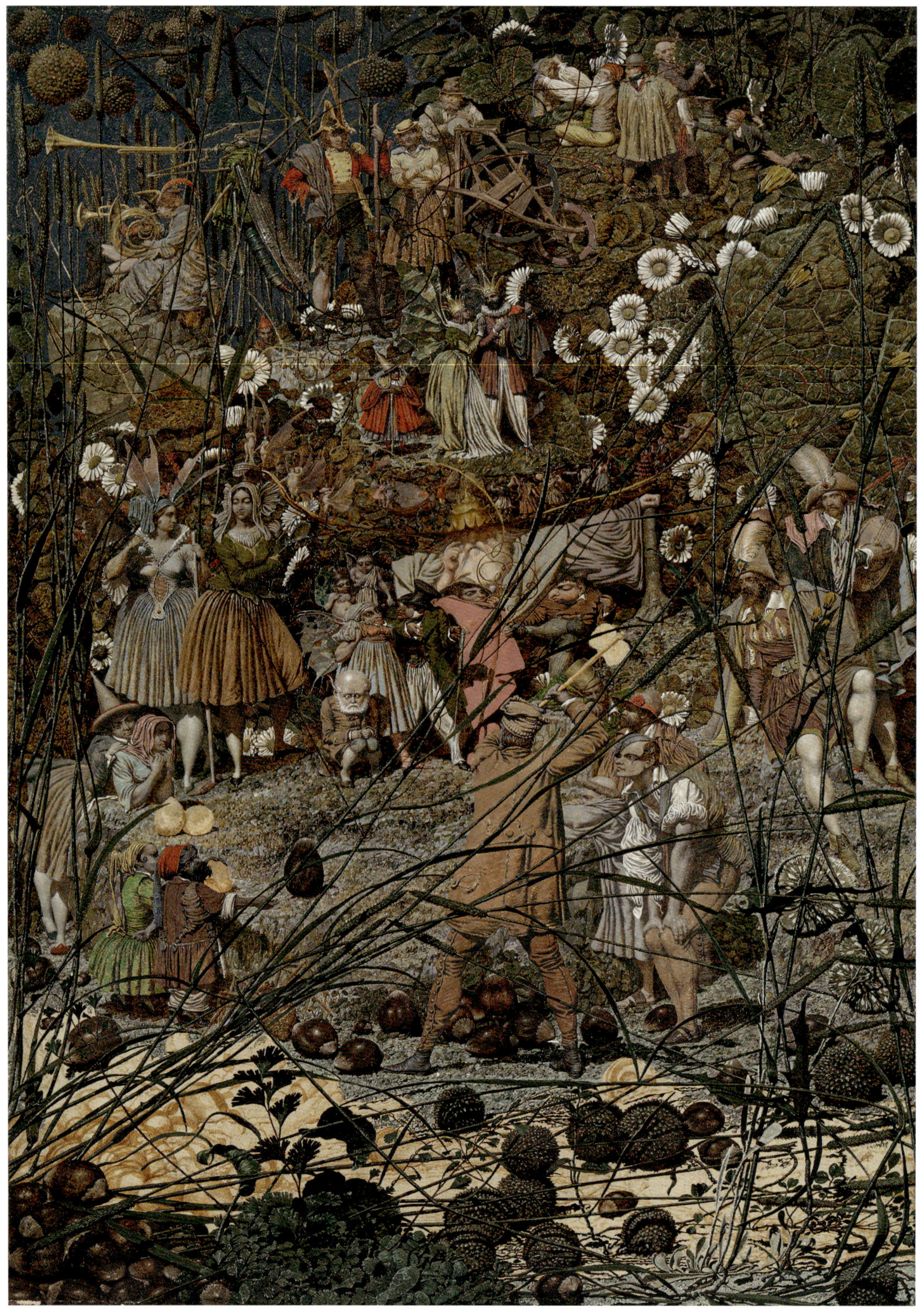

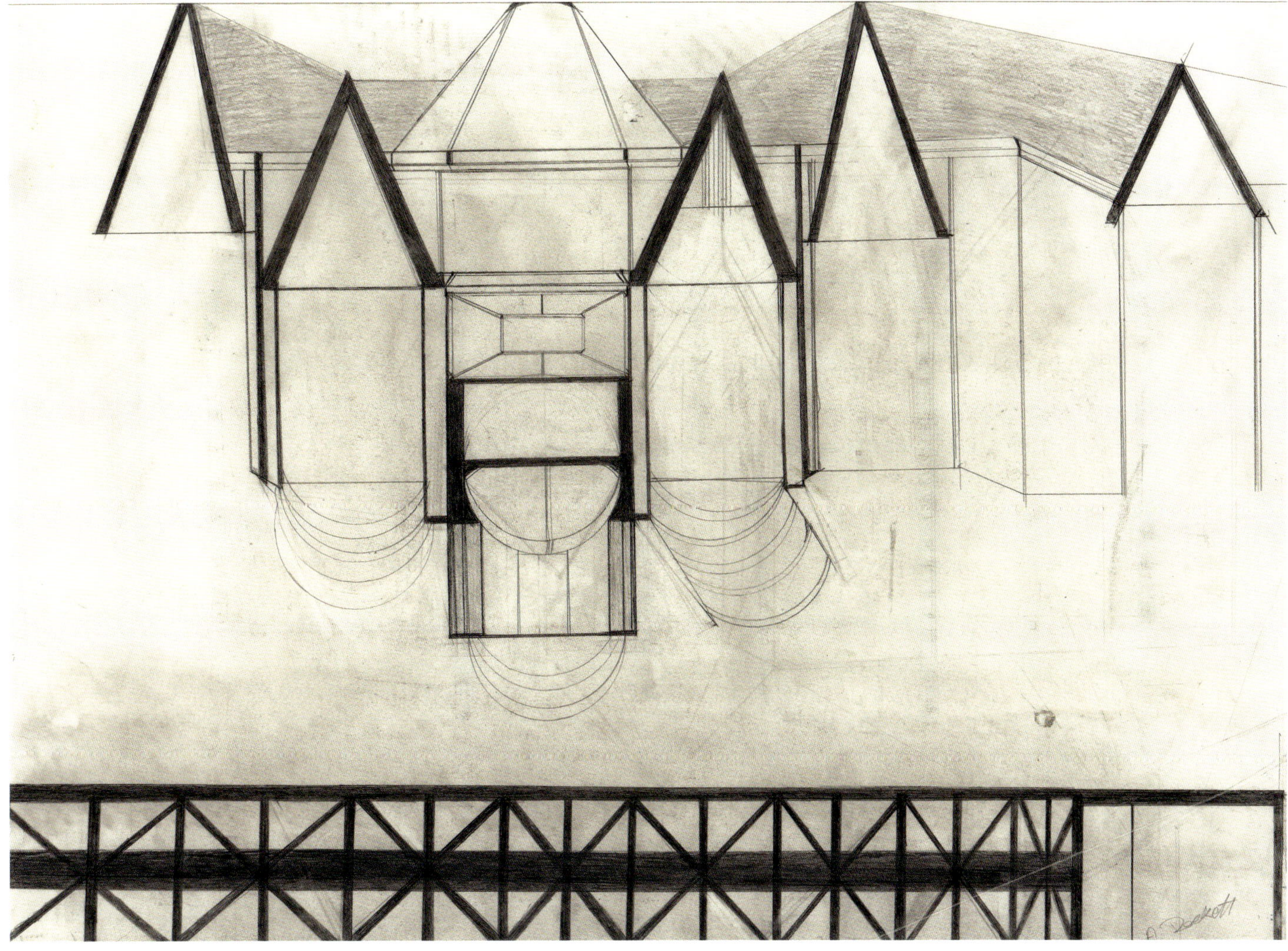

Richard Dadd
The Fairy Feller's Master-Stroke
1855–1864
Oil paint on canvas
54 × 39.4 cm

Albert Rackett
Building 3
2009
Pencil on paper
82 × 106 cm

asylum. It can provide a space for retreat as well as treatment, a chance to look inside and explore the wellsprings of your being. Historically, creativity was often down to the individual and their ability to access materials, with the support of family and staff. Artists such as the Victorian Royal Academician Richard Dadd (1817–86), who was held at the Bethlem Hospital after killing his father, found the opportunity to realise their inner worlds in these spaces. Appreciation of Dadd's work has increased over time as evidenced by numerous exhibitions of his work and it is interesting to consider his growing reputation next to his non-incarcerated peers.

Buildings dominate Albert's work. He is the architect of his inner visions, creating spaces he would like to inhabit. Albert has been supported by the Bethlem Gallery in London and was first exhibited at the Outside In National Exhibition in 2009 at Pallant House Gallery. He has developed significant standing as a contemporary artist and now has works in several important private collections. Albert has spent a large amount of his life in institutions and there is something about the atmosphere of these spaces in his highly worked drawings. Looking inward has led Albert to create uninhabited dwellings, spaces where sometimes carefully erected fences protect the property. You might consider whether the fence is there to keep us out or to keep whatever is inside in (though Albert has attested to the lack of symbolism in the fences in his work). Asylums and mental health institutions, with their focus on the treatment of mental health issues, either through medication, restraint or therapy, often encourage work that reflects the internal experiences of the patients and can also operate as a powerful subtext through their lives and creativity.

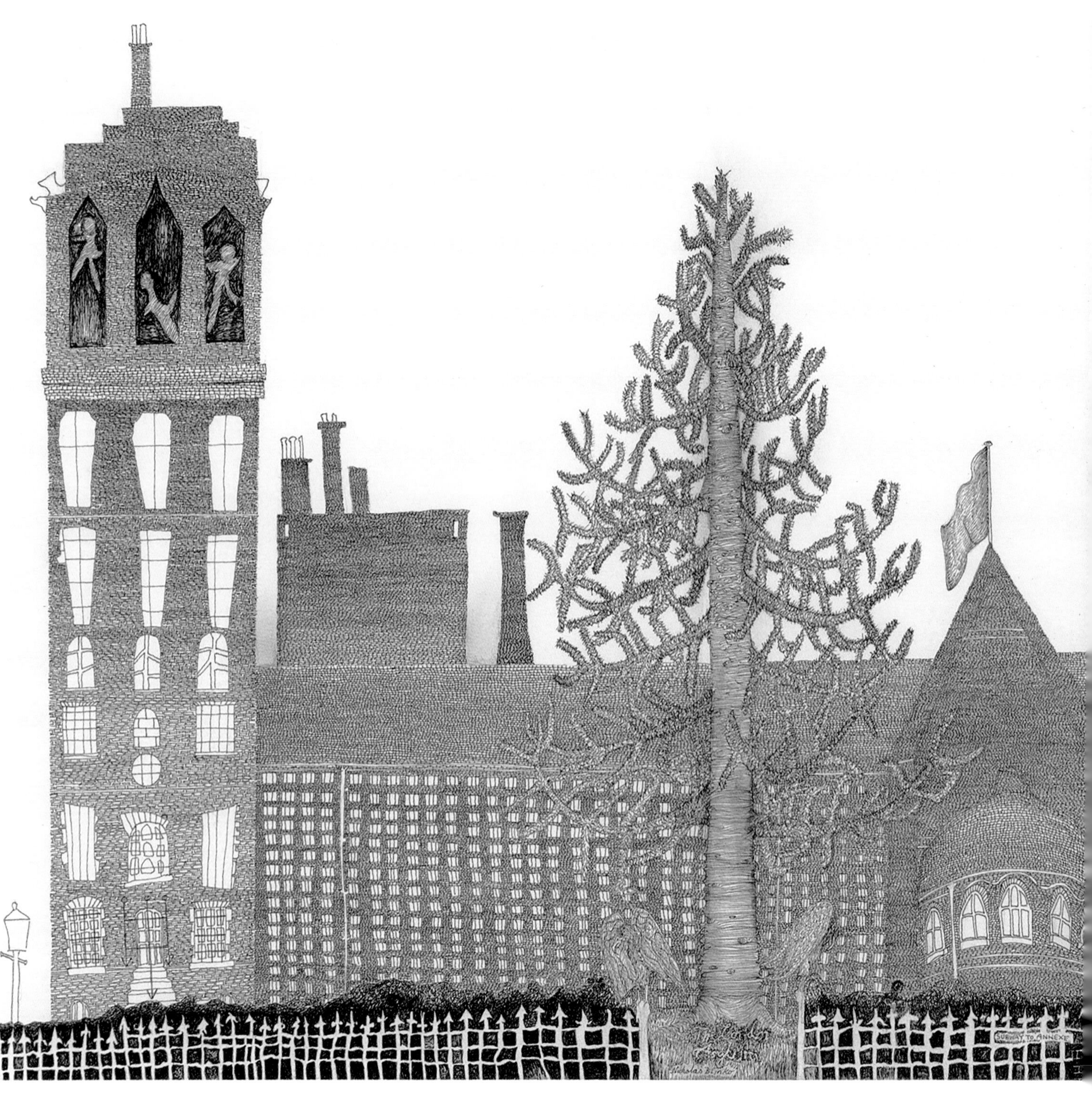

Nick Blinko
London Asylum
2002
Ink on paper
30.5 × 66 cm

The artist, musician and author Nick Blinko has spent time both working and as a patient in asylums, and they feature strongly in his semi-autobiographical novel *Primal Screamer*,[13] and in all his work. *The London Asylum* is a drawing of a sinister building with a fence of arrows in front, with the only gap being blocked by an imposing monkey puzzle tree. The asylum seems impenetrable and removed, shrouded in a half-mist. It is an image which, in his words, 'confirms the notion that the psychiatric set-up is like a grim parody of the illness itself'.[14]

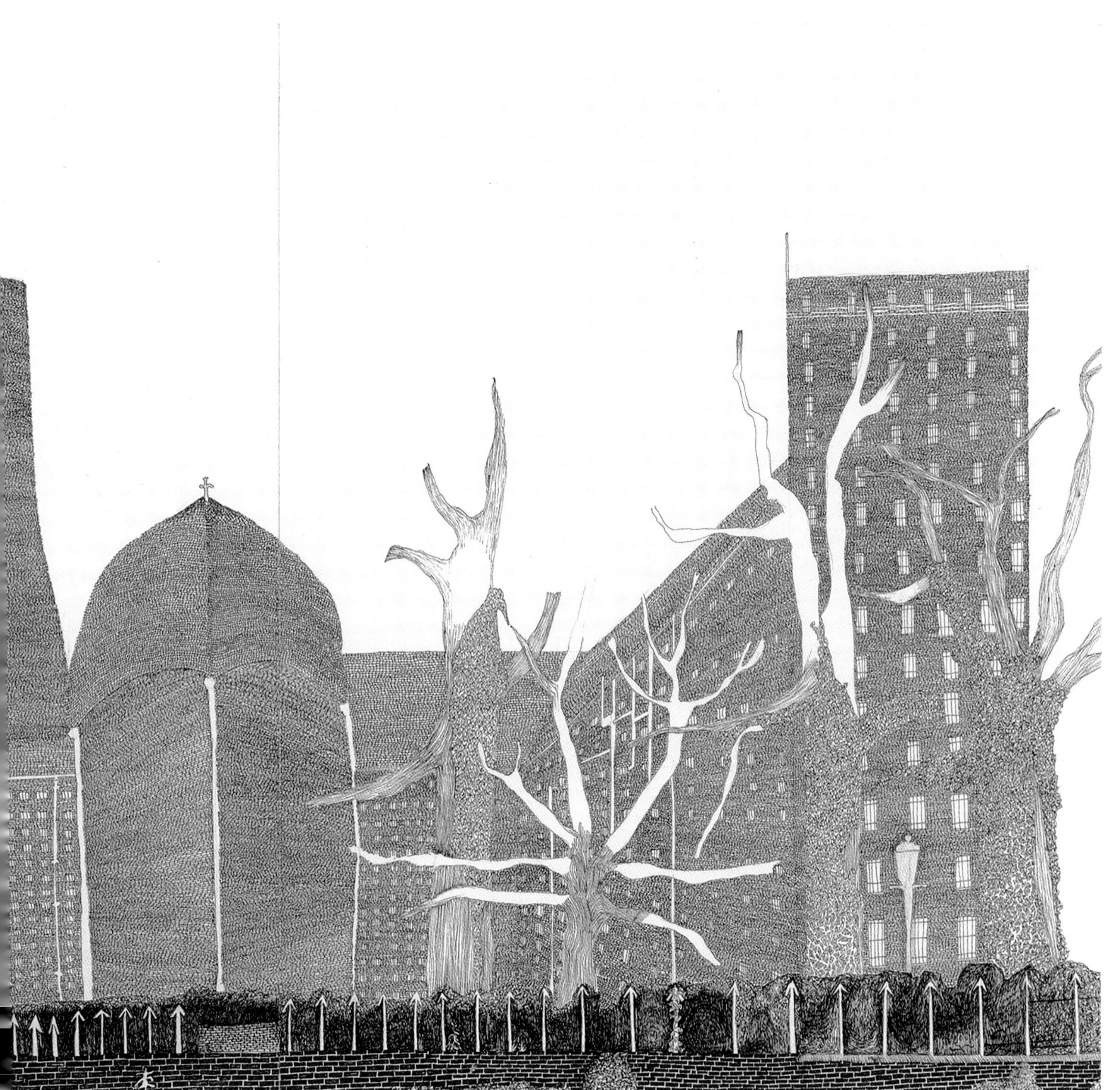

Prisons could be seen as comparable to asylums, their inmates removed from their communities for the safety of wider society. There is also a predominance of mental health issues in prison populations. A recent report by Dr Graham Durcan showed that '45% of adults in prison have anxiety or depression, 8% have a diagnosis of psychosis, and 60% have experienced a traumatic brain injury'[15]. Tyrome Jordan (dates not known) was incarcerated in a jail in Texas, where he created a remarkable series of drawings. The works were shipped to

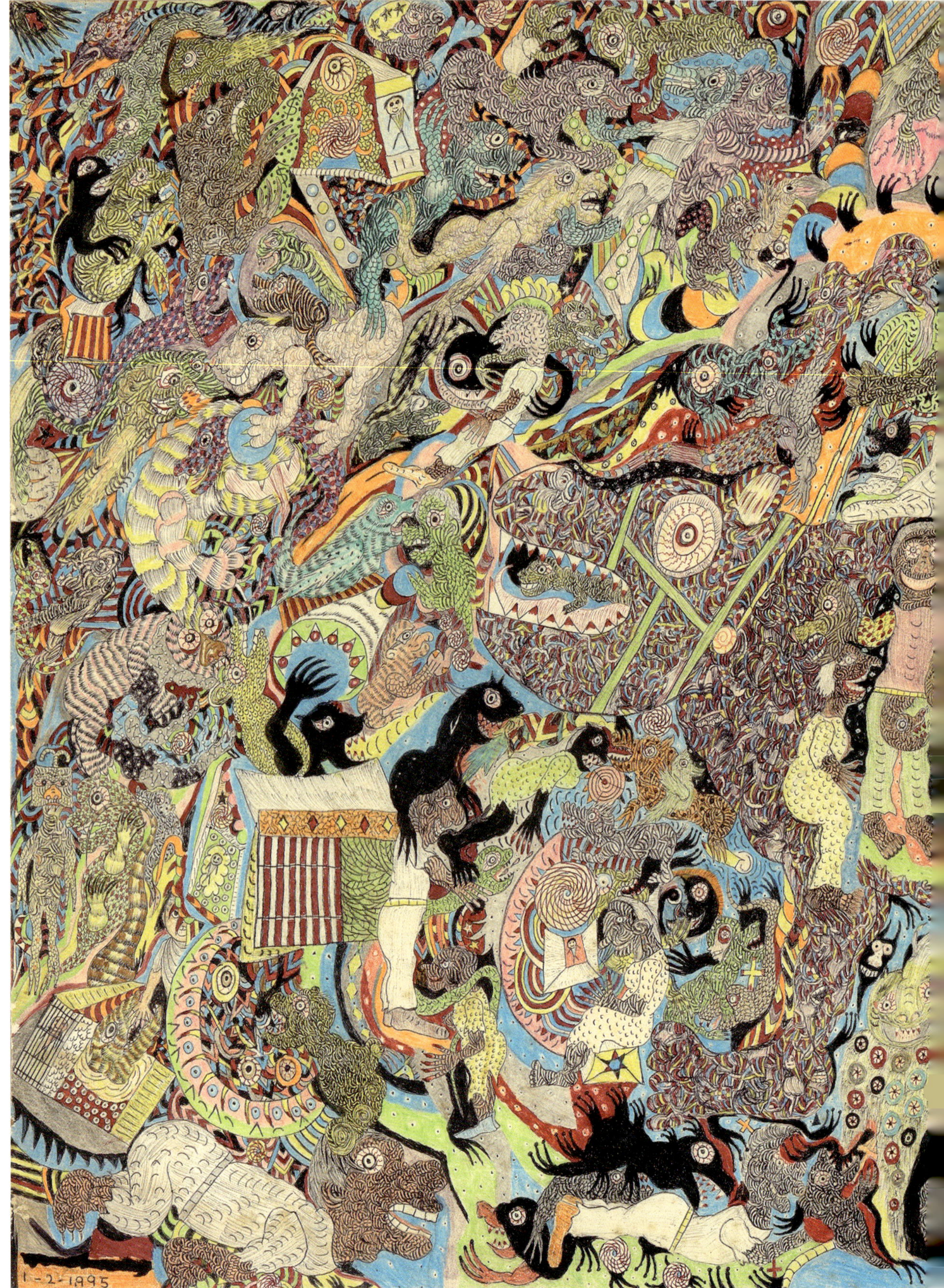

Tyrome Jordan
United States
Overlook Me 1
1995
Pencil, ink and crayon on paper
56.5 × 44.5 cm

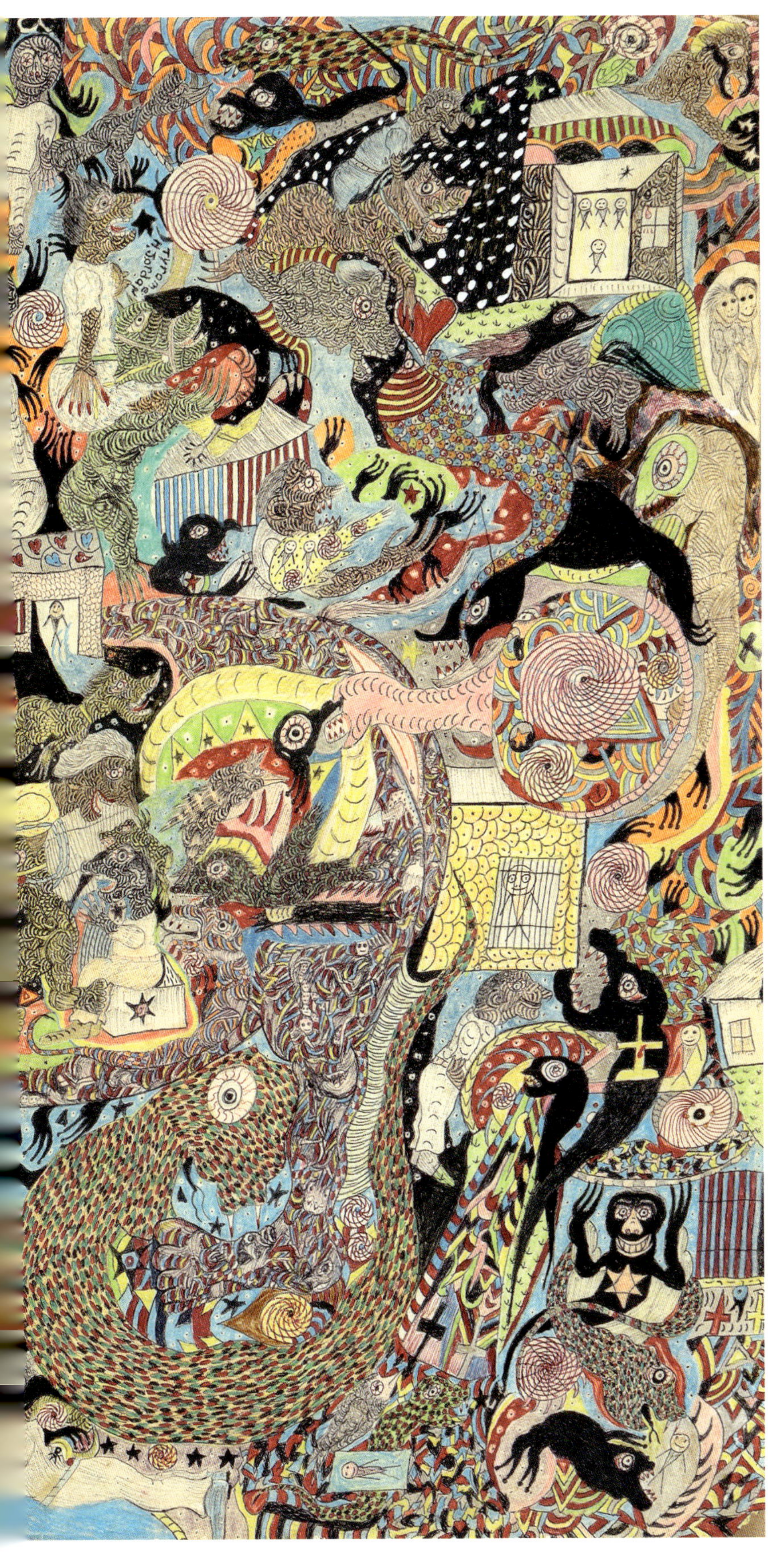

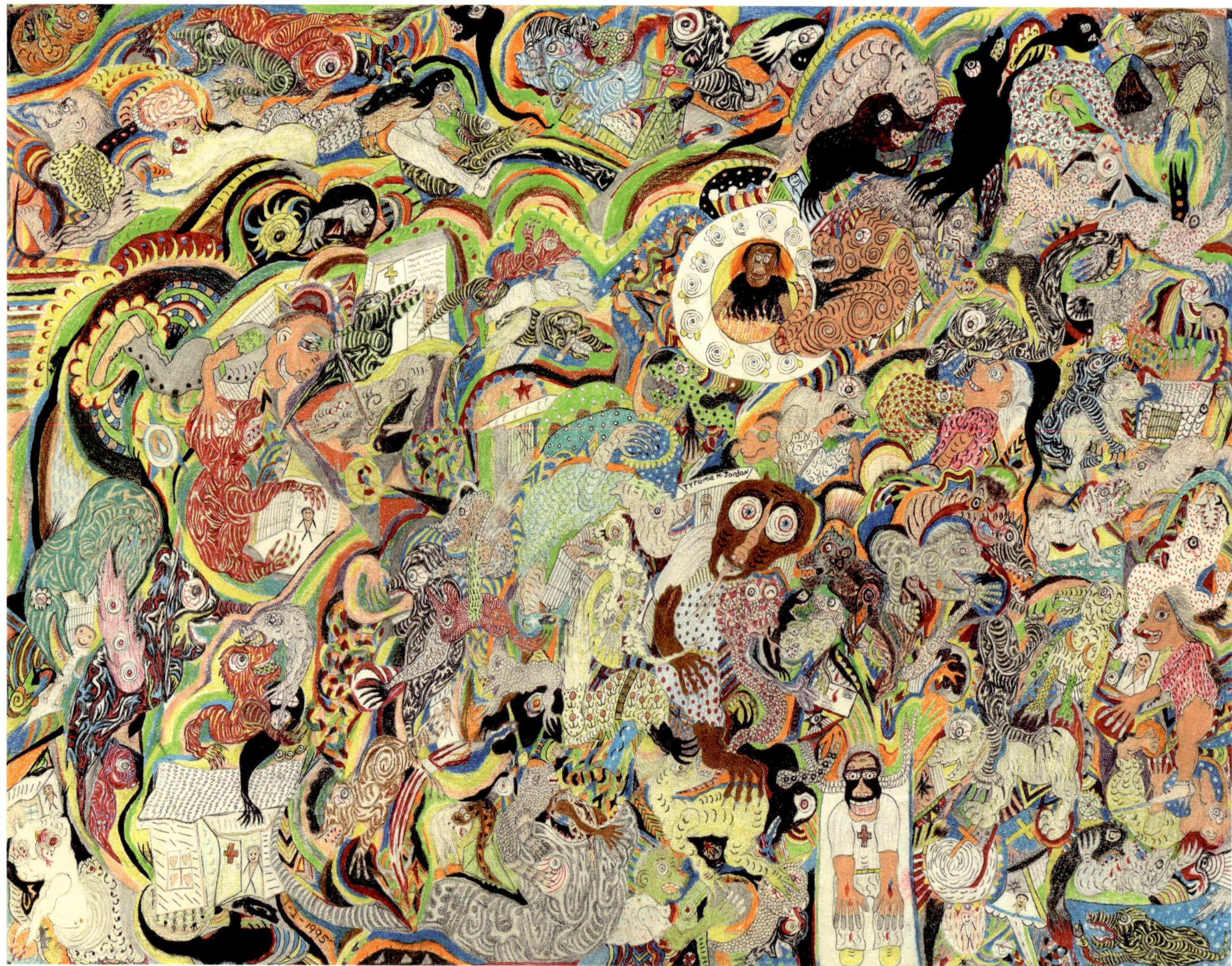

Tyrome Jordan
United States
Overlook Me 2
1995
Pencil, ink and crayon on paper
56.5 × 44.5 cm

the UK in a cardboard folder in the 1980s to be entered for an exhibition, but it seems they remained unexhibited and are currently the only known works by the artist. Very little is known about Tyrome apart from his circumstance, but he displays an incredible creativity and imagination. Delving into his imagination, he created work that is as highly detailed as a medieval bestiary, full of strange beasts and figures engaged in various sexual acts. Interspersed throughout the work are drawings of a lone figure inside a prison cell, seemingly an image of the artist. Held in his colourless cell he is surrounded by the colourful and terrifying demons of his subconscious, Bosch-like[16] in their capacity to torture their victims for their various crimes.

As well as the settings and institutions informing and inspiring creativity, in many instances artists have used the buildings to express themselves. There are many examples of graffiti and drawings on the walls of prison cells and hospital walls. Much of this will never have been documented, but there is something moving about the attempt to assert the self often in the face of a hostile environment and the march of time. Somehow these marks seems to carry the presence of the maker, in ways that a finished sculpture or carved lettering never quite does.

Julius Klingebiel (1904–1965),[17] rather like the artist Gary Williams (see p.36), used the space in which he lived as the canvas for his creativity. Klingebiel was held in the asylum at Göttingen

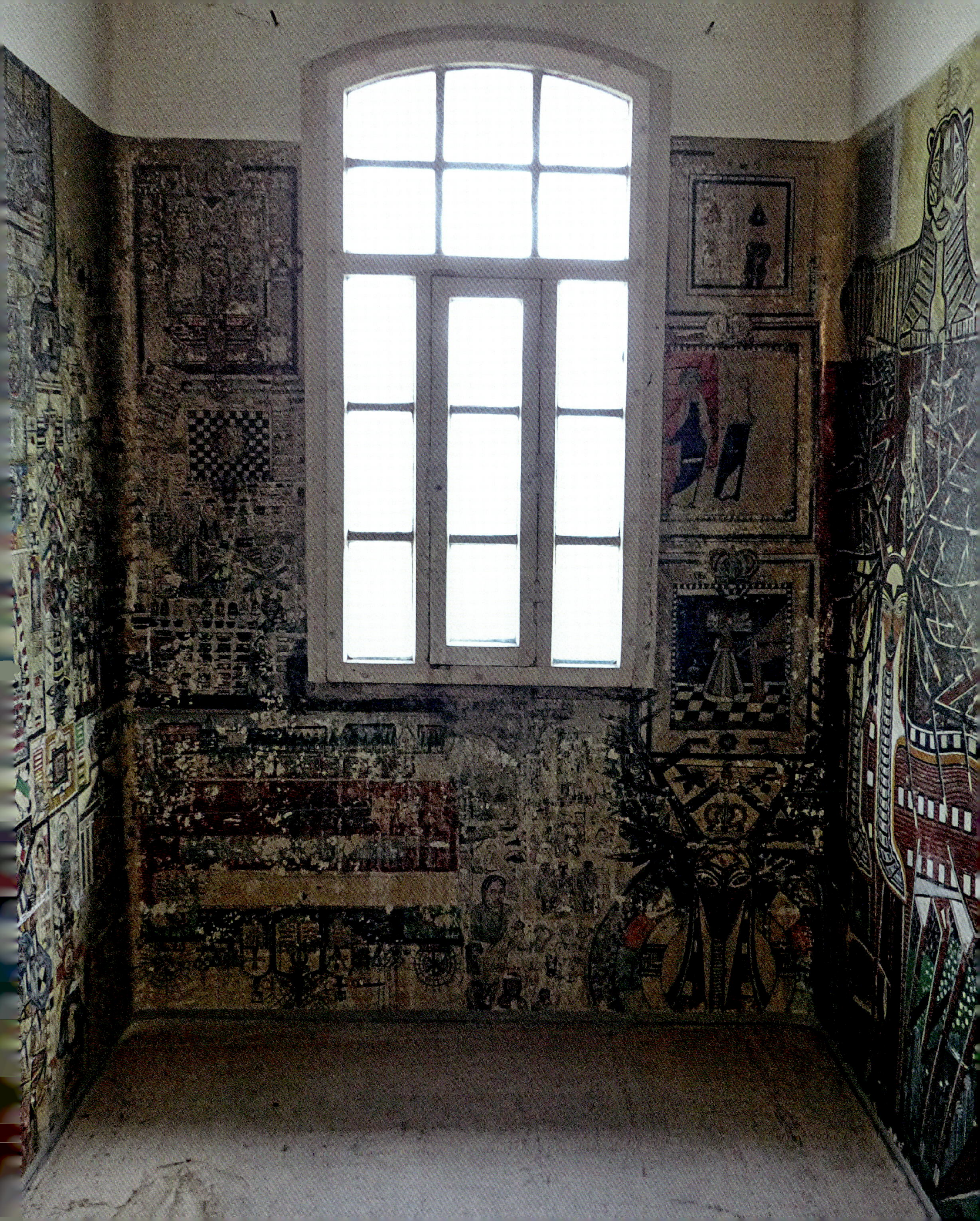

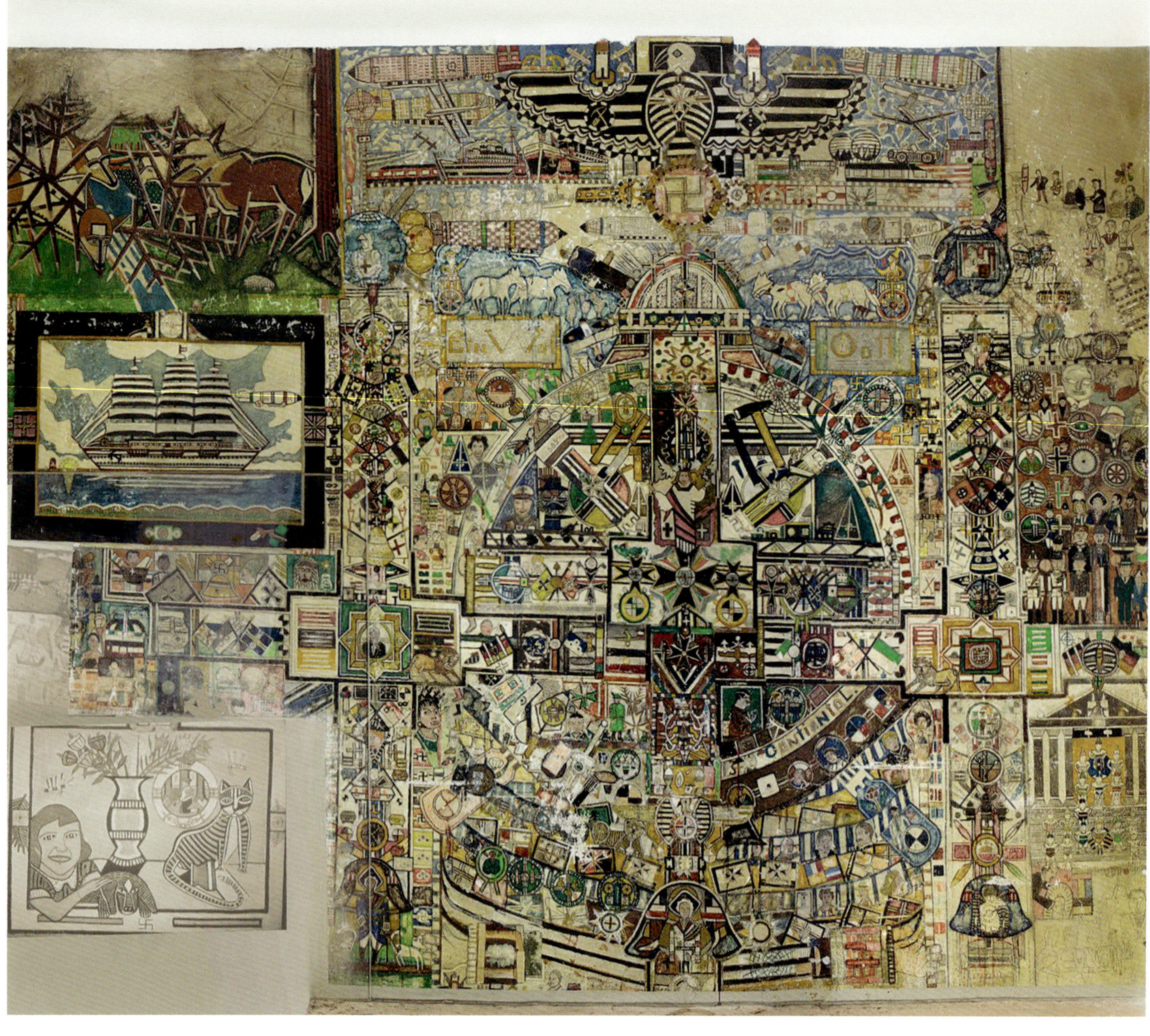

previous
Julius Klingbiel
Image of Julius Klingebiel's cell in the daytime (photo taken 2013)

Julius Klingbiel
detail of his cell

in Germany from 1939 until his death in 1965. He was forcibly sterilised by the Nazis in 1940 as part of their campaign to prevent people with mental health issues and disabilities from corrupting the German race. During his time at Göttingen, he decorated the walls of his cell with fantastic paintings of landscapes, often with stags and forests. He painted frames on the works as if they were hanging on the wall and often painted over his work. As well as the landscapes, he also painted people, technology, and numerous historical and political symbols.

A nurse at the hospital commented: 'Soon after his introduction to cell 117, he began to sketch with stones or sticks from the courtyard, with burnt pieces of wood or toothpaste on the white walls. He had to wash off these "smears" repeatedly, but it was soon noticed that he became calmer and more concentrated as he drew.'[18] It is interesting to read of the calming effects of drawing for Klingebiel, reminding us that the act of creating is therapeutic in and of itself, as noticed by Adamson and Hill in their development of art therapy.

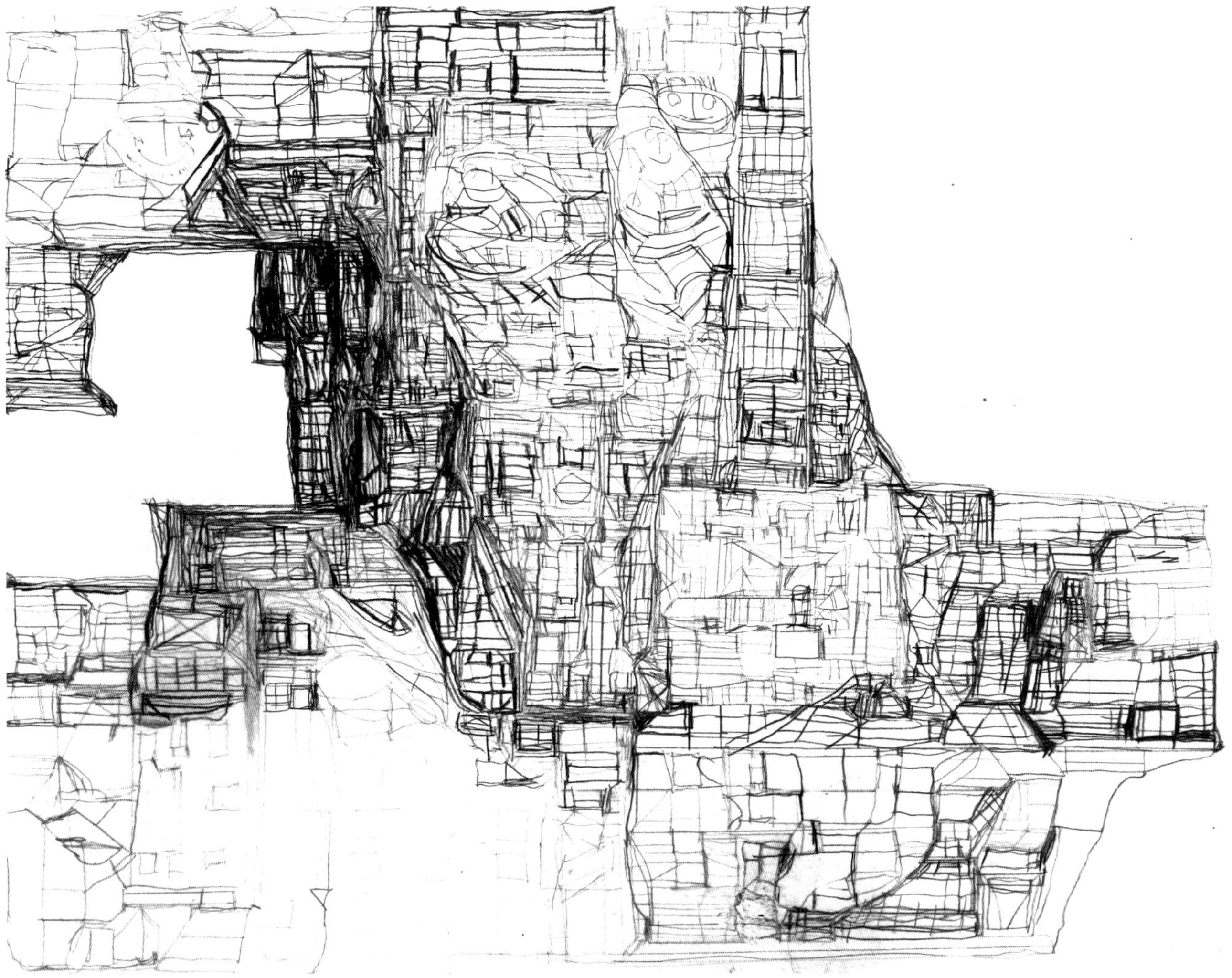

Matthew Beadon
Untitled
2014
Pencil and ink on paper
59 × 42 cm

Buildings can be places of security or danger, providing the refuge of the family home or the private and secret setting for abuse. In dreams, a house can represent the self[19] with ghosts in the cellar and something terrible in the attic. Houses have been presented as the stuff of nightmares, as seen in the 1982 film *Poltergeist* or the 1959 gothic novel *The Haunting of Hill House*. Matthew Beadon (b.1961), who is supported by the Community Art Project in Darlington, creates pictures of buildings. He draws them from an inner compulsion, tapping into an archetype of what a home is at a deeper level. His work was exhibited in *The Outside and the Inside*, at the Lightbox in Woking in 2018, an exhibition of works from the Outside In and Ingram collections. As realisations of impossible spaces, they share something with the work of Albert and also that of Friedensreich Hundertwasser[20] (1928–2000) in their organic structure. Matthew builds his houses carefully, line by line, creating drawings as sensitive and as beautiful as any contemporary artist. These buildings are definitely homes, seemingly safe spaces, but in some drawings, you can see figures and faces seemingly trapped in the structures: they seem happy, but subsumed by the building that surrounds them.

Messages

Restrained and contained within establishments, artists have sometimes resorted to developing secret codes and forms of communication that are often impenetrable to their captors and staff. It could be seen in the work of the woman known as Case 2 (see p.50) that she developed a technique partly to hide herself from the prying, analysing eyes of the psychiatrist. The work of Oskar Voll (1876–1935), an artist included in the

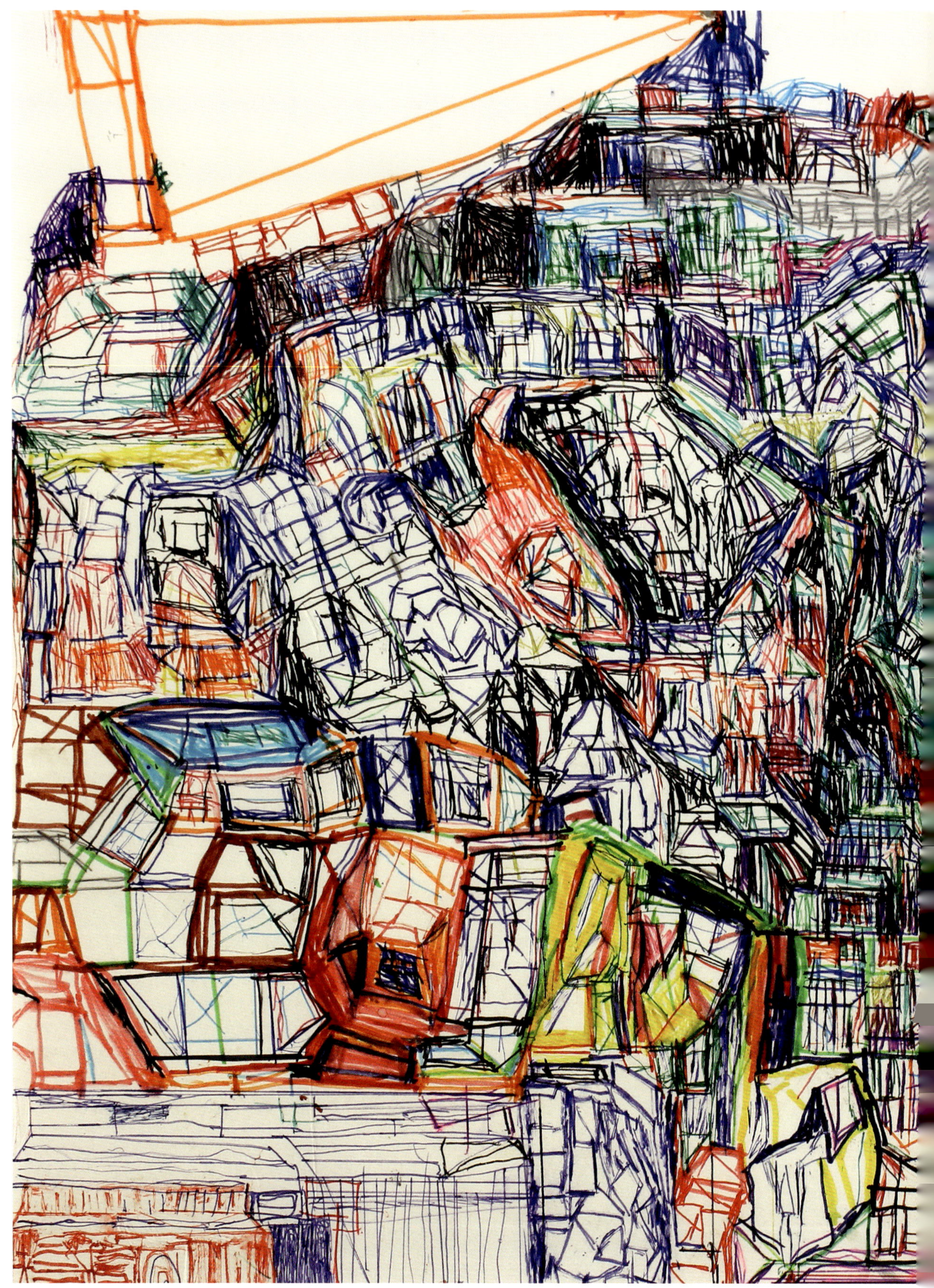

Matthew Beadon
Untitled
2016
Fineline pen on card
50 × 40 cm

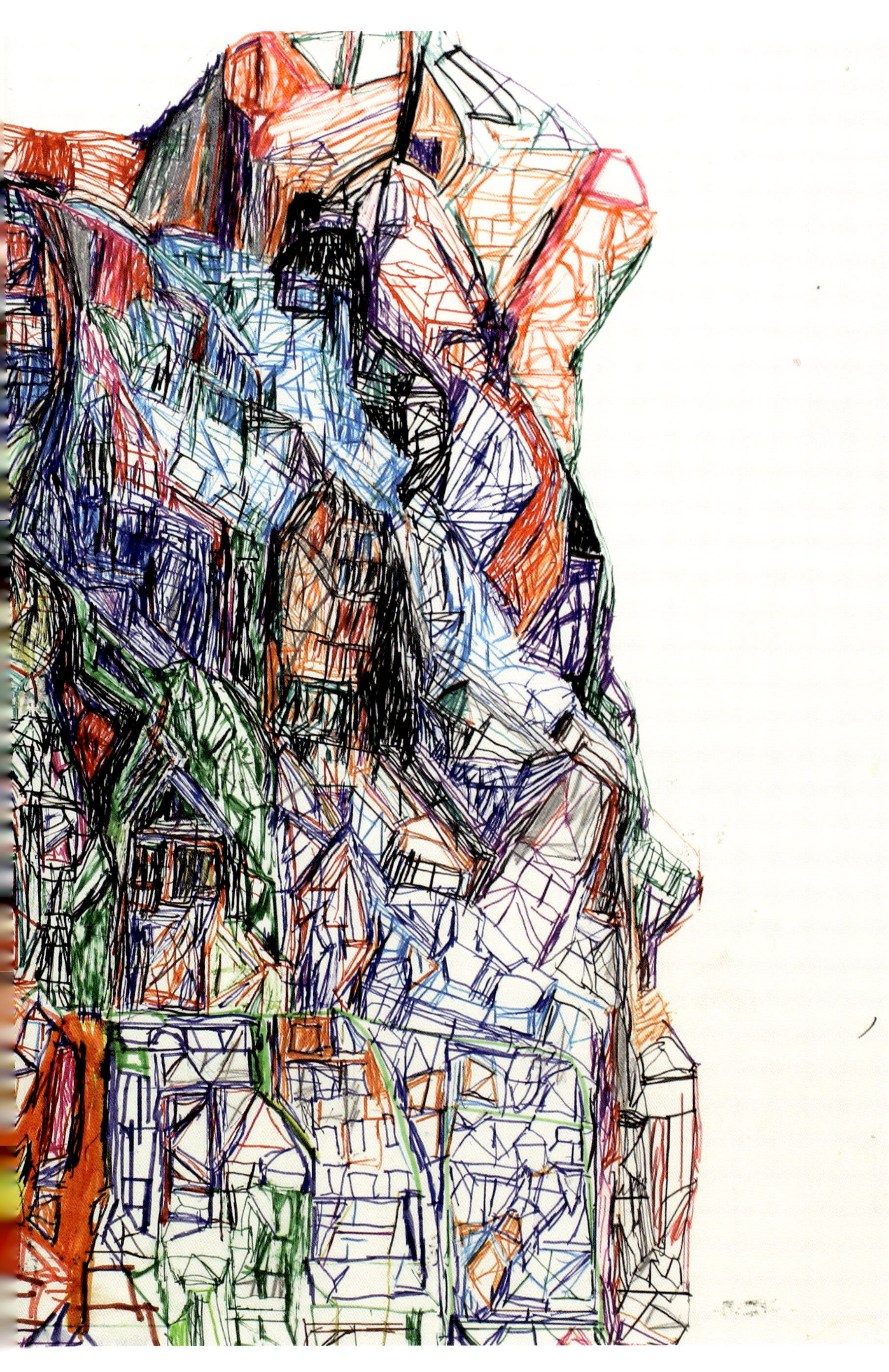

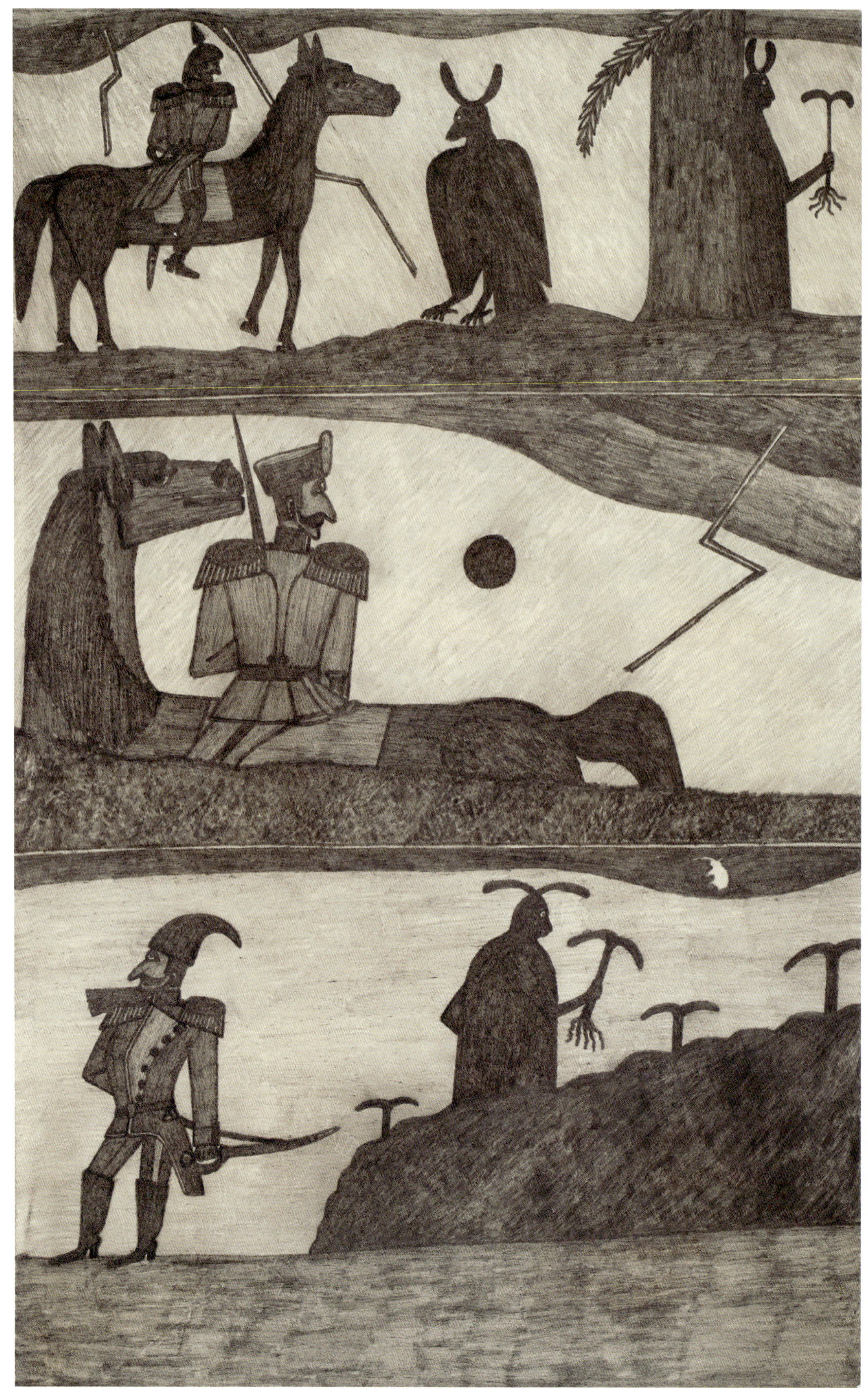

Oskar Voll
Untitled [Notebook 9], before 1921. Inv. No.360, fol.19
Pencil on paper
32.9 × 20.6 cm

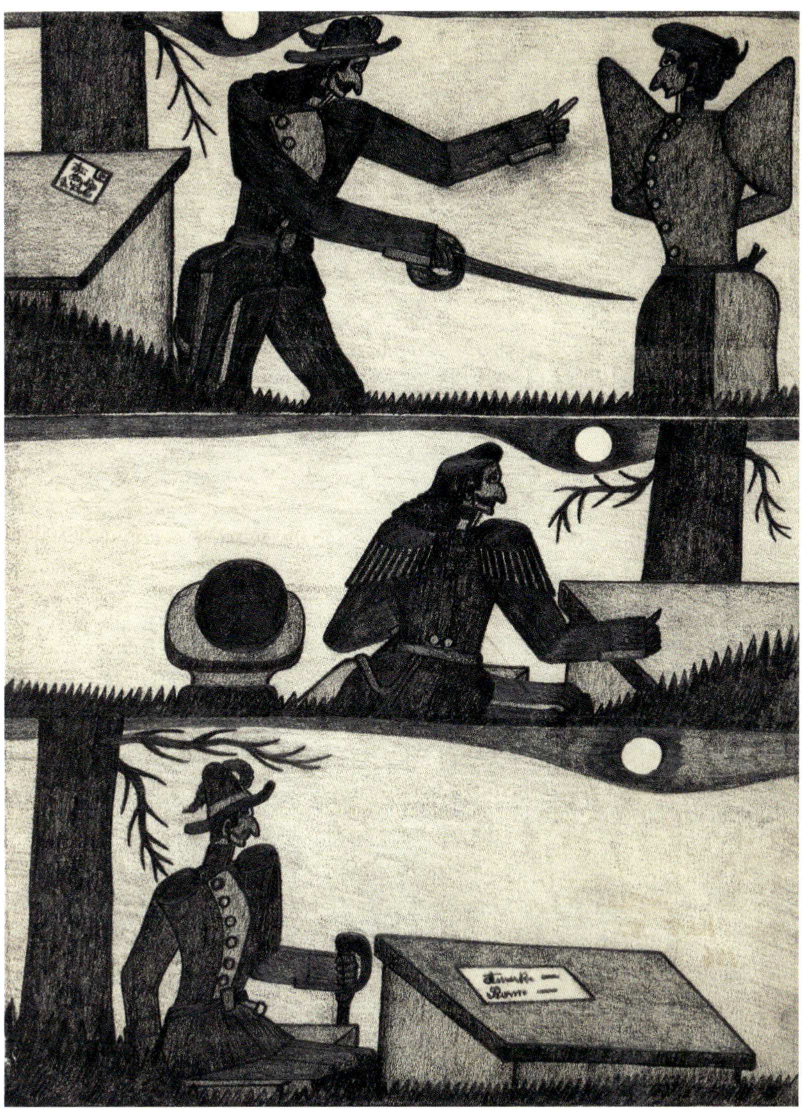

Oskar Voll
Drawing [Notebook 7], before 1921. Inv. No.344, fol.3
Pencil on drawing paper
27.9 x 21.5 cm

Prinzhorn Collection, is deeply mysterious and impregnable. His highly worked drawings often show 19th-century military figures in various postures, seemingly on some moonlit night-time military campaign. They are presented sequentially, hinting at a narrative, often two on a page and one drawing above the other. There is a stillness and otherworldliness about them, the drama having taken place offstage. As well as soldiers, he includes empty castles, indecipherable text and symbols in his work. Roger Cardinal[21] said of his work: 'We have, as it were, stumbled upon an art of enigma whose secretiveness frustrates normal interpretation. We find ourselves peering as through a glass darkly, absorbed in the trappings of secrecy, its elaborate indirection, the flourishing of the vanishing trick.'

Mary Frances Heaton (1801–1878) entered the West Riding Asylum in September 1837 aged 37. Her only crime was to publicly challenge the Rev. John Sharpe, vicar of St George's Minster, Doncaster, for not paying her for teaching his daughter. She called him 'a whited sepulchre, a thief, a villain, a liar and a hypocrite'.[22] Over her 40-plus years in the asylum, Mary made numerous samplers as part of an early attempt at art therapy,[23] one of the best a testimony of her treatment and perceived injustice at the hands of mostly male protagonists. Unlike Oskar Voll, she sought to communicate to the world outside the asylum, once escaping briefly and at another point sewing a message into the stays of a patient about to leave the asylum. Subverting the tradition of samplers and occupational activity, she sought to make them into a means of telling her story and righting an injustice. Their production was encouraged, and they must have been therapeutic in the making. Perhaps like Julius Klingebiel, she felt calmed by being creative and saw it as an opportunity to express and release the emotions she felt. The few pieces of her work that have survived stand, like a lot of the work in this book, as a lasting testimony, with the voice and the experience of the maker echoing through time: art made out of an inner necessity in a less than perfect world.

For artists like Oskar Voll, the need to keep their inner worlds and work secret made it difficult or impossible to decipher. It is as if they were creating a protective barrier preventing unwanted intrusion or analysis. The secrets their

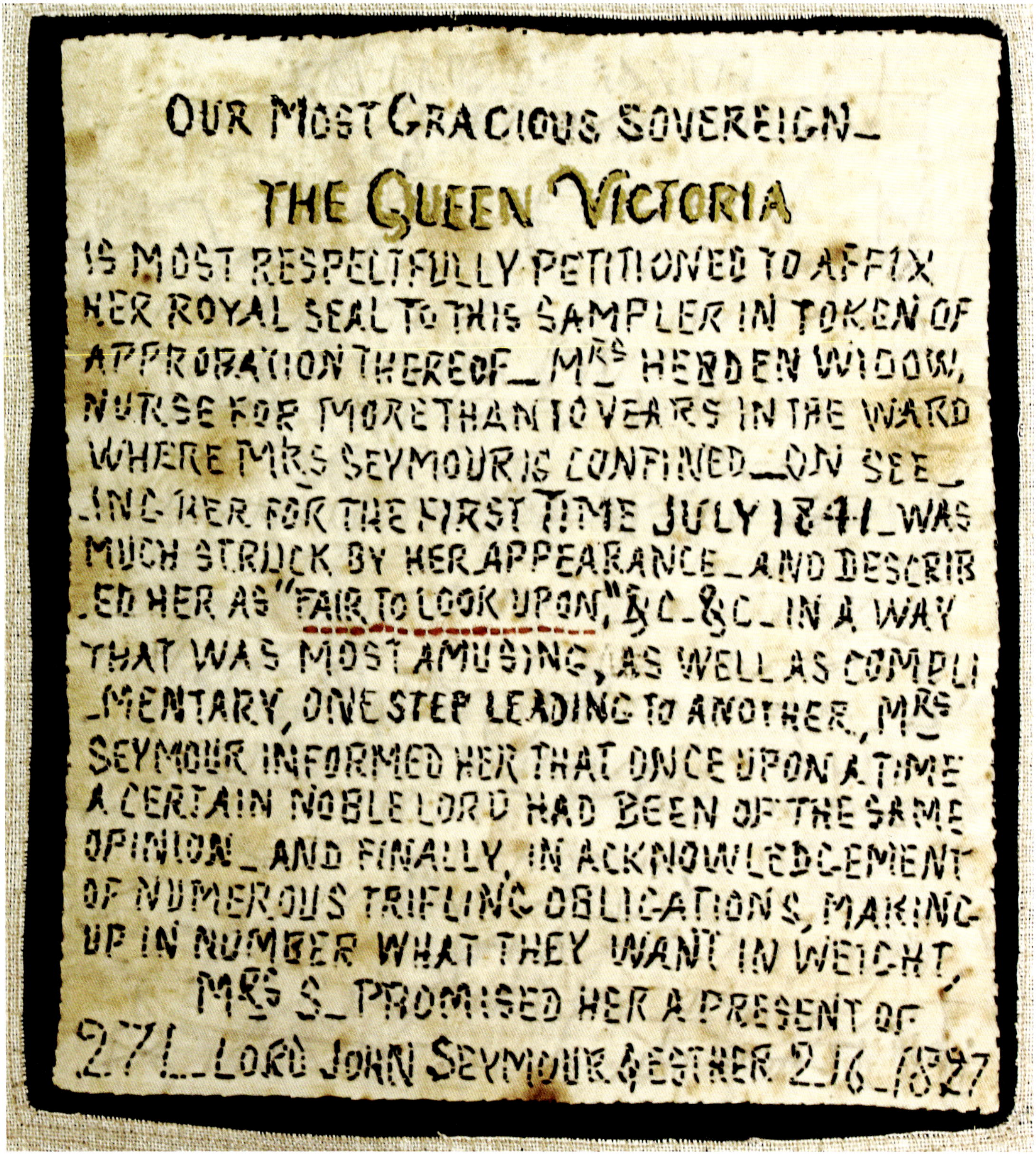

OUR MOST GRACIOUS SOVEREIGN_
THE QUEEN VICTORIA
IS MOST RESPELTFULLY PETITIONED TO AFFIX
HER ROYAL SEAL TO THIS SAMPLER IN TOKEN OF
APPROBATION THEREOF_ MRS HEBDEN WIDOW,
NURSE FOR MORETHAN 10 YEARS IN THE WARD
WHERE MRS SEYMOUR IS CONFINED_ON SEE_
_ING HER FOR THE FIRST TIME JULY 1841_WAS
MUCH STRUCK BY HER APPEARANCE_AND DESCRIB
ED HER AS "FAIR TO LOOK UPON," &C&C_IN A WAY
THAT WAS MOST AMUSING, AS WELL AS COMPLI
_MENTARY, ONE STEP LEADING TO ANOTHER, MRS
SEYMOUR INFORMED HER THAT ONCE UPON A TIME
A CERTAIN NOBLE LORD HAD BEEN OF THE SAME
OPINION_AND FINALLY, IN ACKNOWLEDGEMENT
OF NUMEROUS TRIFLING OBLIGATIONS, MAKING
UP IN NUMBER WHAT THEY WANT IN WEIGHT,
MRS S_PROMISED HER A PRESENT OF
27L_LORD JOHN SEYMOUR & ESTHER 2.16_1827

Mary Frances Heaton
Untitled (Queen Victoria)
1827
Hand stitch on cloth
21 × 24.4 cm

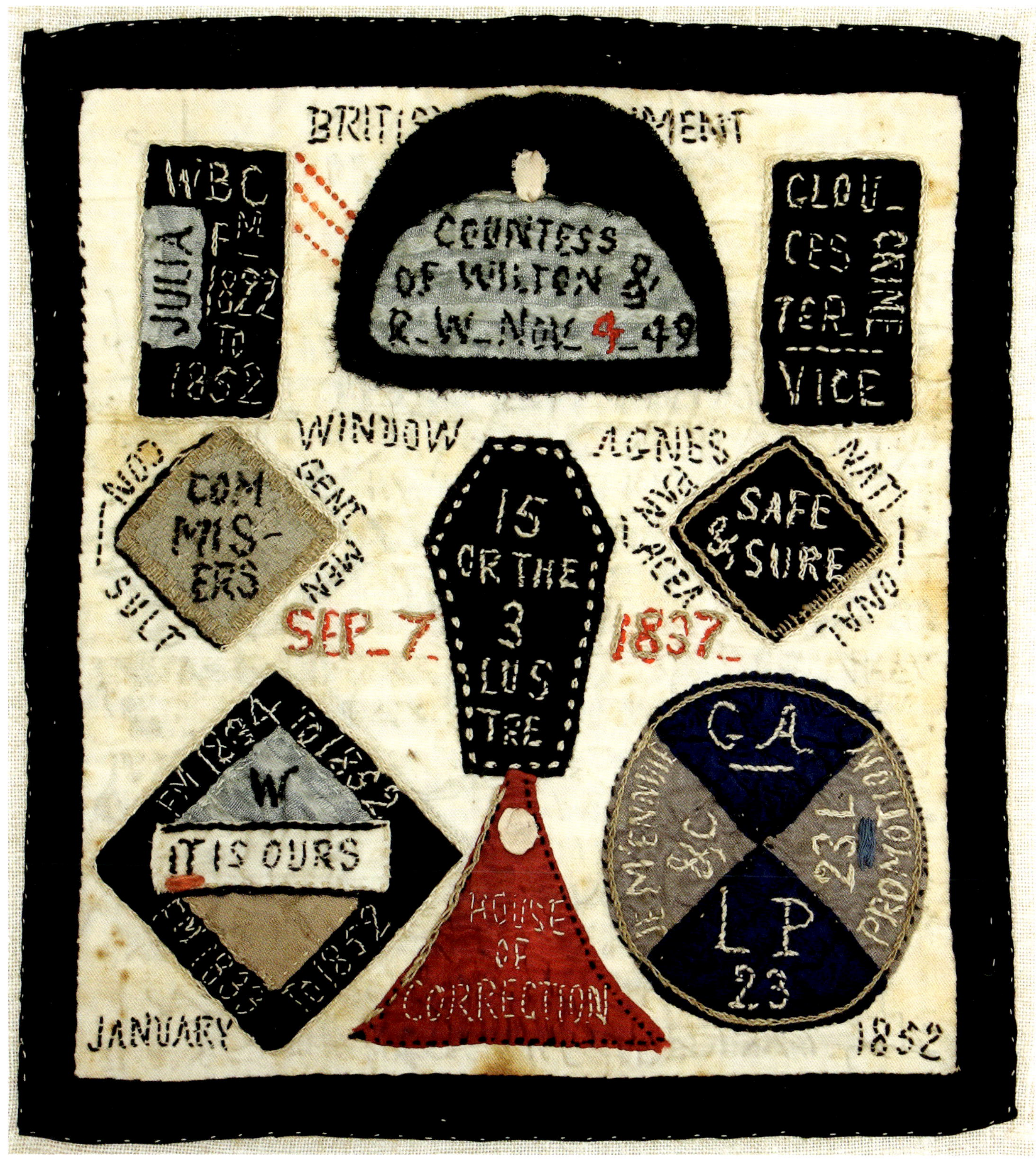

Mary Frances Heaton
Untitled (Sampler)
1852
Hand stitch on cloth
22 × 24.4 cm

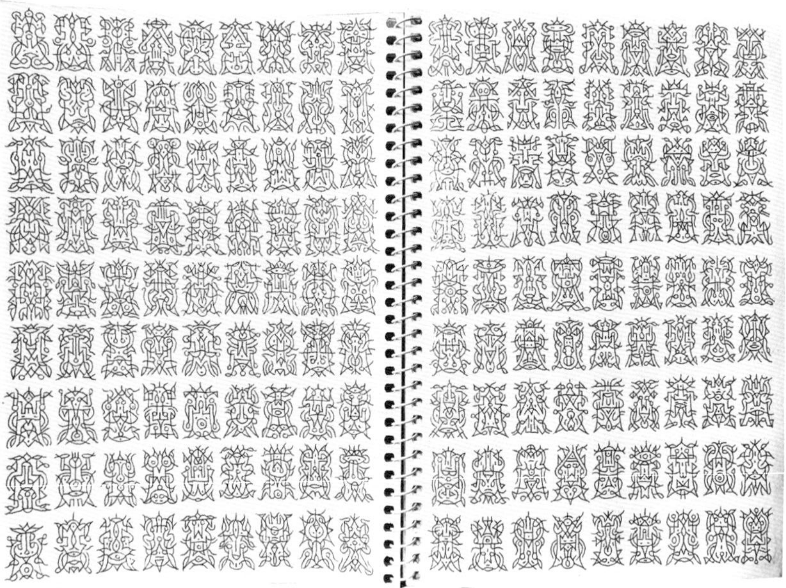

work holds remain hidden, such as with the Voynich manuscript,[24] created during the Renaissance, whose purpose and content remain a mystery to this day. Holding and giving power, sometimes the purpose of these works is to influence lives and the wider world by the seemingly magical properties the artist has invested in them, as is the case with Neal Pearce (b.1967).

Neal exhibited *The Infinite Codex, Book 12* in the 2009 Outside In exhibition at Pallant House Gallery. He has embarked on an ambitious lifetime project titled 'The Infinite Codex or Tera Computartum'. The codex consists of page after page of carefully hand-drawn glyphs, each one different, in a series of A5 sketchbooks. So far he has completed 16 books of a planned series of 115 volumes. Once completed, the codex will comprise 531,441 glyphs. He describes the Codex as:

> An essay and lesson in the beauty and underexplored potential of all that's unfixed/flexible: all that's free-flowing and evolving; that's shifting, teeming and dividing. All that's not held back or contained by all our 'anchoring', humankind's obsession and unhealthy reliance on set ideas, fixed thinking, religious and political ideologies, tramline focus and strategies, not to mention hard-and-fast rules. Because all of these not only hinder our exploration and future development, they move in and around us like strangling vines and are the root of all internal and external conflict.

Neal Pearce
The Infinite Codex
1996 – ongoing
Pen on paper
(A5 Sketch Book)
21 × 29.7 cm

Martin Phillimore
Untitled
2009
Pencil on paper
15 × 19 cm

Channelling his unconscious self through his language of glyphs, he believes that the completion of the 'Infinite Codex' will reveal a hidden message of universal significance. He has spoken of using a fingerprint scanner to scan all the glyphs to find its hidden message: 'Inspired by the Tao-te-Ching '"The Infinite Codex" sets out to prove that through defocus – concentrating on nothing – something under our noses and yet elusive is revealed.'

Obsession

An obsessive need to create can be found in many artists' lives and works, a compulsion to create, which can be fleeting or last a lifetime. Sometimes this can be seen in the works themselves, in obsessive mark making or the dramatic use of scale, such as in the works of Richard Dadd and Nick Blinko. There are other artists whose lifestyle or mental health has led them to evolve an ongoing and singular approach to their art making – Martin Phillimore (1960–2017), David Puttick (b.1963) and Friedrich Nagler (1920–2009) being prime examples. But when does obsession become a problem? We value the obsessive, as can be seen by the fetishisation of Vincent van Gogh (1853–90), whose life and work became universally known, and Frida Kahlo (1907–1954), a disabled artist. Tokens and talismans of their work adorn jewellery and countless objects. They are remindful of the tokens collected by religious pilgrims when visiting the shrine of a venerated saint. But bought for what purpose? Is it to heal or to show an affinity with the artist, or to signal to others one's values and good taste in art? At some level their work has become so far removed from its creation that they have become a glyph or a cypher of the original. The concept of the 'mad genius' does not truly exist. It is in moments of lucidity that most art is created. The idea of a separate race of artist-genius-obsessives does nothing but perpetuate this myth and the stigma attached to madness. In fact, Van Gogh only worked between his bouts of illness and Nick Blinko similarly only worked when not medicated.

Martin Phillimore created highly detailed drawings, organic and evolving, as if they have a life of their own, growing like a bacterium on a Petri dish. His skill was to use a pencil in such a way that it never breaks the surface nor is erased.

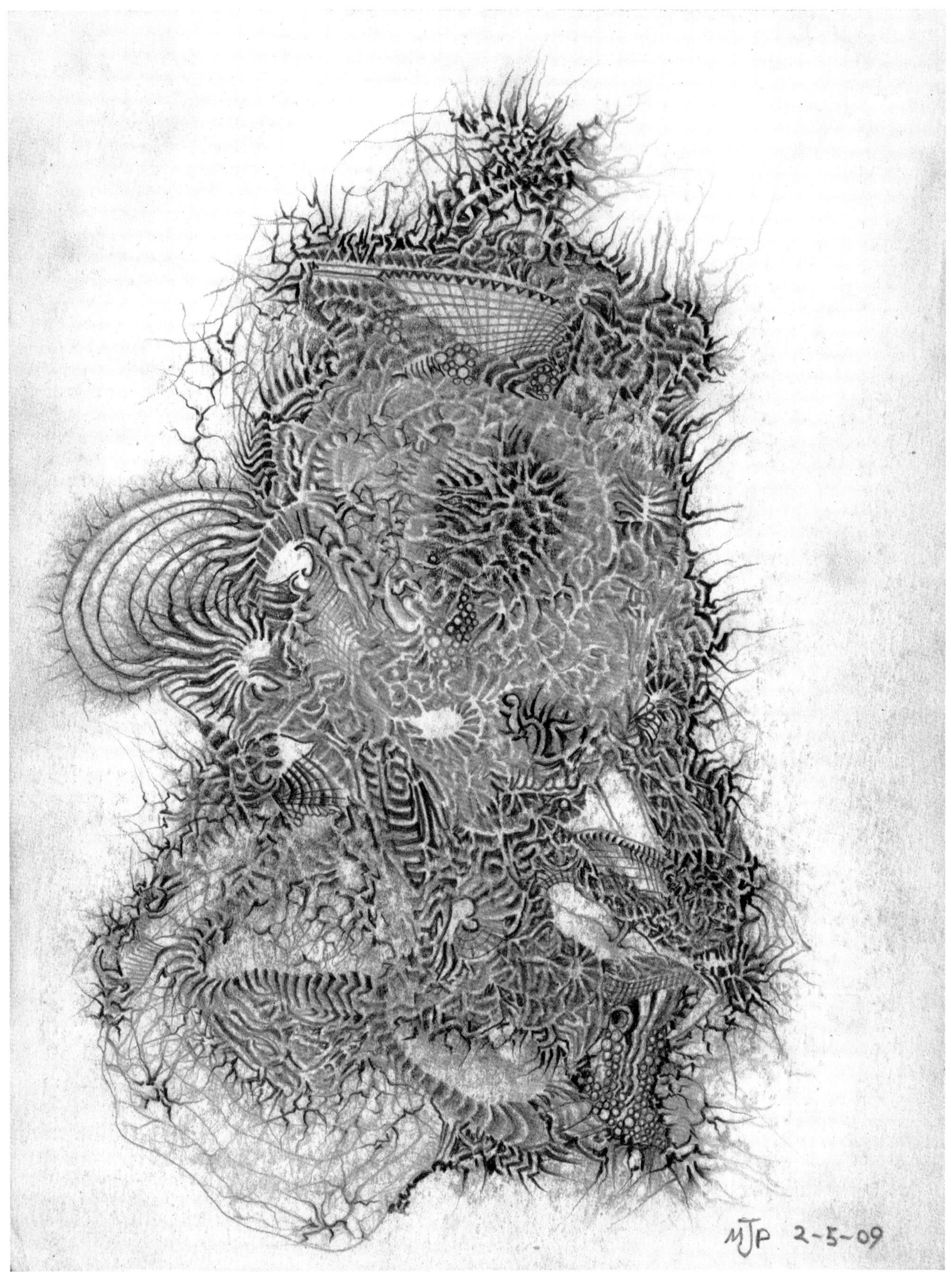

Introspection

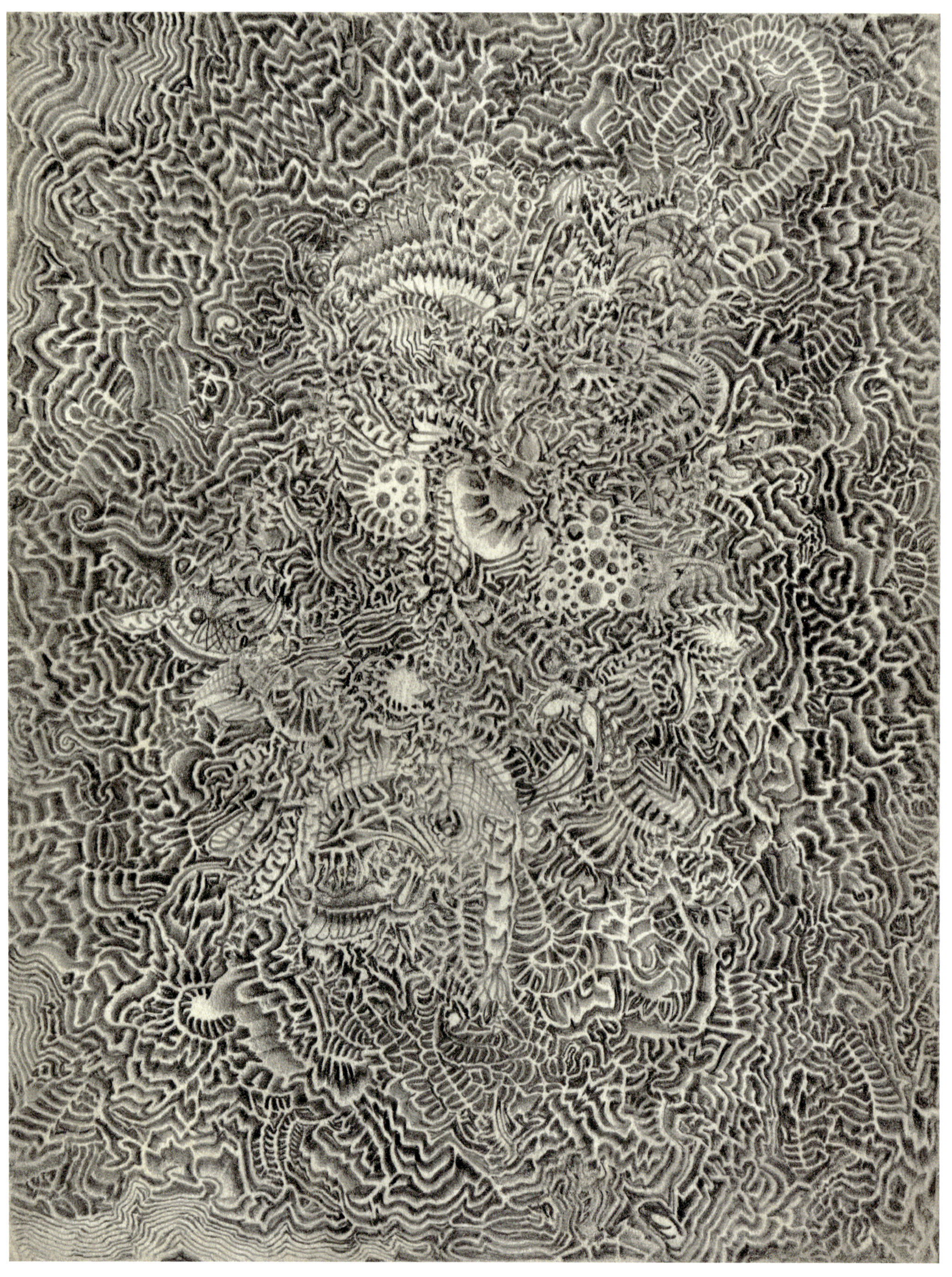

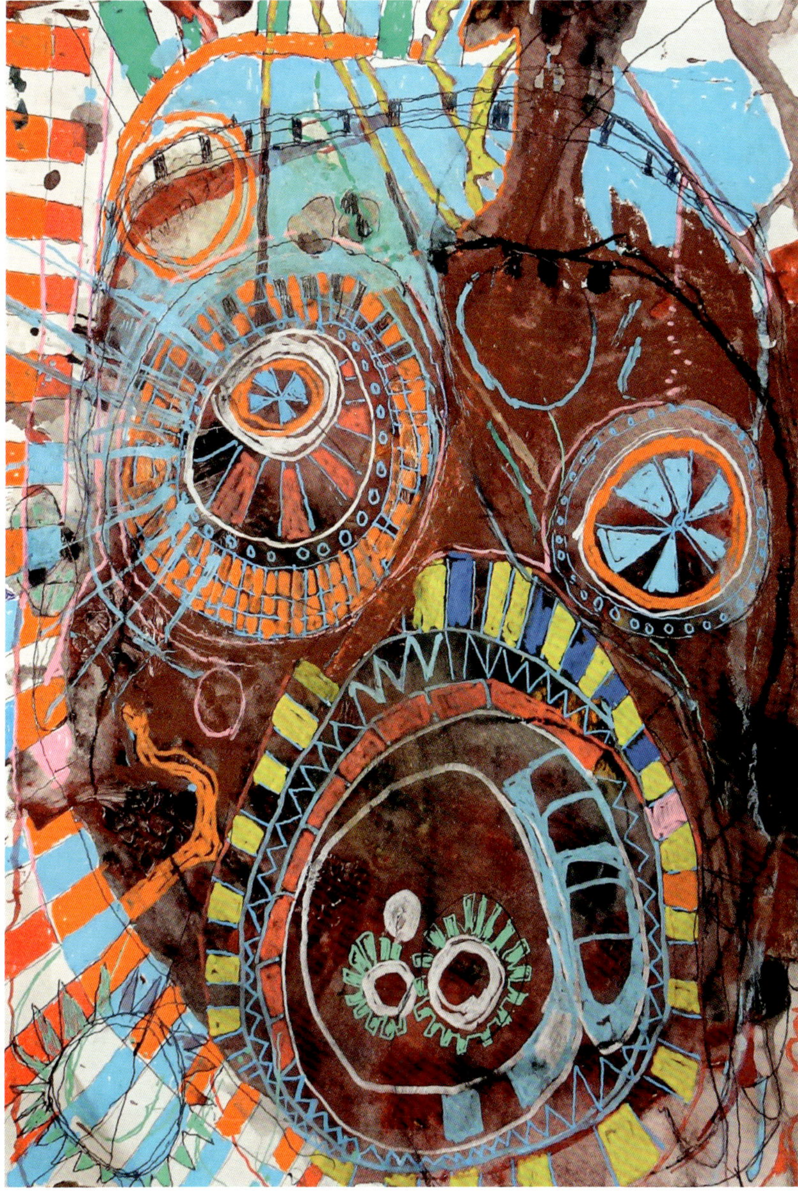

Martin Phillimore
Untitled
date unknown
Pencil on paper
16 × 19 cm

David Puttick
Untitled
2022
Mixed media
40 × 30 cm

There is something similar to the drawings of Oskar Voll in how the ubiquitous pencil becomes a distinctive and powerful medium in the hands of these artists. Connecting with the unconscious, the drawings sometimes suggest animals or people, but never completely reveal themselves. The use of the undrawn negative space is striking in his perfectly poised compositions, balancing the negative and positive. Some of his works were made on Edwardian and Victorian calling cards that his wife acquired through her work as a cleaner. These, and others using recycled paper, have an additional charge, as if they have arrived from another age. Martin's work is also informed by his experiences with hallucinogenic drugs and magic mushrooms. In his words:

> My interest in art was always there as a young child. When I was in my early twenties, I became involved with illicit substances, mainly hallucinogenic, including magic mushrooms. I found myself expressing what was going on in my mind by doing many pieces of art one after another. I found the intensity of what I was producing a reflection of my subconscious and also what I was feeling from the heart.

There is something similarly organic and experimental in the obsessive work of David Puttick. The content, colours and composition arrive during the process of their making, an introspective process, tapping into his subconscious through their creation. What is remarkable is the consistency and quality that he creates in his work. David said about his process of making: 'The monotypes are made by using a process that just makes a mess, and the paint is applied by hand and then water and then laying paper on top to repeat an image then more water, using biro felt-tips pastels on top when it has dried out'.[25]

It is powerful work, darkly expressive. He is a magnificent colourist, using a fantastic range of marks, which are layered and complex. He describes the initial motivation for his work: 'when I started to locate faces in marks in the floor and started to make drawings which I called "ghosts picked up from the floor"'. His work warrants close scrutiny, as its possible interpretations emerge over time. David has found his art to be a solace during the challenges he has had to face in life: 'My paintings are something I can depend upon; they have always helped me through'.

The artist Jonathan Pettitt's (b.1952) artistic practice is different to the introspective intuition of David Puttick and Martin Phillimore, but it is no less an internal process. His work arrives from a belief in spirits and mediums, and it is their guidance that leads to the startling, colourful visions he creates. When he is well, he meditates in the early hours of the morning, around 3am, when the world is calm and everyone is sleeping. He sits with a blank canvas in front of him, says a prayer for guidance and with his brush in hand completes his painting in one sitting. Jonathan regularly consults mediums

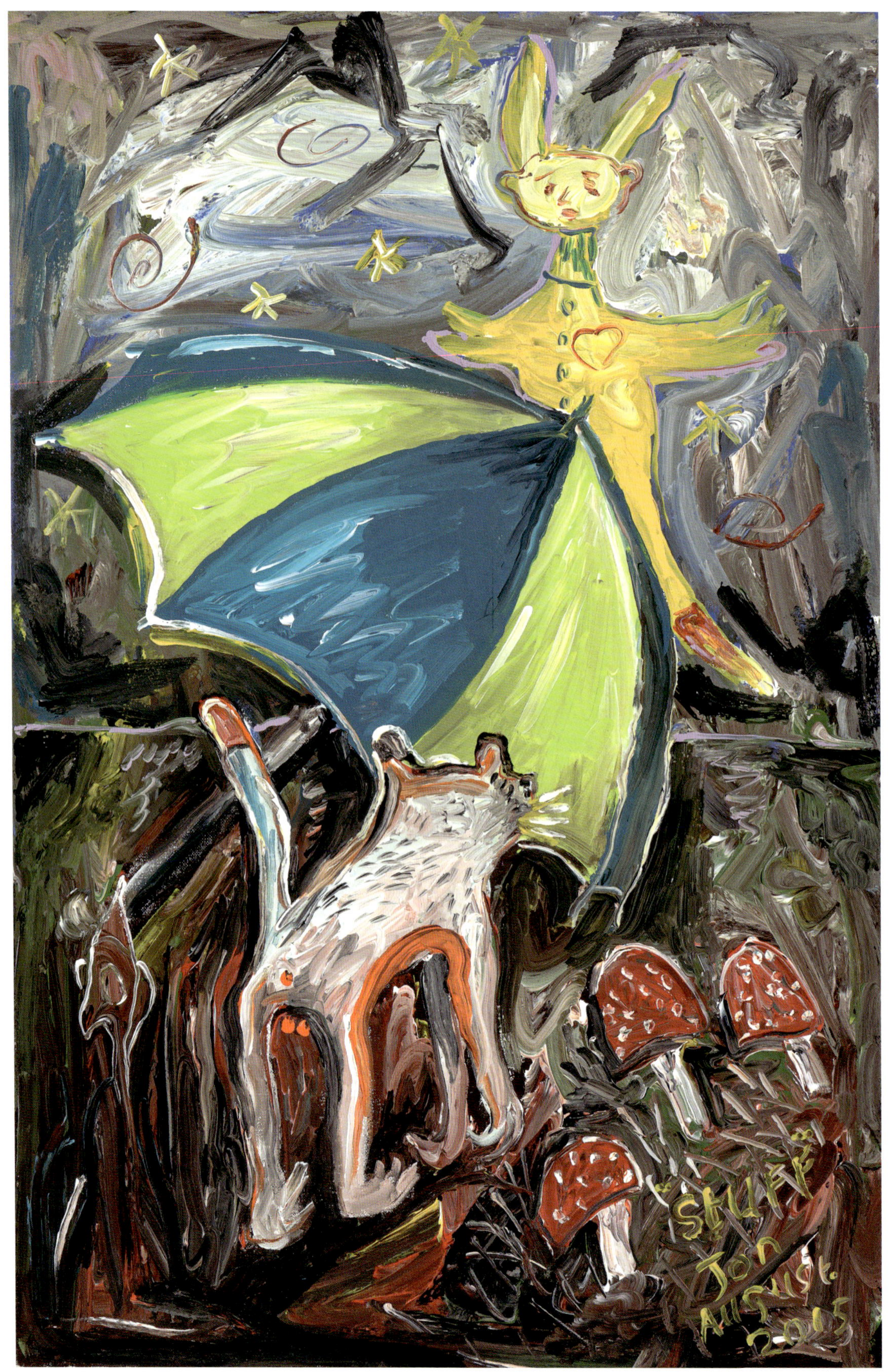

Jonathan Kenneth William Pettitt
Stuff
date unknown
Oil paint on canvas
50 × 70 cm

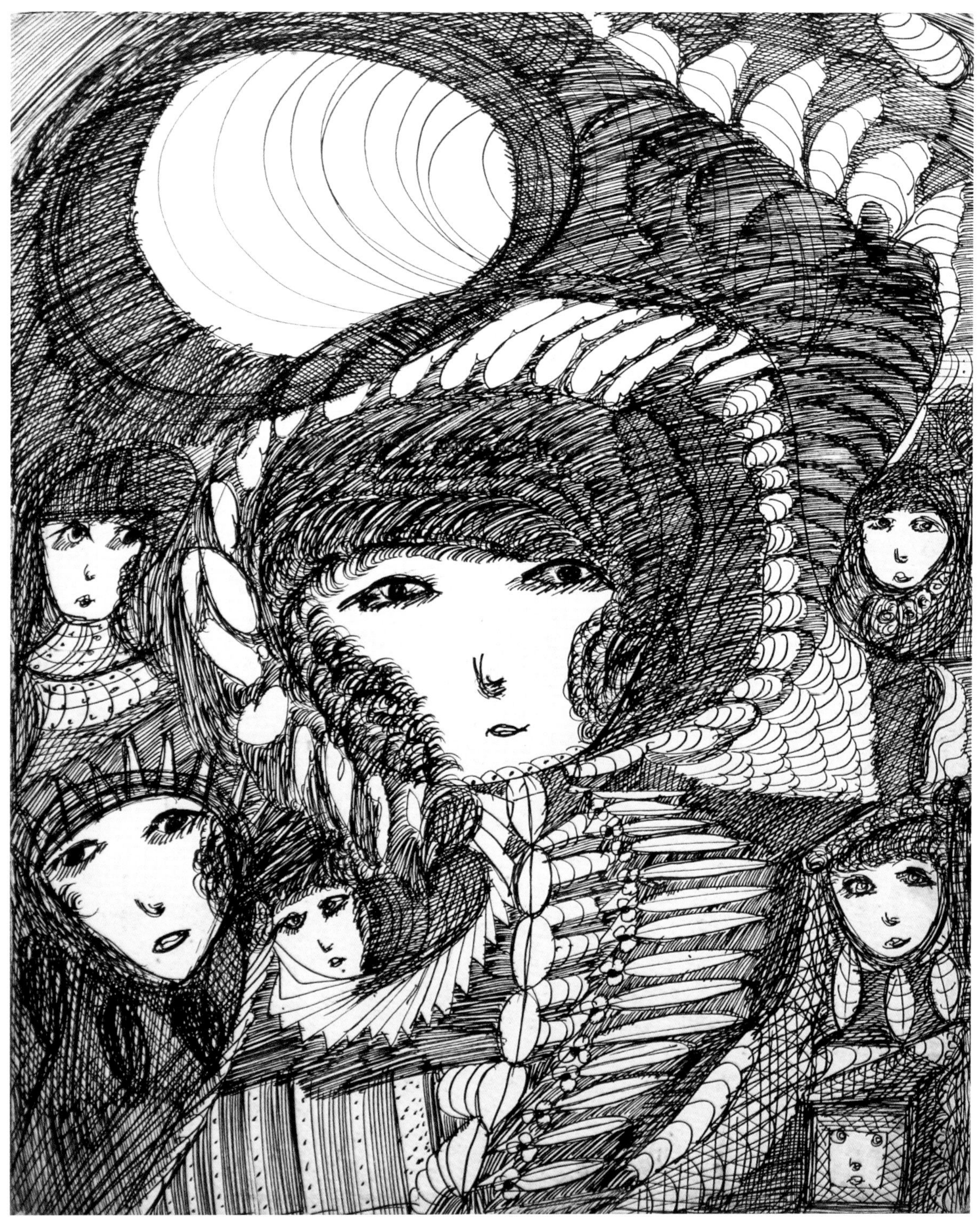

Madge Gill
Untitled
date unknown
Ink on paper
25 × 31 cm

and attends the Corinthian Church & Healing Association in his local town, preferring to be guided by them rather than the world of psychiatry and psychiatrists.

As with the British artist Madge Gill (1882–1961), Jonathan Pettitt's work connects with the world of spiritualism and mediums, but unlike Madge Gill, who was guided by a spirit she called Myrninerest', he is guided through a medium who connects him with the 'Great Unseen'. There is something of William Blake (1757–1827) in his work – the ability to see spirits and fairies in the everyday, a parallel world in which there are other forces at play.

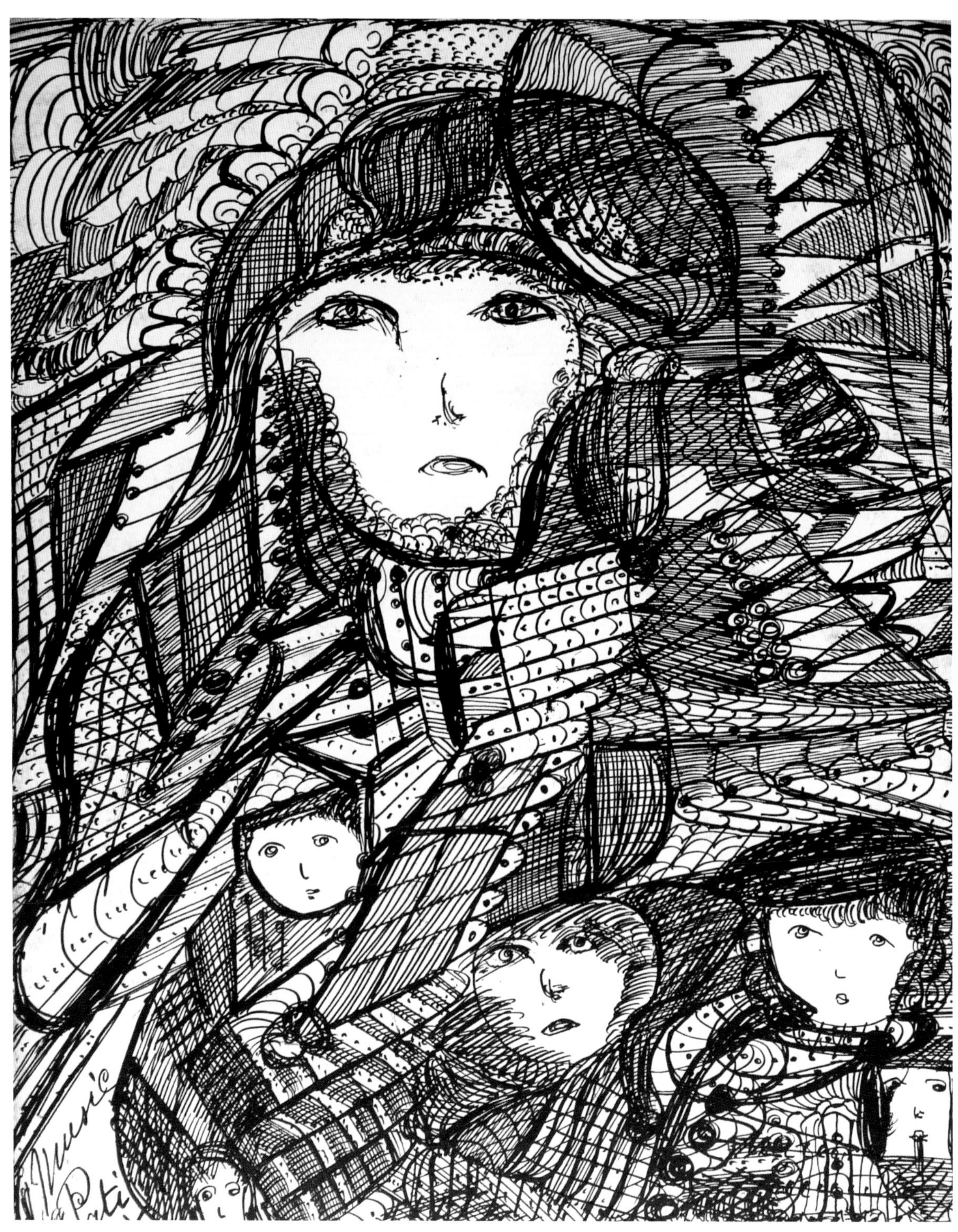

Madge Gill
Untitled
date unknown
Ink on paper
25 × 31 cm

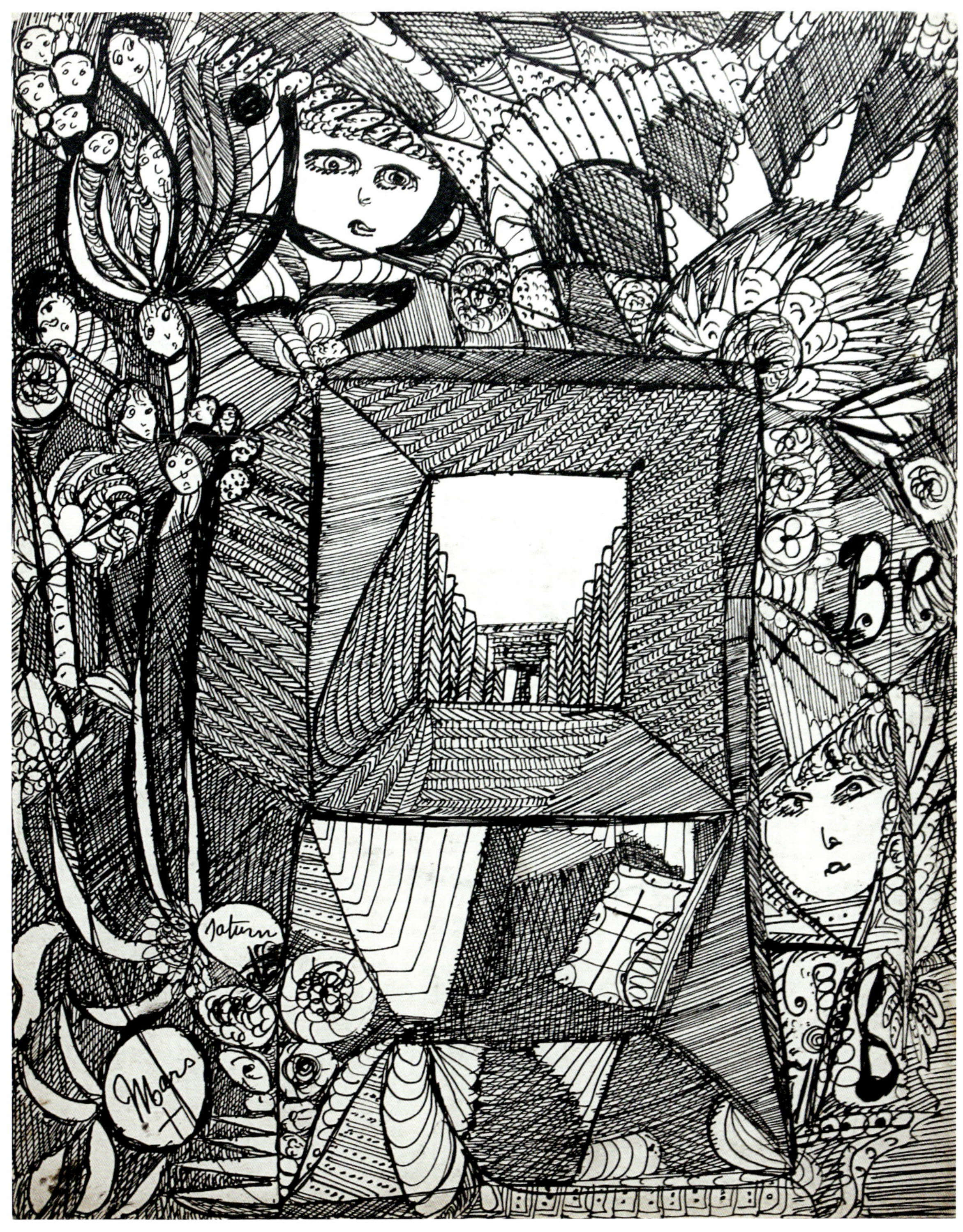

Madge Gill
Untitled
date unknown
Ink on paper
25 × 31 cm

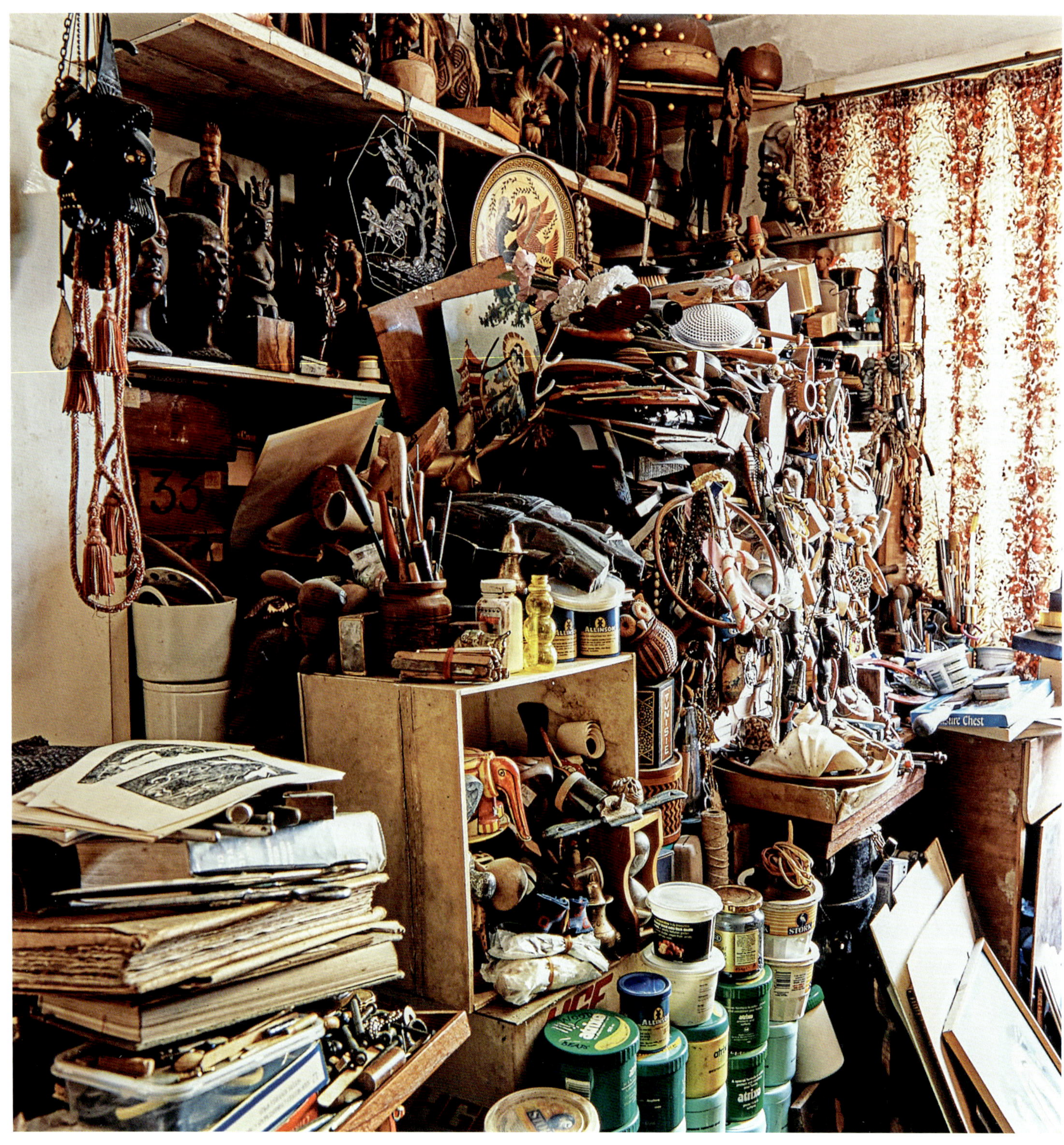

Friedrich Nagler
Artist's home

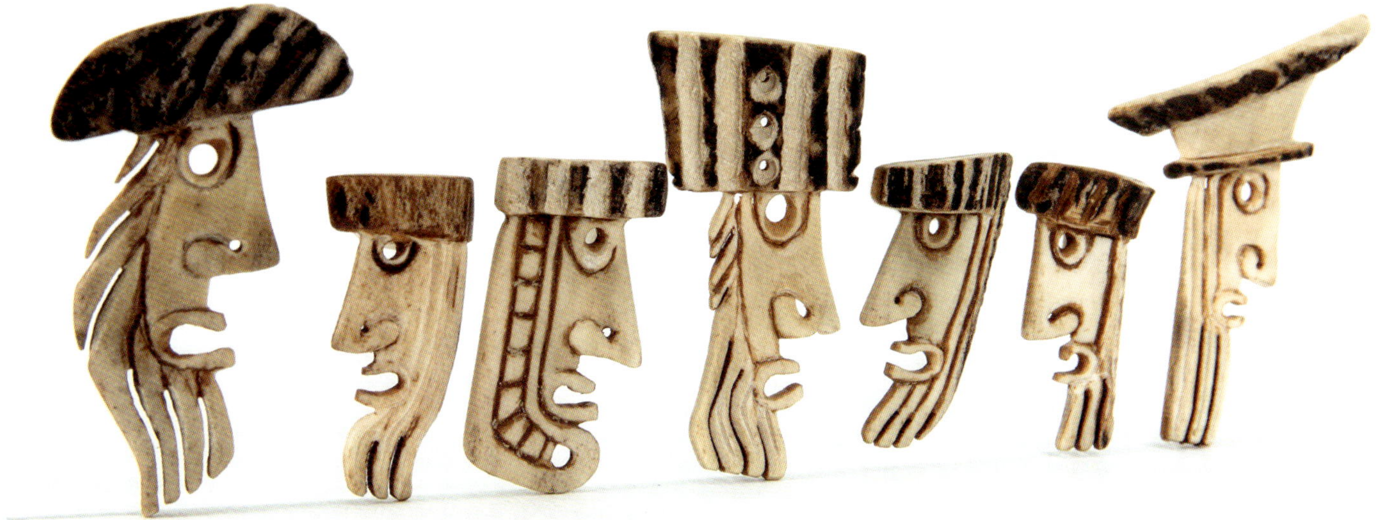

Friedrich Nagler
Untitled
mid to late 1970s / early 1980s
Bone
5 × 4 cm average

An obsessive approach to creating can take other directions, such as the use of unusual materials and scale of production, as can be seen in the work of Friedrich Nagler and Ian Sherman (b.1961). Their preoccupation with experimentation, and the ability to adapt and use a vast range of materials, marks them out as highly original creators.

Friedrich was an émigré artist born in Vienna. He escaped Nazi occupation in 1939 aged 19 and eventually settled in Petersfield, Hampshire. He always considered himself an artist and dedicated his life to producing a prodigious artistic output, working with a very wide variety of materials. He also kept a record of his thoughts in the form of 42 books of poetry. He refused to either sign, sell or exhibit his work during his lifetime.

Along with all the materials he collected, Friedrich produced so much art that it occupied most of the house he shared with his wife and two sons. He never stopped making. He worked late into the night, listening to classical music, sleeping on the kitchen floor and then getting up to go to work. On one occasion, when his wife was on holiday, he spent all the money she had left him for food on some old piano keys so that he could repurpose them into his art.

Friedrich's work alludes to a dark and tragic subtext: as a young Zionist in Vienna, he experienced first-hand the rise of fascism and there is a sense that he is repopulating a lost history and heritage in his art. The need to keep his work together and for it to not be dispersed; the creation of hundreds of boxed tribes and families; and the diversity of materials and faces all speak of the motivation for Friedrich's art, the Holocaust. Whether or not he was conscious of these parallels or of its psychological benefit, he found his 'art therapy' and through it he was able to express and hopefully integrate some of the emotions he carried.

As Charlotte Oliver said in her article on Friedrich:

> Many faces evoke a strong Jewish influence, especially those that depict bearded men with peyot and shtreimels. One only has to learn of Nagler's history – he narrowly avoided Nazi capture and he lost many of his loved ones in concentration camps – to surmise that, on some level, he was obsessively replacing the millions killed during the Holocaust.[26]

Ian Sherman has been making assemblages since 1991 and has gone on to create multiple mysterious and complex structures, all still in his possession. Similarly to Friedrich, Ian enjoys using

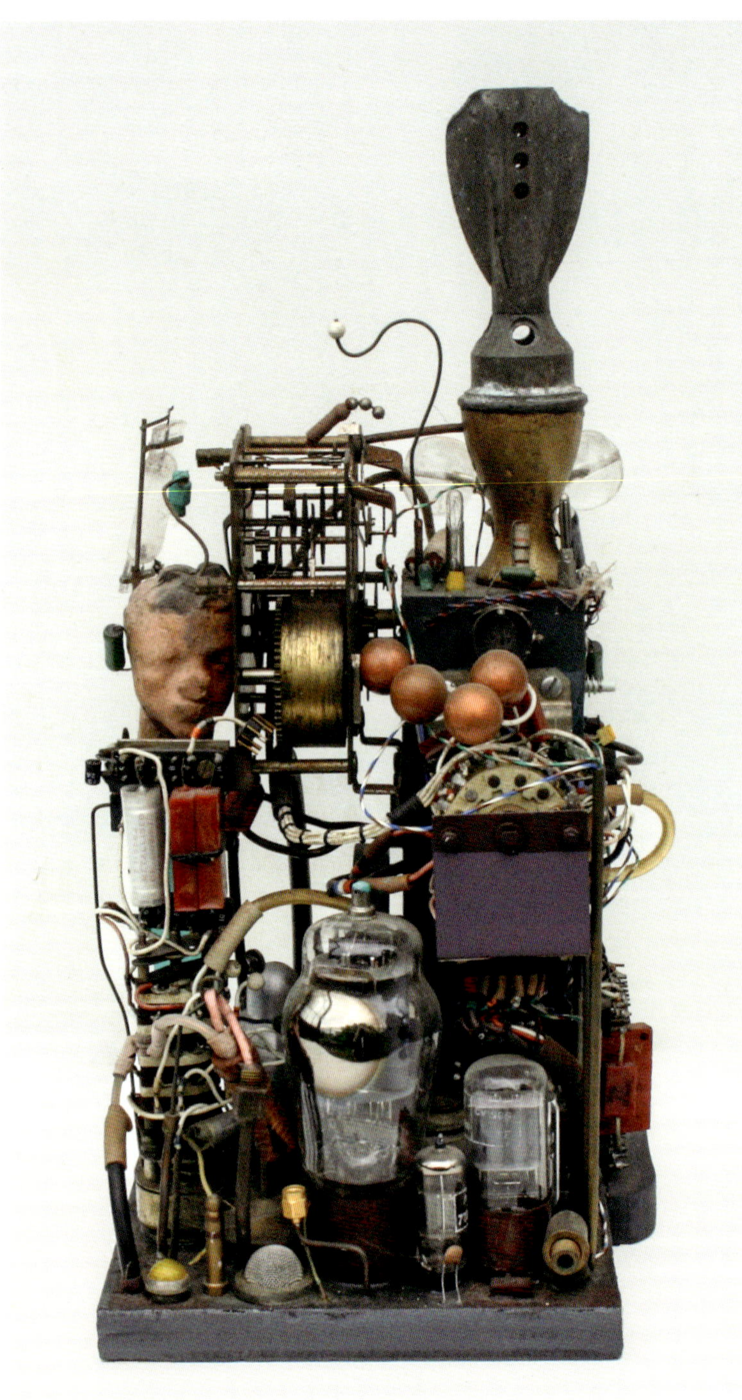

Ian Sherman
Despotic Tribulator
1999
Assemblage
40 × 18 × 18 cm

Ian Sherman
Monument to Time
1997
Assemblage
52 × 43 × 32 cm

and experimenting with an array of materials and making multiple related objects. 'In 1991 I threw some molten wax into cold water. The resulting solid was complicated and fragile, which I later covered in clear resin. Soon found objects were being included in assemblages on wooden bases,' says Ian. He had the idea of creating 'a large room filled with eerie objects that tended to evoke silence', describing how a found object is 'usually a "worthless fragment" which can be "ennobled" by the assemblage'. Each of the assemblages holds a special meaning and their titles, such as *Apparatus for Perpetual Meditation*, are often philosophical, surreal and humorous.

The accrual of objects and materials allows him to channel the unconscious in his work, as if fishing in the dark, not knowing what he will catch or its initial purpose. The materials Ian uses to build his monuments include melted aluminium, wood, papier mâché, plastics, resins, glass, glues and plaster. Together his works are a remarkable achievement, each worthy of contemplation, and a time will come when they will be gathered in a room to disturb audiences and leave them quietly contemplating their meaning.

As the art shown in this chapter makes clear, creativity can be used to connect with and manifest the unconscious. These artists demonstrate that making and creating is inherently therapeutic. While making art we operate differently: with our verbal and dominating ego put to one side, we can act instinctively, tapping the unconscious. Art therapy and art as a means to gain insight and understanding could be seen as one and the same. But often the work produced by artists whose work manifests their inner worlds, sometimes due to their mental health, or whose work is labelled as 'therapy', is not given the same standing as more conventionally produced art. There is a lot to learn from this work, with its link to our inner worlds. When it is stumbled upon by the art world, such as with the Surrealists, it has validated their ideas and led them to create in ways they might not have had the courage to do otherwise. This has in turn influenced and inspired artists, encouraged exploration and continued art's ongoing embrace of new ideas and movements. In the words of Bruno Bettelheim: 'Relying once more on the insights of psychoanalysis, we may say that the unconscious is the source of art, the mainspring from which it originates'.[27]

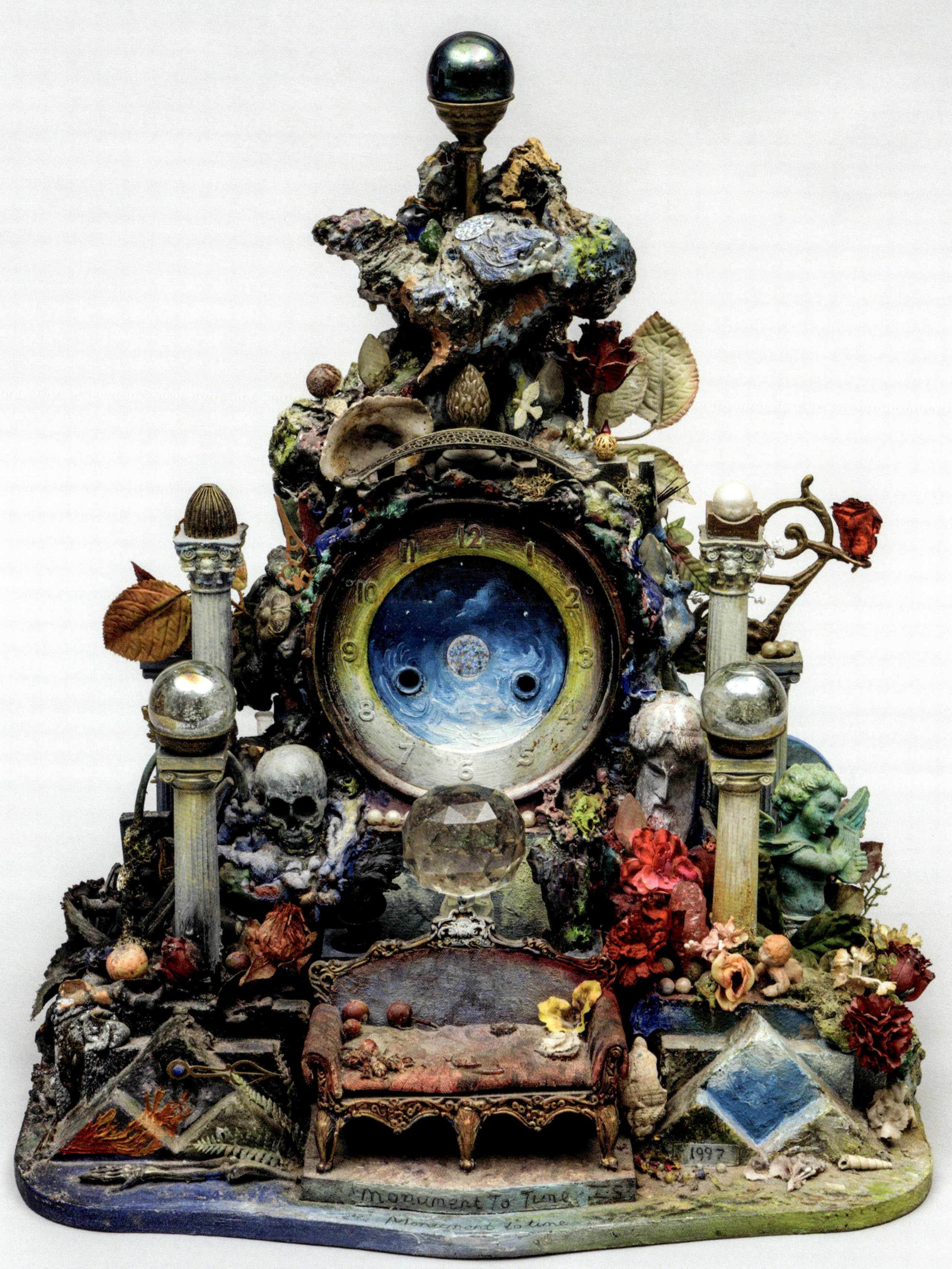
Monument To Time
Monument to time
1997

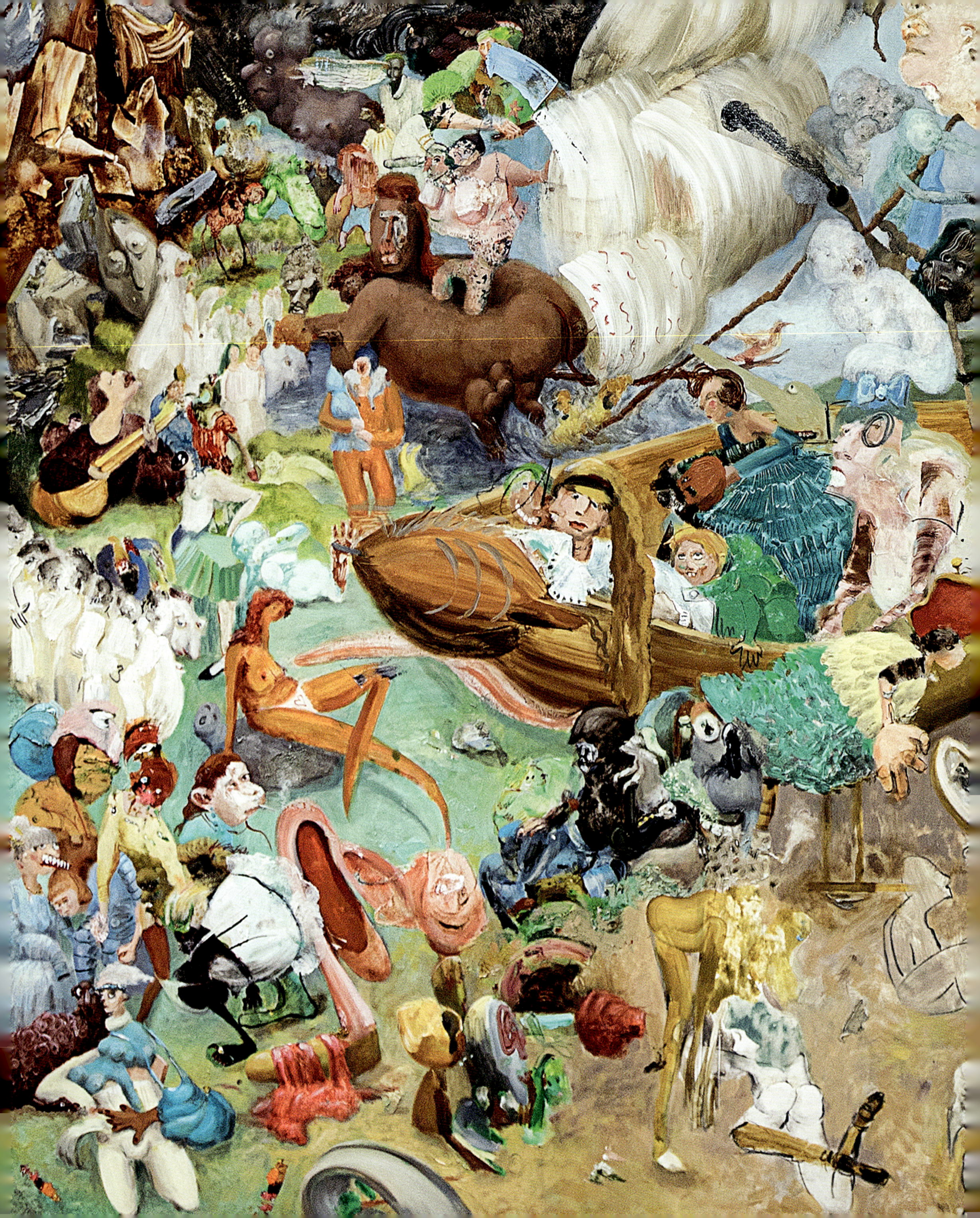

Chapter Three

Insight

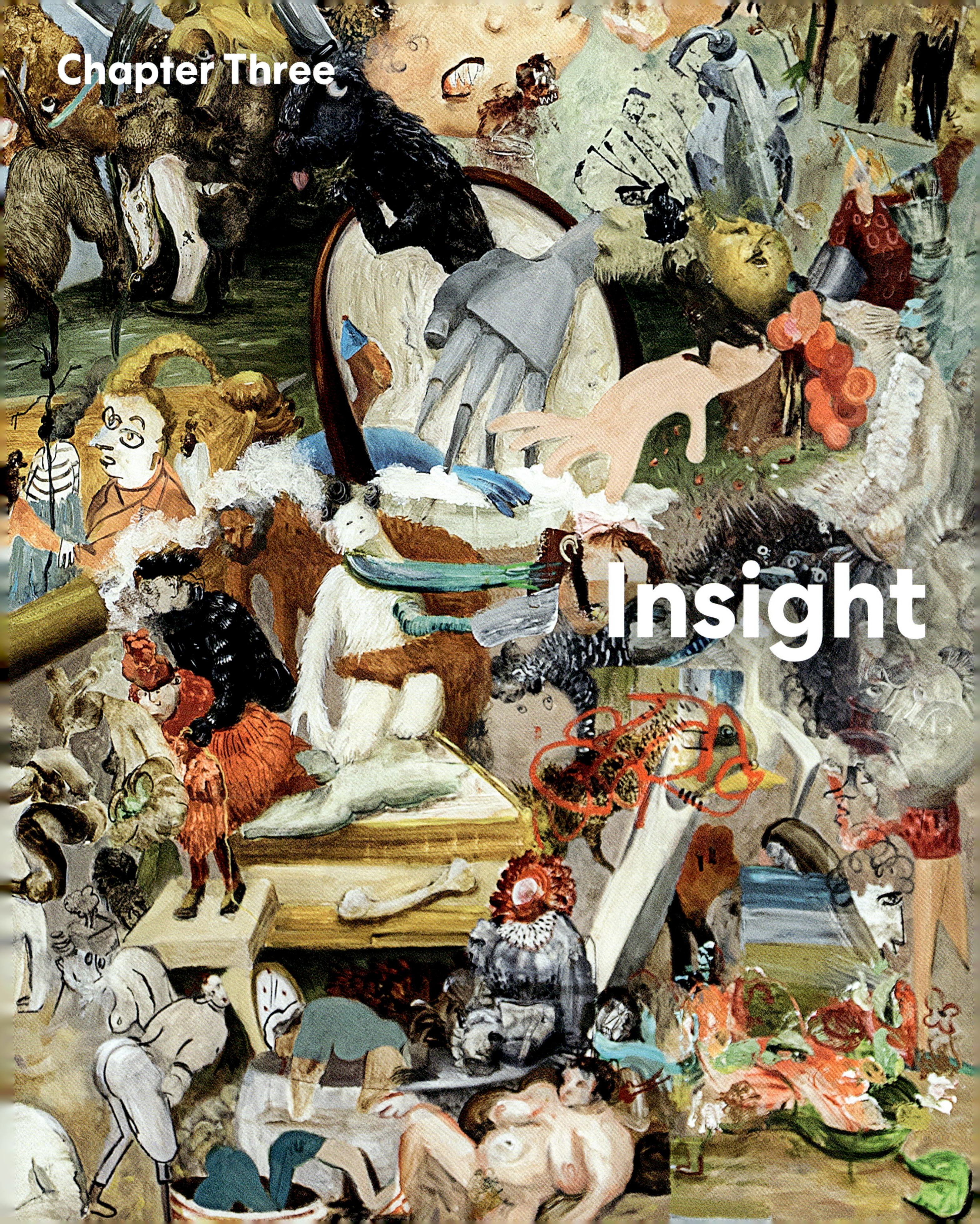

Life holds many challenges, some too difficult to face or even understand, but we can carry our creativity into these dark places as a means of recording our experiences, sharing our story and healing our psyche in the process. These testimonies can be stark reminders of humankind's cruelty as in the work of Wilhelm Werner (1898–1940) and his portrayal of his forcible sterilisation during the Nazi regime and eventual euthanasia during its Aktion T4[1] programme, or the record of a traumatic life experience such as the near-death experience of Drew Fox (b.1965). These artists are seeking to share their experiences, to tell their story. They are the journalists and documenters of the soul, venturing into the bleakest of places to shine a light and share the things they have beheld. It is too simple to describe this art as merely cathartic as it carries an intention to communicate, to enable others to understand and for the artists' voices to be heard.

In essence, all art is therapeutic, as by its nature it allows the artist to convey, and audiences to experience and share the emotions of the creator and the subjects they portray. Michelangelo's *Pietà* is a powerful evocation of a mother's grief at the death of her son, with the emotions clear to see. Elsewhere, Matthias Grünewald's depiction of a torturous crucifixion in the *Isenheim Altarpiece* is a reminder of the weakness of the flesh, and human mortality is made visceral and real.

Much of the art in this chapter can seem cathartic – a 'purification and purgation of emotions'.[2] It can help heal the creator but also the viewer, leaving them able to process the emotions on display. It might be considered that dwelling on strong and sometimes negative emotions poses its own risks. The artist's work, caught in a cycle of repetitive negativity, can seem a wilful and destructive act. It takes courage to face life's demons, an act of defiance and expression of the self in the face of the sometimes seemingly insurmountable challenges life throws our way. Being creative can enable us to understand and slay the demons that can torment us, sometimes providing healing and resolution. The series of prints by Francisco Goya (1746–1828) known as *The Disasters of War*, created between 1810 and 1820, are some of the starkest images ever created, showing man's inhumanity to man, produced after Goya had become deaf due to illness and witnessed first-hand the horrors of the Napoleonic Wars. Similarly, Titian's *The Flaying of Marsyas* – one of the most shocking images ever realised – is an evocation of cruelty and suffering. It can seem very dark this space, but art, as with life, is not always about beauty and escapism; we cannot have one without the other.

The experience of being disabled was the primary driver for the Disability Arts Movement, started in the late 1970s. Vic Finkelstein (1938–2011) was a major figure in the development of the social model of disability, first expressed in the short booklet *Fundamental Principles of Disability* published in 1975.[3] The social model believes that it is society that prevents disabled people living their lives 'normally' and not their disability. The lack of adaptations in the built environment and the inherent prejudices in society create the barriers to their inclusion. The artists associated with the Disability Arts Movement focused on their experience of being disabled and the injustice towards disabled people in wider society. The social model has many echoes in the attitudes held in the art world, where the exclusion of disabled and non-traditional artists is often due to the inherent structure of the system in place, and its definitions of what constitutes art and who is considered an artist.

David Hevey – CEO of Shape Arts, a disability-led arts organisation that works to improve access to culture for disabled people – summarised the movement:

> In a sense, the art of the Disability Arts Movement has been a journey off the body-as-problem to society-as-problem, but with many artists playing with much of the space in between, too. In this way, the Disability Rights Movement very much learns from and echoes other political-art movements who also did this move off-the-body as site of problem to making art about society being the problem, such as the Black Arts Movement in the UK in the 1990s and beyond.[4]

Lived experiences

The majority of the artists in this chapter base their work on their lived experiences, including their health, disability, mental health and social circumstances. Similarly to the Disability Arts

previous
Dannielle Hodson
Triumph of Life (detail)
2022
Oil on canvas
190 × 180 cm

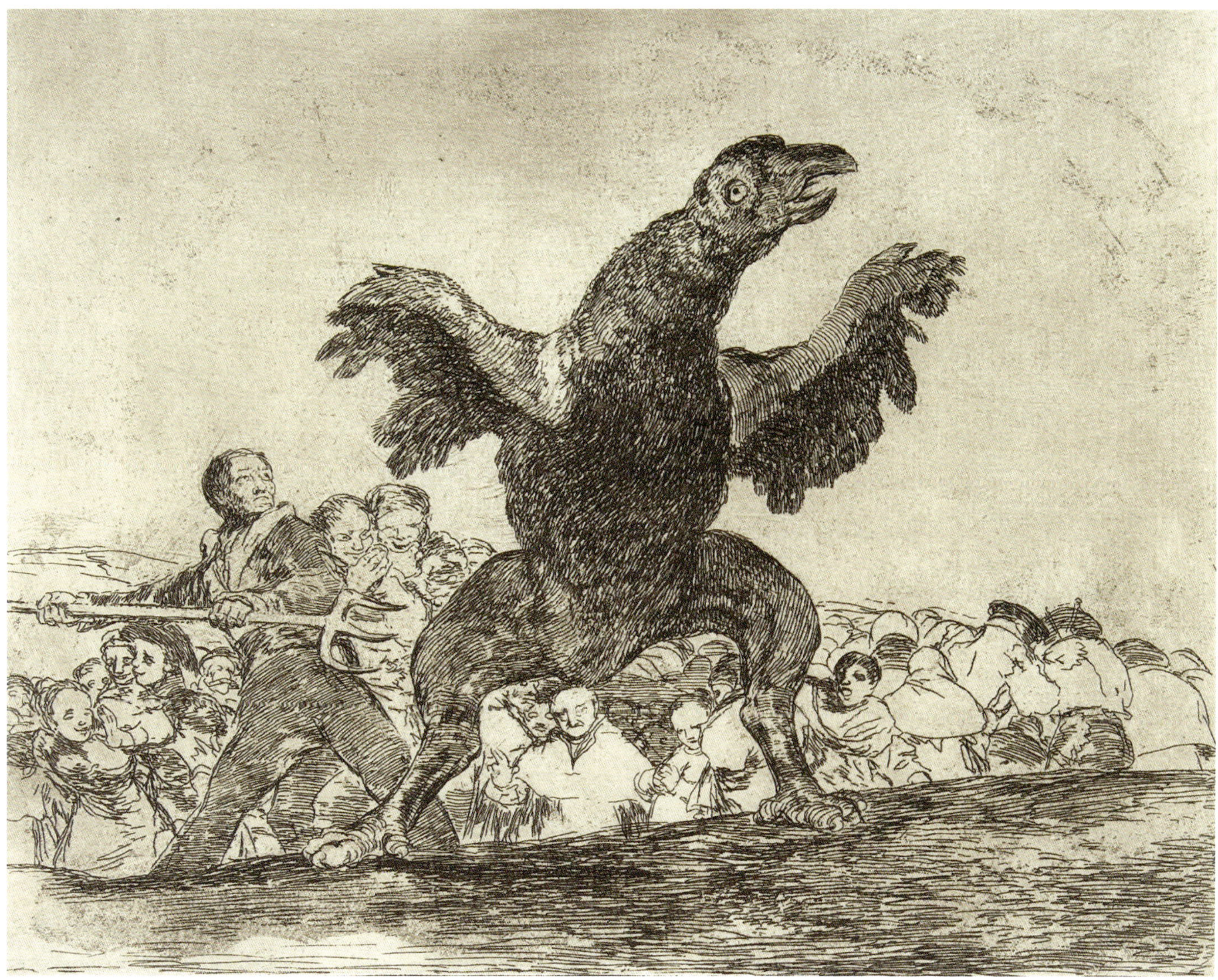

Goya
Los Desastres de la Guerra No.76. El buitre carnívoro
1814–15
Etching
17.7 × 22.1 cm

Movement, some, such as James Lake (b.1974), refer to their disability and the issues disabled people face; others such as Corinne (b.1990), Drew Fox and Andrew Hood (b.1967) produce work which either focuses on or expresses their life situations and mental health. It could be said that a lived experience is one of the most important motivations for creativity. The sharing of lived experiences enables art of purpose and integrity, its primary intention being to share and communicate. Unlike art created as commodity, or to please, it has a charge and force all of its own, speaking powerfully to the viewer.

Dannielle Hodson (b.1980) is an artist whose work strongly evokes her life experiences. Her award-winning painting *Swallow* was exhibited in the 2009 Outside In National Exhibition at Pallant House Gallery. She painted it whilst in prison and it is a powerful expression of how she felt during this period of her life. She discovered painting as a way to express what she was feeling, an outlet in a time of extreme stress. Dannielle describes how she felt her life had been turned upside down and she had to leave a successful career, and, as the image so clearly shows, it was a bitter pill to swallow. Dannielle's award was to have a solo show at Pallant House Gallery which she has described as a life-changing event and eventually led to her undertaking an MA in Fine Art at Central Saint Martins and becoming a trustee at Outside In.

Dannielle's work has continued to be informed by her life and her response to PTSD. She describes

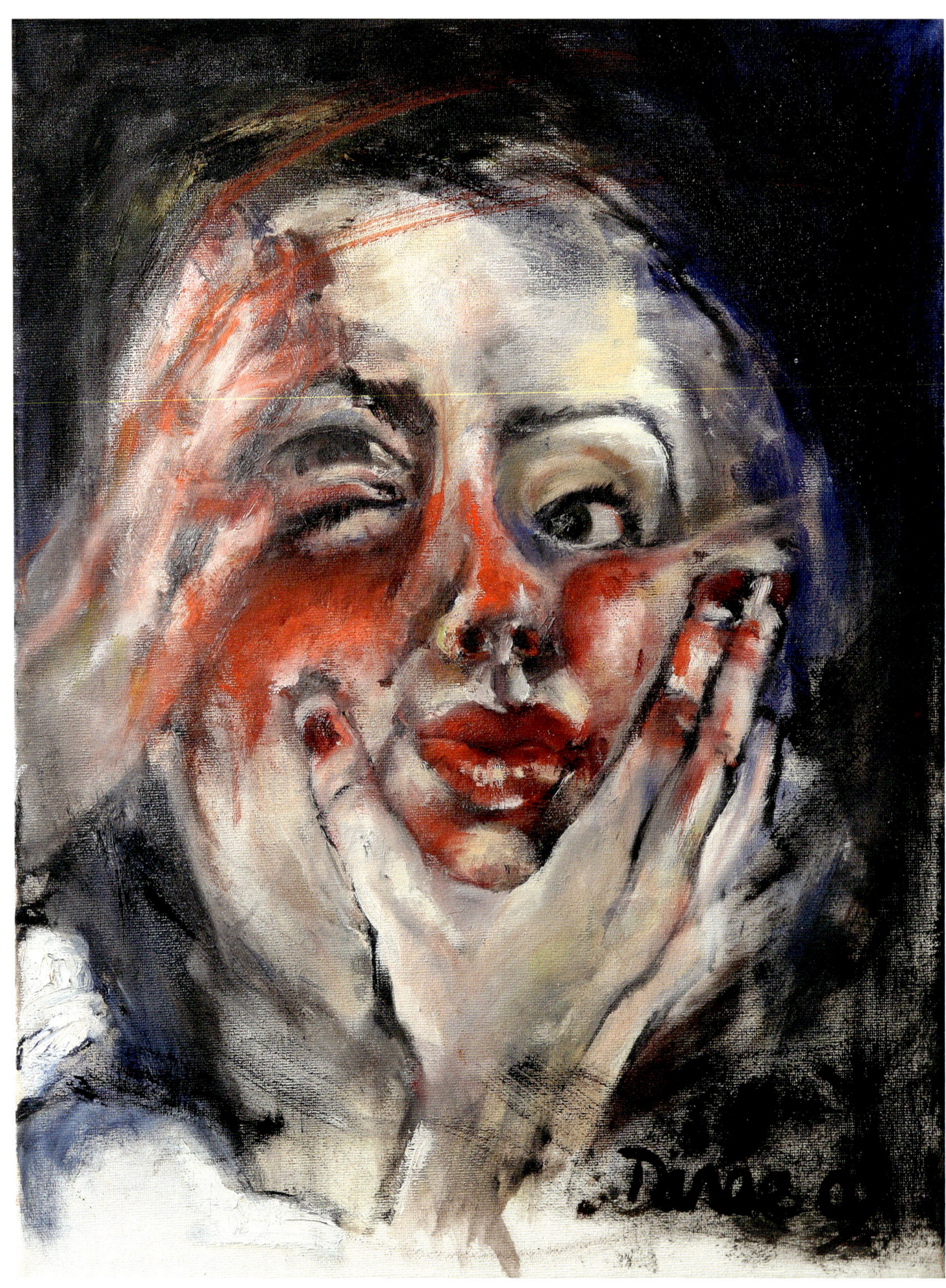

Dannielle Hodson
Swallow
2009
Oil on canvas
approx. 60 × 50 cm

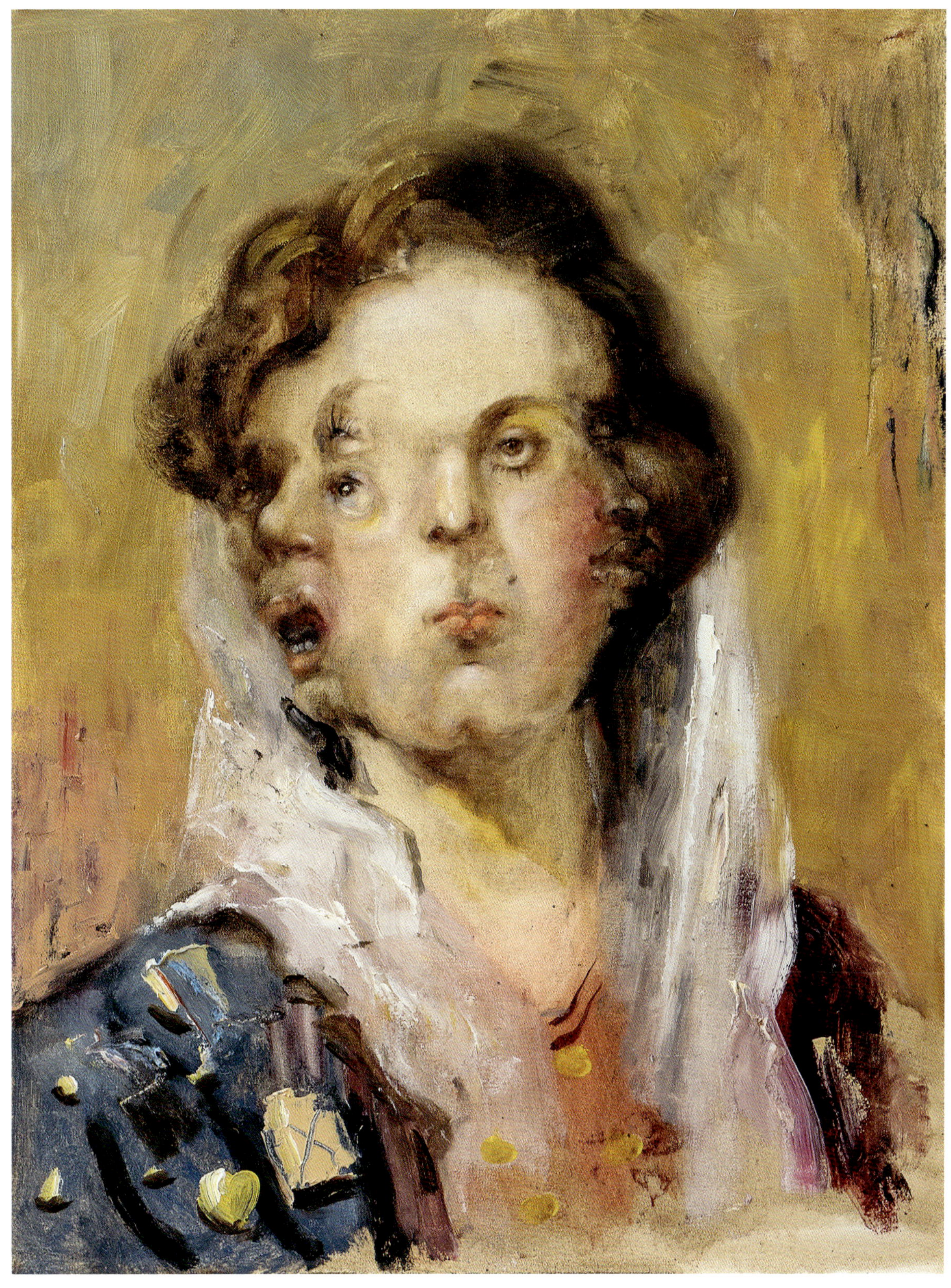

Dannielle Hodson
Inner Turmoil
2021
Oil on canvas
60 × 50 cm

making art as a release, a means to be yourself and be in a safe space. Moving from her more 'Confessional Art'[5] approach as seen in *Swallow*, she has evolved a way of working that is both a direct outpouring and an avoidance of making art about something:

> While my large-scale oil paintings teem with physiological details – a grotesquely comic multitude of human and animal eyes, teeth and limbs – these figurative elements evolve out of a kind of primordial abstraction. Each work begins with a process of unplanned, almost automatic mark making, during which I'm concerned not with creating imagery, but rather with channelling energy from the world outside the canvas onto its flat, bounded plane.

This approach to her making can be seen in the large painting *The Triumph of Life*. Referencing Pieter Bruegel's *The Triumph of Death*, it is informed by the challenging life situations she has lived through. Dannielle said of the painting: 'Life of all kinds – winning over death, I saw a kind of a ship in it, that's coming from one place of madness into another strange place, madness is everywhere but we survive it and move on'.

Dannielle's work still channels the trauma and stress she grew up with. She directs it into her work, searching for identity, creating something horrible and difficult so as to externalise her feelings and come to terms with her life experiences. She believes that personal identity is fluid and has powerfully explored this in her recent series of imaginary portraits. There is a painterly quality to these works such as in *Inner Turmoil* and first seen in *Swallow*. The struggle with identity is being explored: '... these works position the individual as something closer to a verb than a noun – a process of mutation and endless becoming'. She describes art as a release, a way to be yourself and to escape a sometimes frightening world, creating a safe space: 'This is something I've had to work on and painting is a good place to do it. I can create stressful situations in paint and keeping them in painting makes life much easier!'

Laila Kassab (b.1985) was born in Gaza, where she still lives. She was supported by Outside In to undertake a co-commission with Pallant House Gallery in 2018 inspired by the work of Scottie Wilson (1891–1972) from the Gallery's collection. An exhibition of the commissioned works, *Colliding Worlds: Scottie Wilson*, was held at the Gallery in the same year. The commission was a significant opportunity for Laila, the first she had undertaken and the first time her work was exhibited in a major gallery. Due to her situation, Laila was unable to see her work on display, as she explained: 'As Gaza is under blockade, it is extremely difficult and rare for anyone, including artists, to be able to leave, even for urgent medical treatment. However, I still hope, and I am determined that one day I will be able to attend an exhibition of my artwork outside Gaza. I would love to travel to the gallery and hear the visitors' impressions and their views about my paintings.'[6]

Laila has determinedly pursued her interest in art despite a lack of support or recognition. Being creative plays a significant part in her life. 'For me I was born on the day I discovered art, when for the first time in my life I painted on white paper. I was eight years old. Then the sun rays of art began to shine upon me. I carried the pencil and began to draw everything my eye fell upon and discovered my passion and gift for art.' She has also described the creation of her work as like a Caesarean section, bringing something new into the world, but not without its challenges.

Art is a means to express the challenges of her situation. Her drawings are beguiling in their bright and joyful colouring, belying the content, which is often shown through symbols. Her drawing *Love and Passion* was produced as part of the co-commission. It shows a tree with the face of a woman, presumably Laila, bending and protecting three apparently grief-stricken women in Palestinian dress, with a dove sweeping in to seemingly take a heart from one of the women.

In her application for the commission Laila said of the work of Scottie Wilson, 'In my opinion, the birds in his work may symbolise the loss of freedom. On the other hand, the fish, which are unable to live outside water, may symbolise the many people who are forced to live in an environment, customs and traditions that kill their soul'.

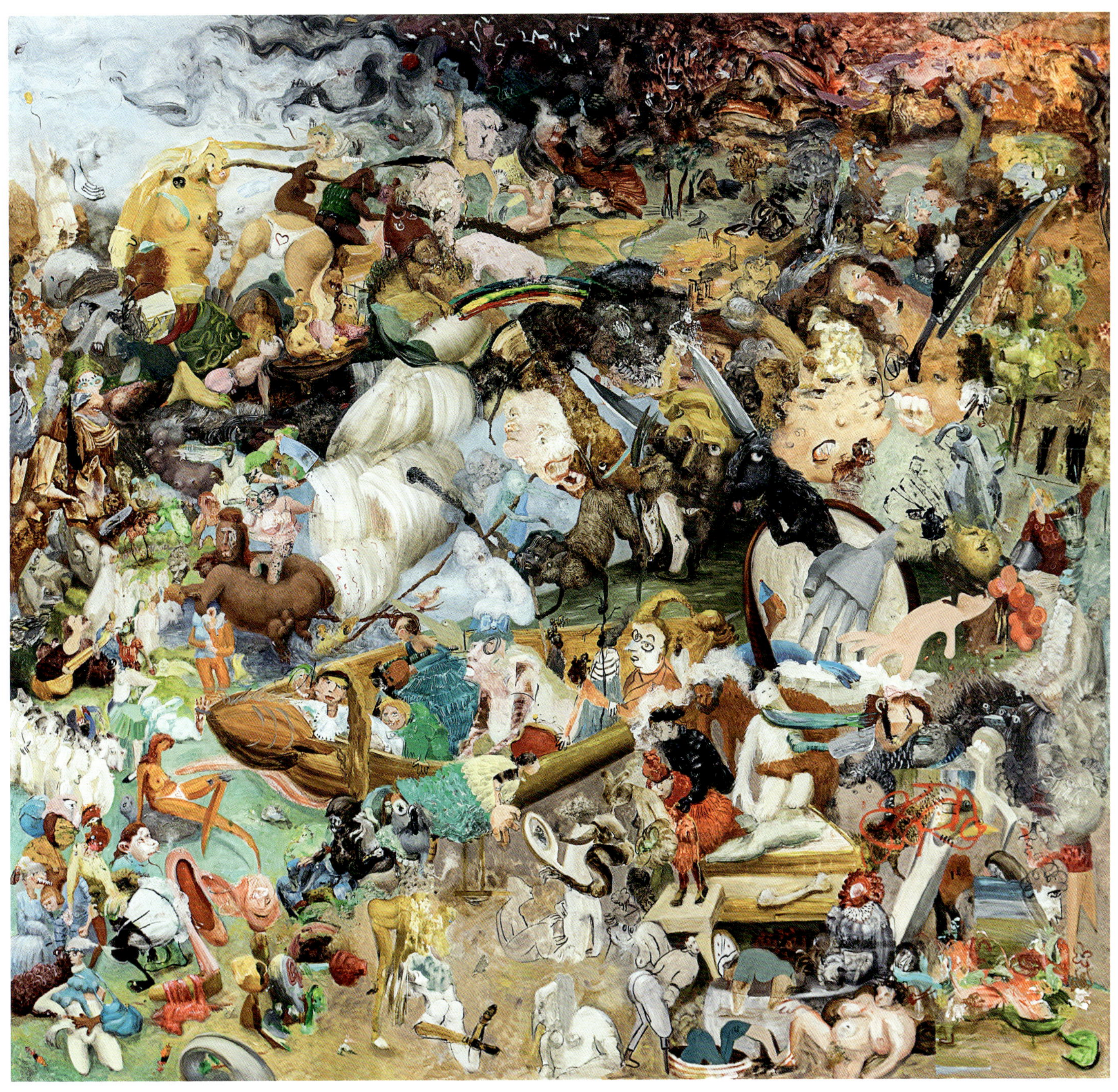

Dannielle Hodson
Triumph of Life
2022
Oil on canvas
190 × 180 cm

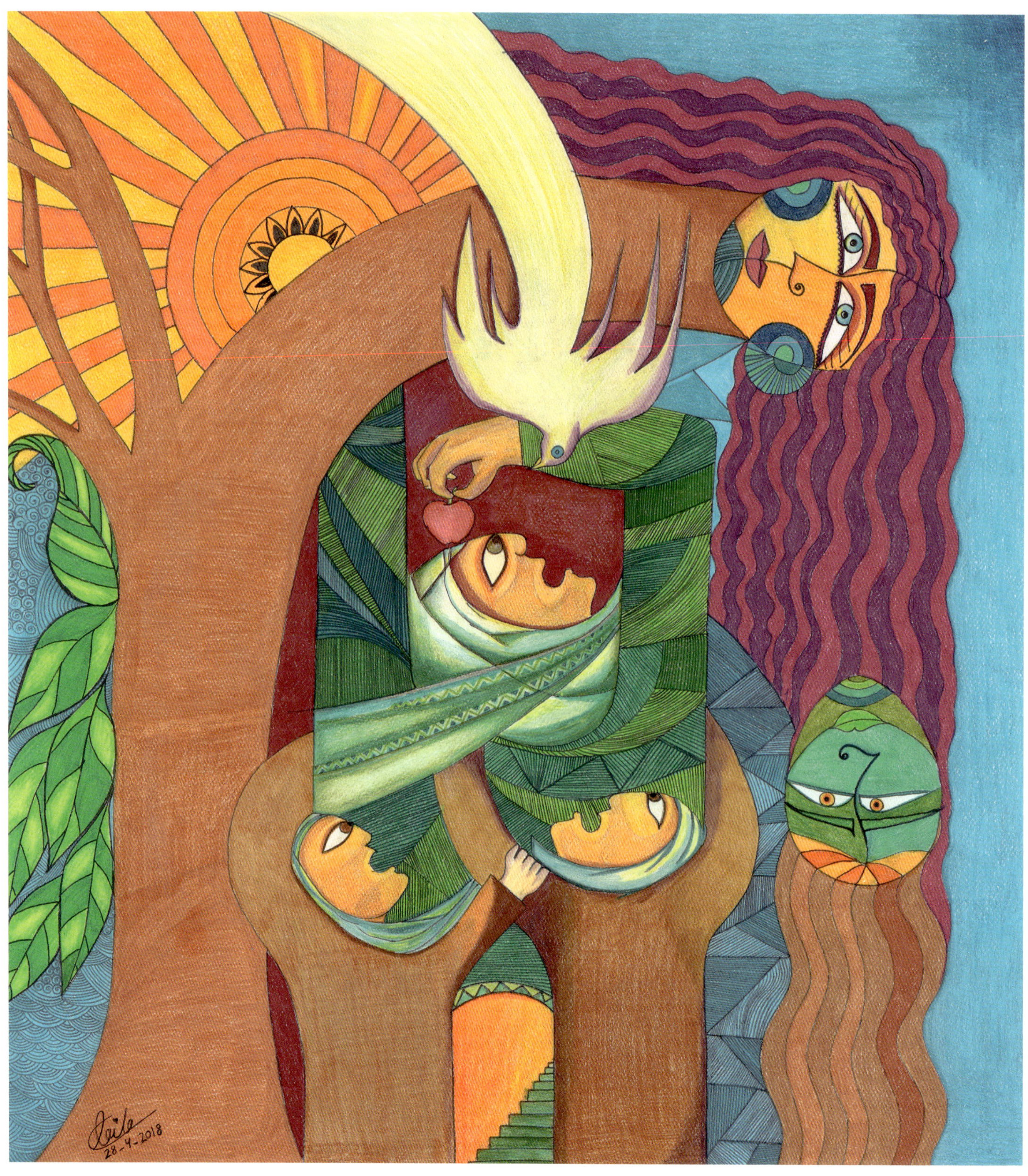

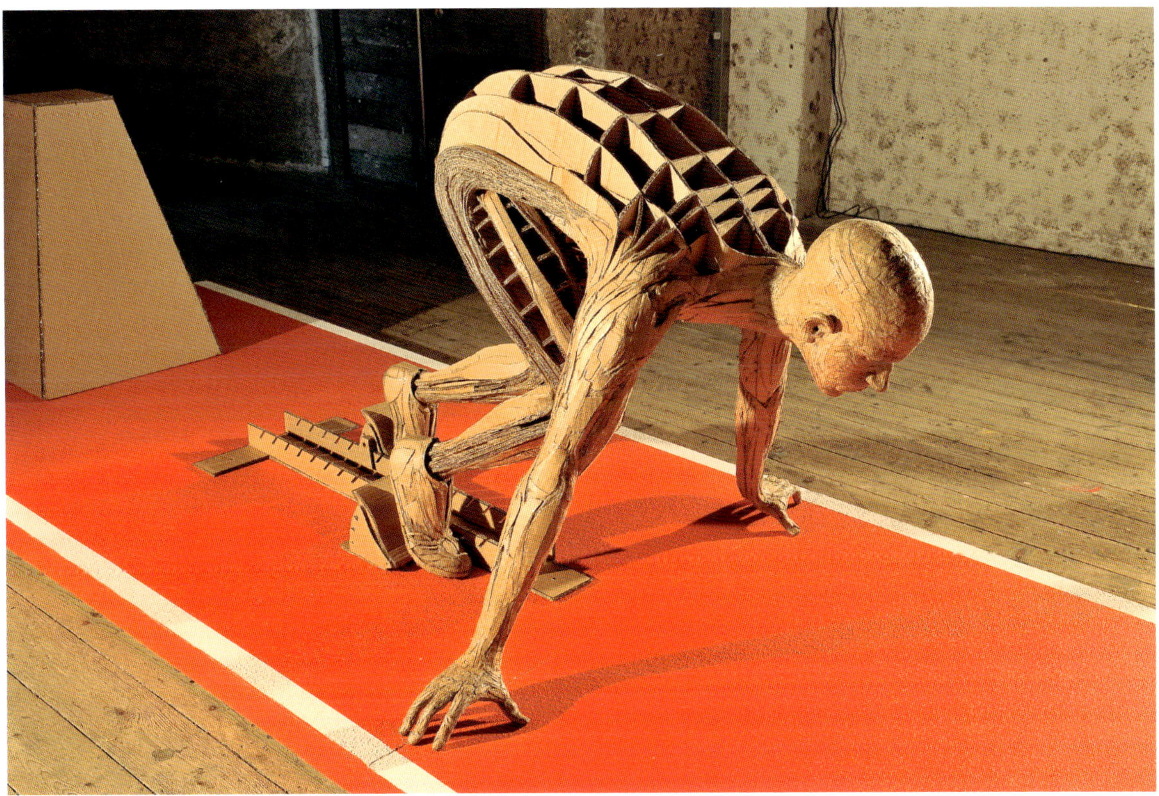

Laila uses her lived experience to produce art that expresses the challenges of her life, both of living in the Gaza Strip and the challenges she faces as a woman. 'While a woman like me is denied the freedom to travel, my defiance is symbolised by having my paintings exiting Gaza.'[7]

As a teenager James Lake lost his right leg to cancer and it was around this time that he discovered cardboard as art material. Lightweight and readily available, it would enable him to realise his desire to make sculptures. Because of its advantages, he uses cardboard to adjust or remove barriers to creativity. He makes monumental sculptures with it. A master of his medium, he has pioneered and encouraged others to take up the material, eager to share its potential as a cheap and accessible means to make art.

In 2011, James was commissioned to produce a stage set and sculpture for Gold Run, a project that brought together Outside In, Glyndebourne Opera House and Carousel, a Brighton-based charity supporting people with learning disabilities. Gold Run celebrated the reintroduction of learning-disabled athletes in the 2012 London Paralympic Games. It was both an opera and an art installation.

James was mentored by Ron Henocq, the former Director of Café Gallery Projects (now Southwark Park Galleries), and the internationally renowned sculptor Richard Wilson to create the work. The installation, *Gold Run: Remix*, was first displayed at Dilston Grove (now Dilston Gallery), a Grade II listed church built in 1911. It was the first poured concrete building in England, and its narrow and tall nave provided the perfect setting. The work had both a personal and wider resonance for James: 'The installation ... places the athlete on the starting blocks of a distorted running track with hurdles. The track curves upwards at the end and at the highest elevation there is an impossible hurdle to jump. The installation presents itself as a race that is not possible to finish. While designing the installation I was considering the idea of "what happens next?" It references disability, art and sport ... with the desire of overcoming significant social and cultural barriers.' From Dilston Grove, a smaller version of the installation travelled to other venues, including: The Lightbox, Woking; Chapel Arts Studio, Andover; and Pallant House Gallery, Chichester.

Laila Kassab
Love and Passion
2018
Coloured pencil on paper
85 × 80 cm

James Lake
The Sprinter
2012
Cardboard
91.5 × 91.5 cm

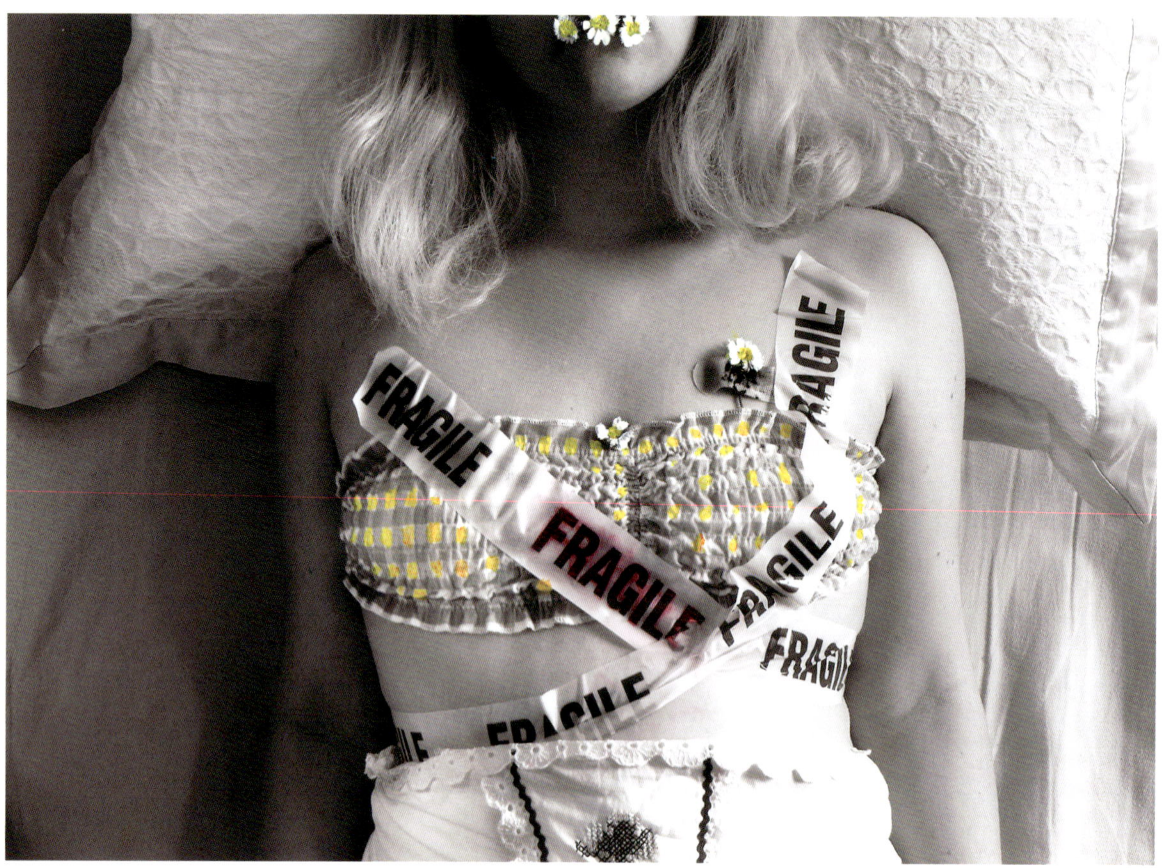

Corinne
A Bedtime Story #6
2020
Black and white photographic self-portrait, hand coloured with oil and watercolour paint.
20.3 × 25.4 cm

Photographing the self

The camera never lies, or that might seem the case, but the use that Drew Fox and Andrew Hood make of both modern and old technology shows that it is possible to manipulate and change what we see into something the artist wants us to see. Modern technology has enabled nearly all of us to take images, the majority of which are selfies – us as we would like to be seen by our friends and the wider world. Bravely these artists have created images of themselves that show how they feel. This work can be difficult to look at, but all the more important for being so. It challenges taboos, such as death and the stigma of mental health, so creating a healthier and more open dialogue.

Corinne has been confined to her bed due to her mental health for five years. 'My distinctively dark and evocative self-depictions intimately reflect my ongoing struggles with mental illness (severe anxiety, depression and auditory hallucinations). My work is created within the same 2 by 1.5 metre space: my bed, the only place I feel safe enough to create.'

Using her body as the means of communication, she carefully arranges props, words and bodily positions that enable her to express her feelings. Some of these images make for difficult viewing as they speak clearly of the challenges she has to face. There is a courage in such openness, a willingness to reveal her innermost self, but this exposure has a powerful impact on both her and audiences. 'My life and art have become inextricably entwined. To bury my struggles deep within would allow them to thrive, but through my use of art as therapy, I'm offered a cathartic release,' she says.

Corinne has been able to undertake a virtual residency and curate an exhibition of the Outside In Collection in 2022 at Paradise Row in Mayfair. Through the support of the charity, she has formed a group of similarly bed-bound artists.

Andrew Hood has also used photography to share and express his mental health struggles, especially in relation to his home environment. He is an image-maker, seeking to convey his inner mental state through manipulating images of the interior of his flat, which are often disconcerting

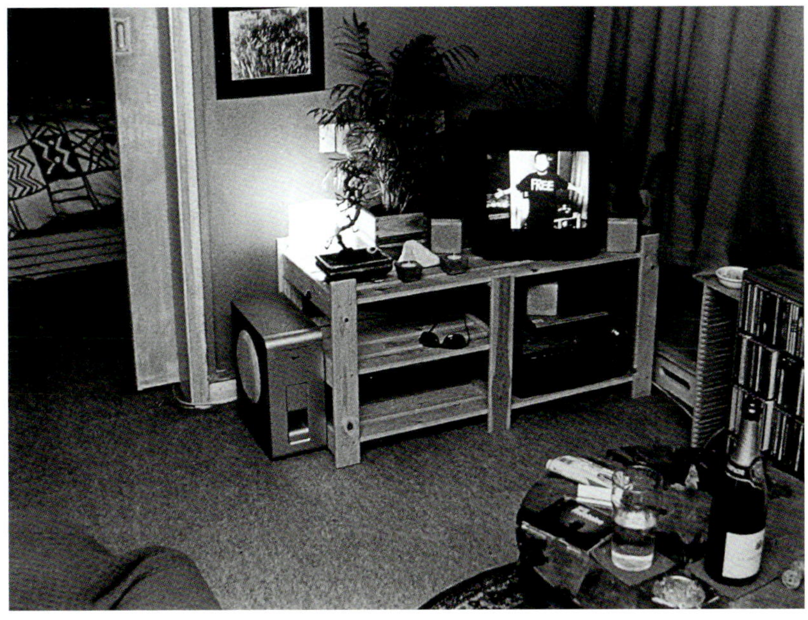

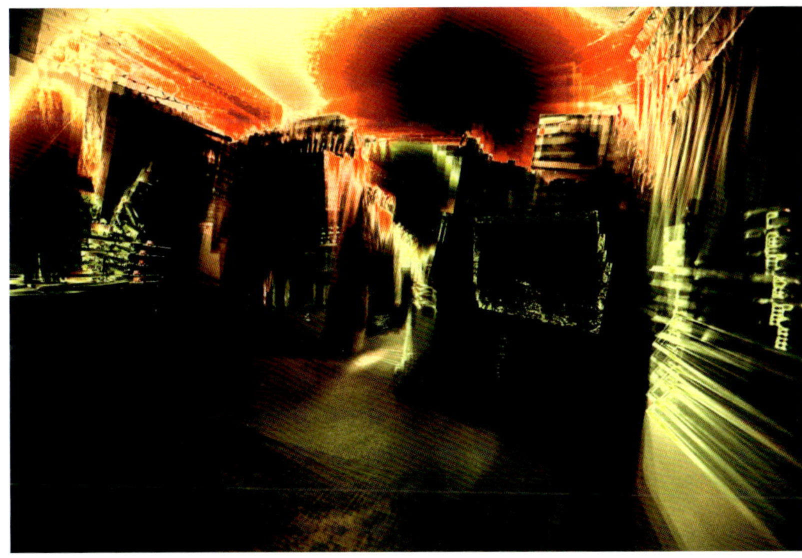

Andrew Hood
Self Portrait
2007
Photograph

Andrew Hood
No Room for the Weak
2016
Photographic
C-Type print
84 × 119 cm

and disturbing, but on occasions humorous. 'I am interested in the space that's around me, particularly inside my home', he says. 'I see space as fractured dimensions that can be free and open, or closed and restricting. The internal and external world merge and flip in space and become reality. It feels like I am unravelling these spaces and merging into another state of consciousness.'

Andrew's early black and white *Self Portrait* was exhibited at the first Outside In exhibition at Pallant House Gallery in 2007. It is an image of Andrew's front room, seemingly empty, until you notice him on the television screen, arms outstretched with 'FREE' emblazoned on his T-shirt. One might wonder what Andrew has escaped from: is it his flat, his mind, or is he trapped in another space?

More disturbing is his photograph *No Room for the Weak*. Taking its title from a Joy Division song, it is a disturbing kaleidoscope. The room shimmers with light and it looks as if there is blood on the ceiling. Using timelapse and manipulation of the image on the camera, he has recreated his room into a shocking environment no one would seek to live in. More recently, Andrew has moved home. He has left his flat and is now living in the country where he has found new subjects and refuge.

Drew Fox is another artist who uses photography but, in his case, to express and make sense of a life-changing event he faced ten years ago which impacts on him and his health to this day. Drew had a major heart attack. Initially pronounced dead, he had to be resuscitated twice. In his near-death experience, Drew felt that he had left the world of the living and visited the land of the dead. When he recovered, he felt compelled to make art that would make sense of his experience and its influence on him, or as Drew expressed it: 'What it felt to be a ghost, a dead man walking in the world of the living'.[8]

In order to find a means to share his experience, Drew researched the techniques of early photography and began making his own cameras out of recycled materials. 'All of my builds are based around biscuit tins and offcuts of wood; at the time I was fascinated with the ideas and experiments that went into creating the first cameras and photographic processes, so I taught myself how to make wet-plate collodion photographs on glass plates.'

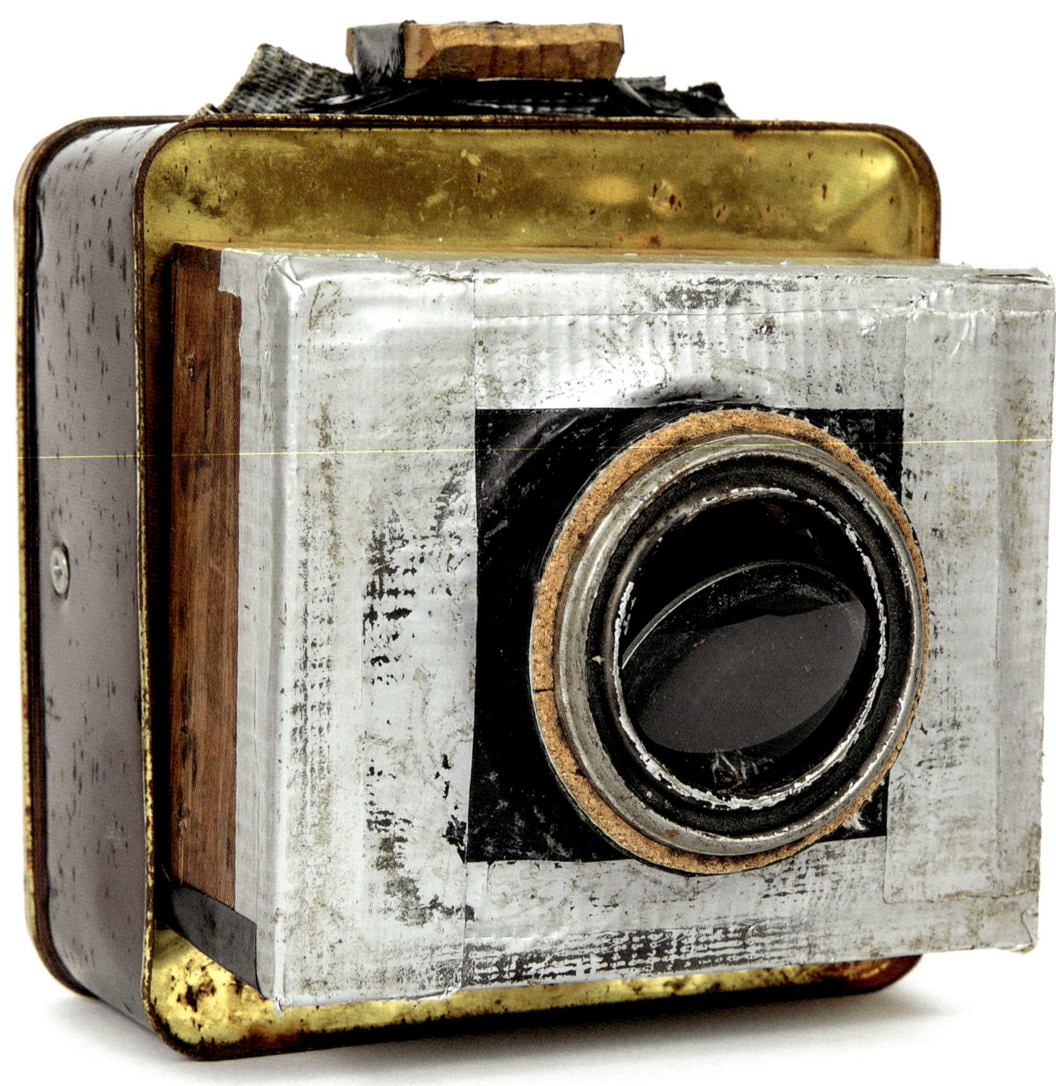

Drew Fox
Camera
2014
Mixed media
16 × 16 × 17 cm

Drew Fox
When water turns to steel (the alchemy of death)
2014
Wet Plate Collodion Photograph
10 × 7.5 cm

Using his self-made camera, Drew produced a series of harrowing images. One in particular, *When water turns to steel (the alchemy of death)*, consists of a series of four self-portraits. The images represent the four stages of his death, each image lighter than the last, fading as he lost his sense of being human. Drew said of these photographs: 'I think these images were the most upsetting to make as they describe my death and how it felt to die'. Ultimately the work Drew produced in response to his life-changing experience has been cathartic and is the foundation of his creative development. 'Art can heal your soul even after you have experienced the most horrific of traumas,' he says.

Unfolding narratives

Some non-traditional artists seek to tell stories, sometimes fantastic and sometimes a reflection of their life experiences, as with the work of Wilhelm Werner. Artists have used existing stories, such the adaptation by David Beales (b.1954) of *A Rake's Progress* by William Hogarth (1697–1764), or adapted formats such as cartoons and comics, as with Charles Devus (b.1962). Others have created diaries to record their lives such as Carlo Keshishian (b.1980). As with the other examples in this chapter, these works reflect the life experiences of the artists, but their use of a narrative engages the audience differently, both as art and testimony, often creating a greater impact on the viewer and reader.

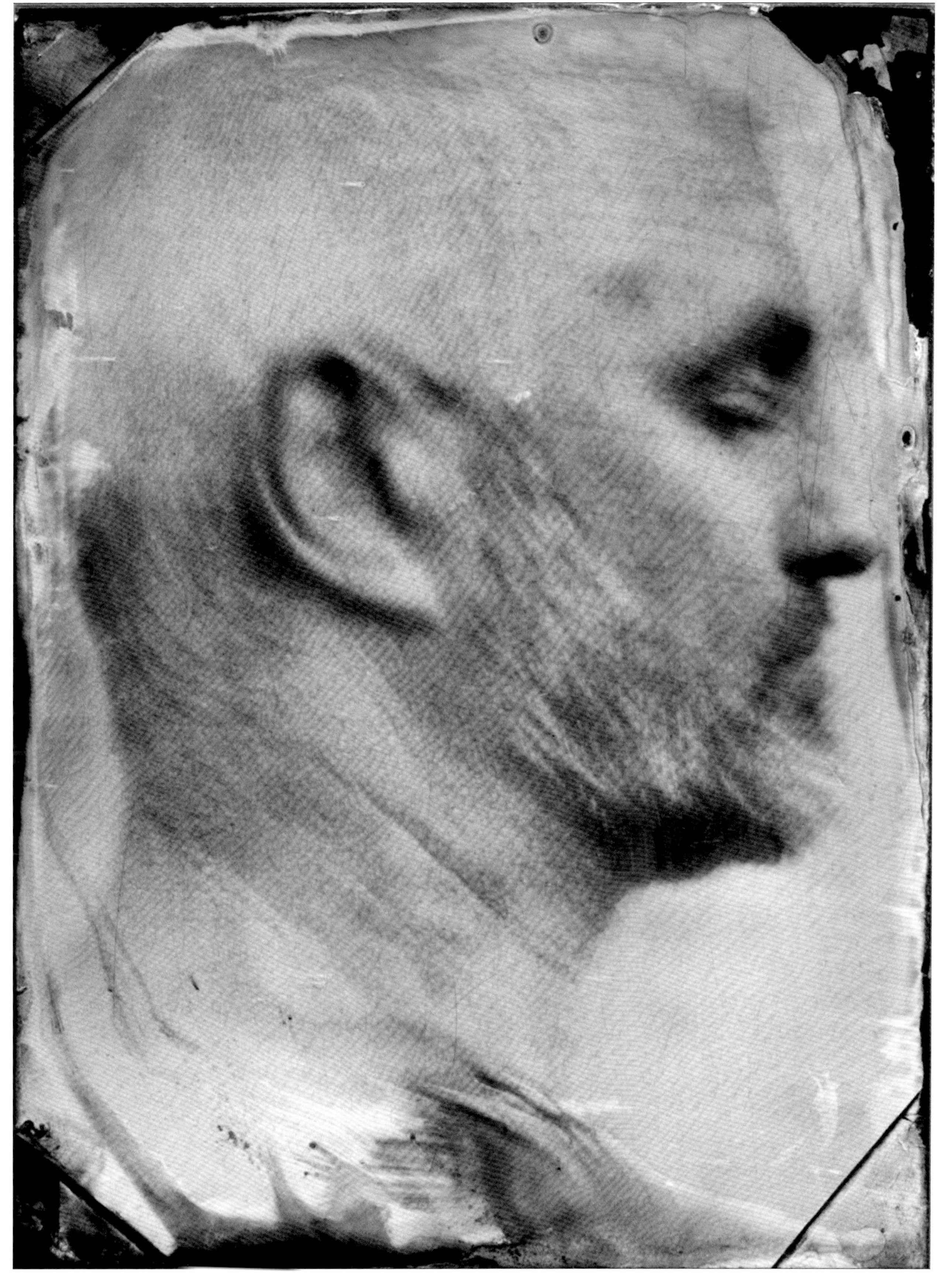

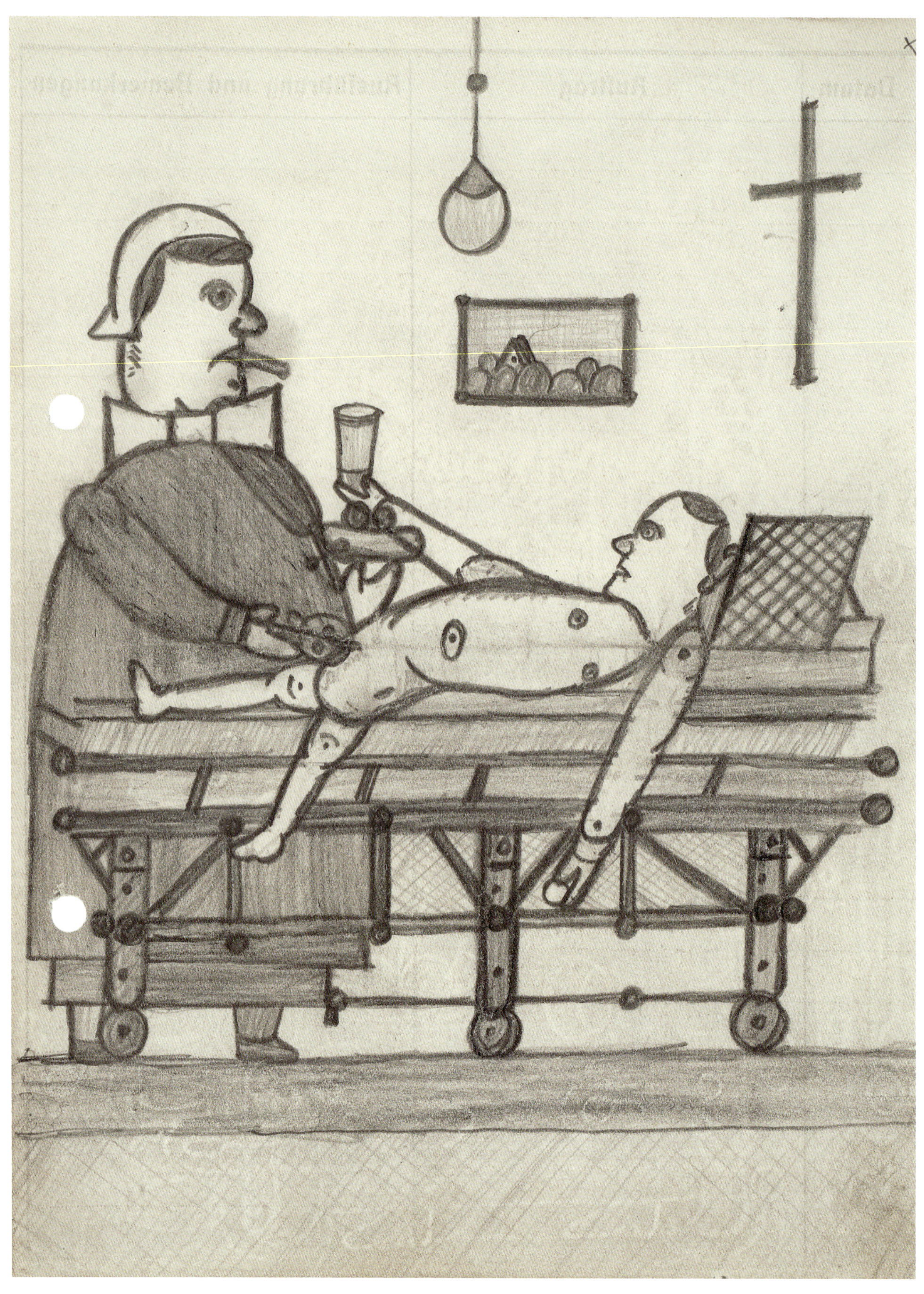

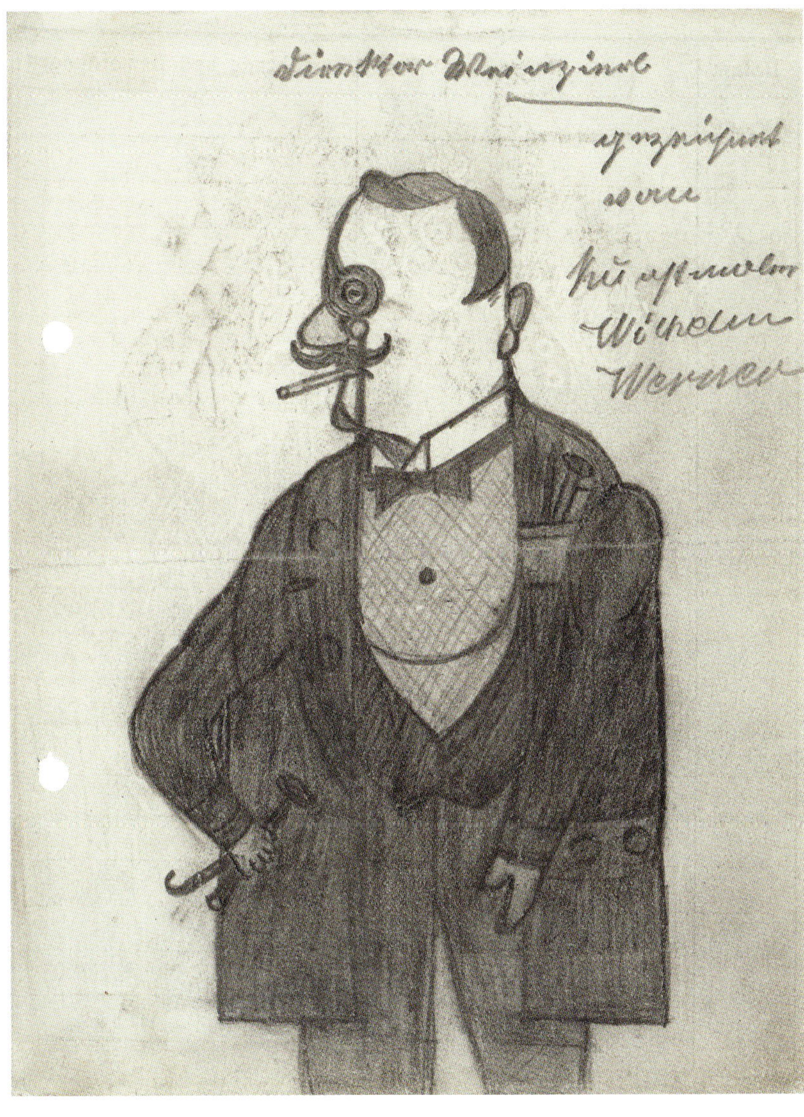

Wilhelm Werner
Untitled, between 1934 – 1938. Inv.No.8083/1
2010
Pencil on paper
20.2 × 15.3 cm

Wilhelm Werner
Director Weinzierl drawn by painter Wilhelm Werner ("Direktor Weinzierl gezeichnet von Kunstmaler Wilhelm Werner"), between 1934-1938. Inv. No.8083/10
2010
Pencil on paper
20.2 × 15.5 cm

Wilhelm Werner was diagnosed with 'idiocy' and forcibly sterilised by the Nazis sometime between 1934 and 1938 as part of their 'NS-Rassenhygiene' race cleansing programme. He was later gassed on 6 October 1940 at the Pirna-Sonnenschein death camp. His only known work is a book of drawings acquired by the Prinzhorn Collection in 2008. The book comprises 44 drawings of which 30 are numbered in sequence. They are a unique documentation of a person with learning disabilities living under the Nazi regime.

On the inside of the book cover, Werner describes himself as the 'orator of the people and theatre director Wilhelm Werner, Werneck Asylum'. There is a theatricality to the drawings – it is as if they are illustrating some bizarre Weimar-period marionette performance. He records his sterilisation without anger, and his characters are like puppets, lacking autonomy and under the control of cigarette-smoking Nazi nurses.

Werner's work seems informed by the Neue Sachlichkeit, the 'new objectivity' and 'return to order' movement that had arisen as a response to Expressionism in 1920s Germany. His style somewhat echoes the art of George Grosz (1893–1959), whose politically informed work was a powerful indictment of German society at the time. Perhaps in his role as 'orator of the people', Werner was commenting on the wider political situation as well as his personal circumstances? In particular, his drawings of the men of authority – the doctors and bureaucrats of his world with their monocles and waxed moustaches – echo the acerbic drawings of Grosz. In one drawing it seems he has turned the tables on these figures of authority and a cigarette-smoking, moustachioed, monocle-wearing man is being castrated. This is an act of defiance and a statement of personal suffering, drawn with great control and bravery.

David Beales's work is a stark reflection of time spent in institutions. He powerfully documents his experience and the everyday life of a patient. David once described himself as 'a revolving door patient', spending a lot of his life in various psychiatric hospitals. David intends his work 'to draw attention to the problems caused by the ghettoization of the mentally ill and the drug users in the community'. His painting *Corridor Conversation* was exhibited at the

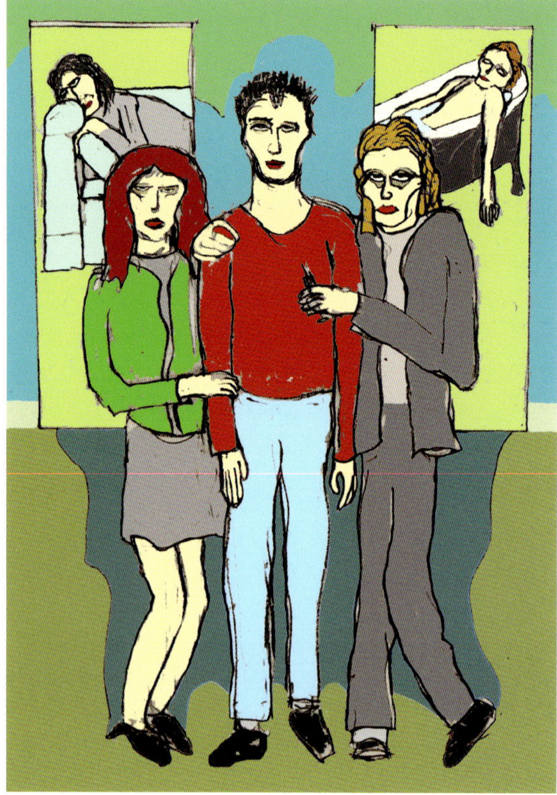

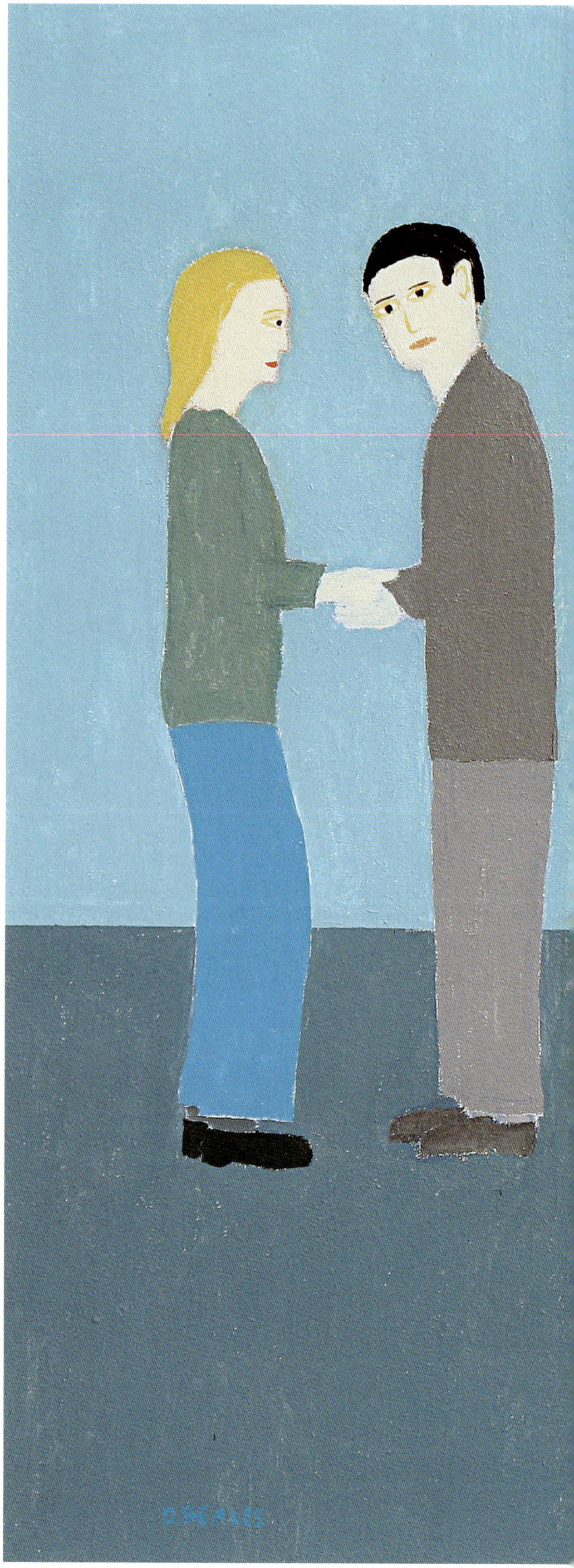

Outside In National Exhibition at Pallant House Gallery in 2009 and shows two nurses in conversation, just out of earshot of the patients looking on. It conveys a strong sense of paranoia and the disquiet felt with partially overheard conversations.

David has also produced a version of Hogarth's *A Rake's Progress*. Hogarth's work is a morality tale told in a series of eight paintings that chart the journey of Thomas Rakewell, an impressionable young man from the country who comes to the city and embarks on a dissolute life, ending up in the Bethlem Hospital for the insane. David has been supported by the Bethlem Gallery in the past which may have provided an added resonance for him. In his retelling of the story the 'rake' is led astray by drug addicts and nurses and ends up in a suicide pact with his girlfriend which he opts out of, leaving her to drown alone. Some of the images depict knife crime and drug abuse and were meant to inform fellow patients of the dangers and perils that might await them should they take the wrong path.

A different but related art form to the narrative paintings of David Beales, comics have been used to entertain, inform and subvert for

David Beales
A Rake's Progress
2004
Digital print
21 × 29.7 cm

David Beales
Corridor Conversation
2010
Acrylic on board
40 × 76 cm

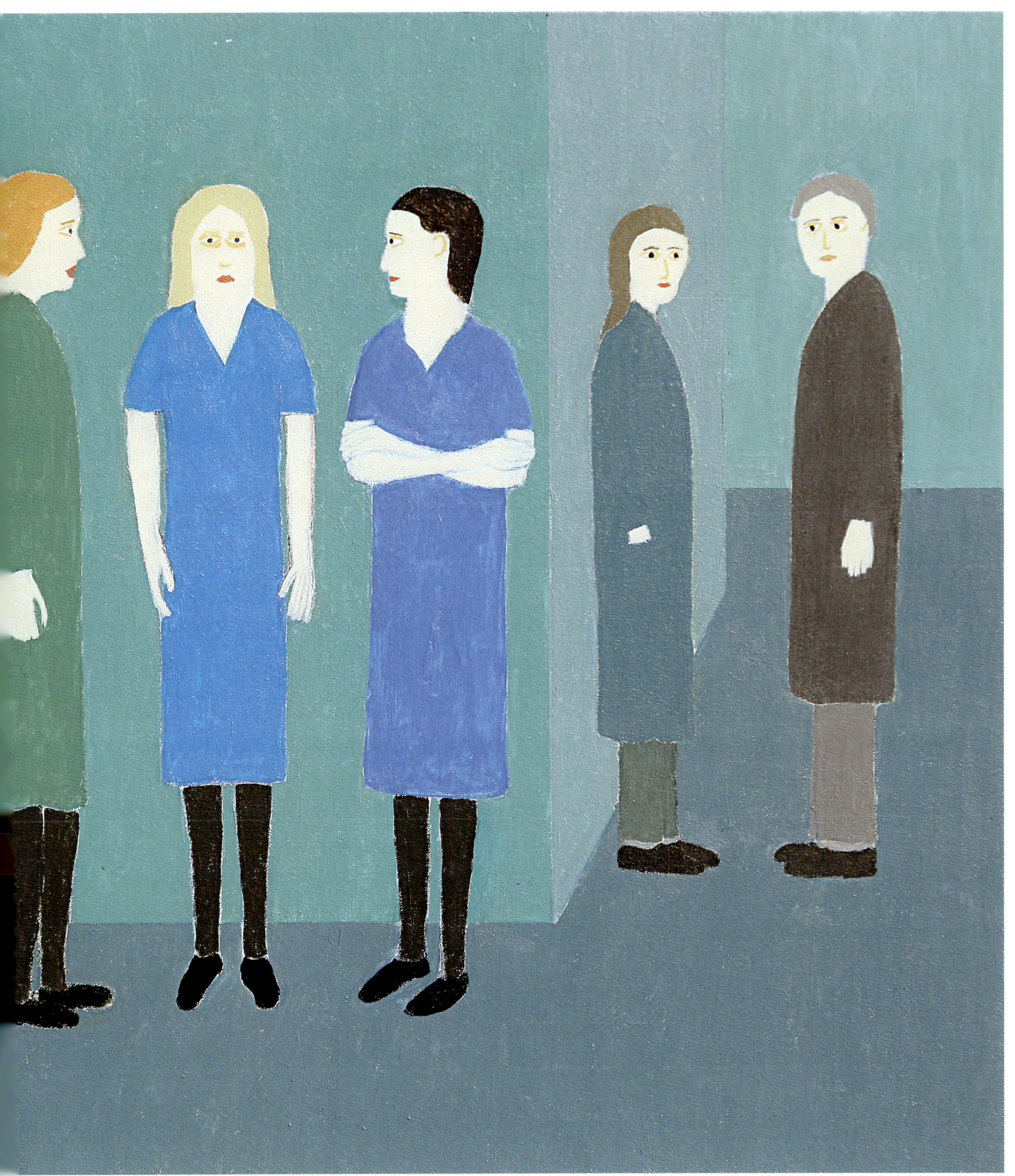

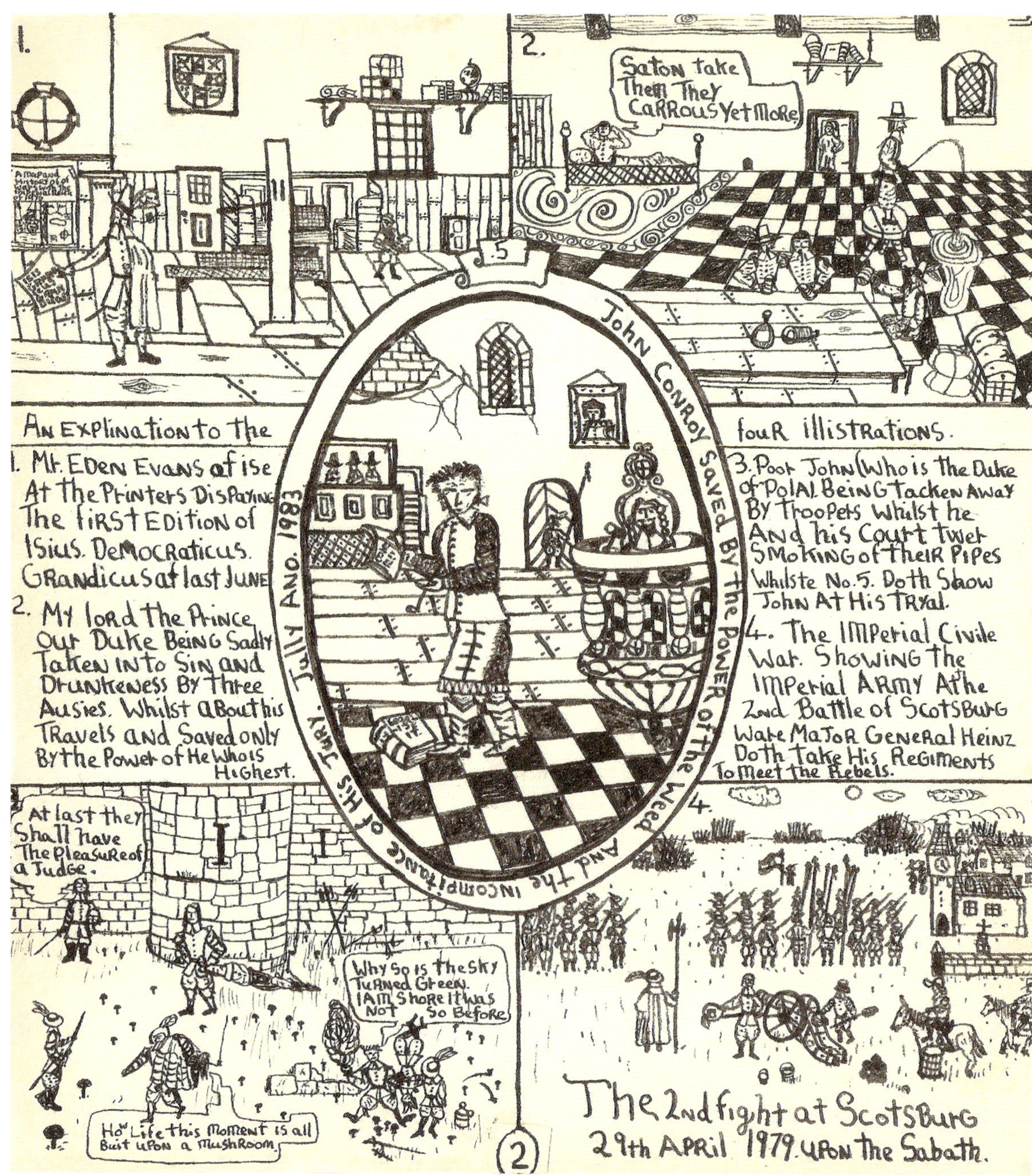

Charles Devus
Mercurius Moronicus No.10
August 1983
Ink on paper
21 × 21 cm

centuries. Many artists have used comics and their characters to inform and populate their work and to share their life experiences. The artist and writer Charles Devus has created a striking and diverse body of work inspired by comics, from his earlier detailed and historically referenced *Mercurius Moronicus* newspapers to his uncompleted graphic novel *Justin Sane*.

The *Mercurius Moronicus* newspapers were created in the 1980s and are imbued with the history and graphic style of 17th-century England and in particular the English Civil War. In developing his work, Charles made regular visits to the British Library, examining in detail original pamphlets from the period. The newspapers chart his difficult relationship with his stepfather: 'The First Series, 1-8, began as a propaganda instrument against "The Man of Blood and War, James Stuart", my stepfather, and relating news of the Empire through the medium of a

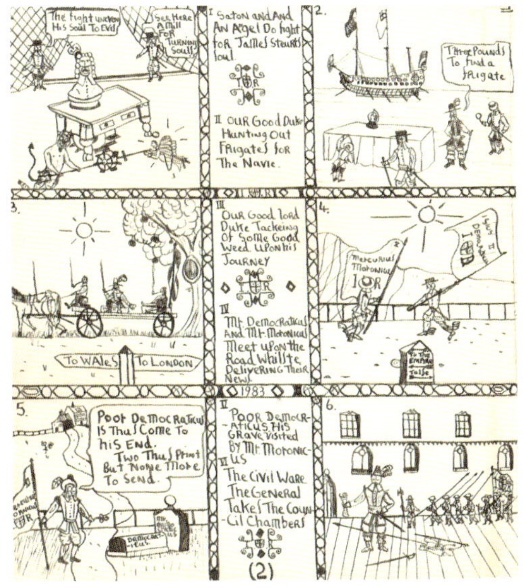

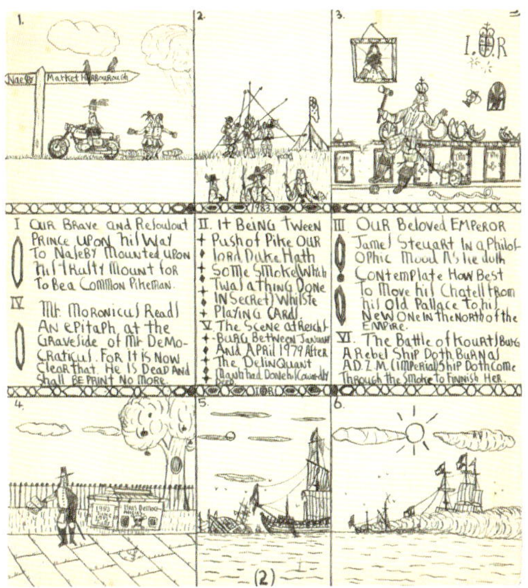

Charles Devus
Mercurius Moronicus
No.11
September 1983
Ink on paper
22 × 21 cm

Charles Devus
Mercurius Moronicus
No.12
October 1983
Ink on paper
23 × 21 cm

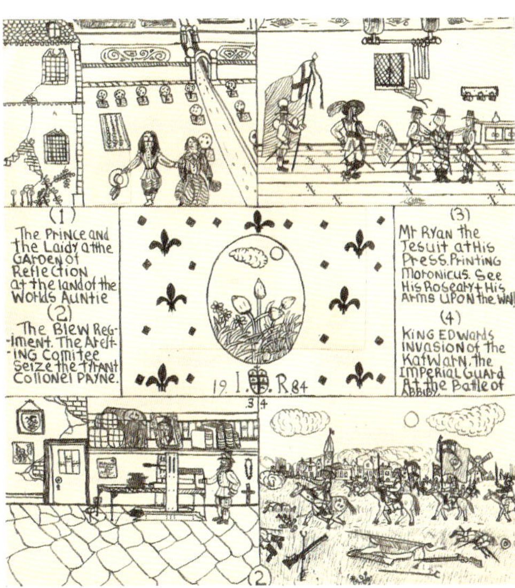

Charles Devus
Mercurius Moronicus
No.13
May 1984
Ink on paper
21 × 21 cm

mid-17th-century newsbook of the English Civil War era. The style was typical of the time and the language deliberately turgid, reflecting the earnest entrepreneurial Puritan authors of such periodicals as *A Piurect Diurnal*, *Mercurius Civicus* and the Leveller journal *The Moderate*.'

Mercurius Moronicus was the mouthpiece for a parallel and fictitious empire which Charles created in order to deal with his difficult home life and his relationship with his stepfather. 'I created the Empire as a means of escape, centred around a large navy,' he says. The battles and stories relate to events in his life, including the time his stepfather destroyed his collection of model boats: 'The sinking of the fleet, known as the Reichsburg Incident, took place on the 11/1/1979 in which 134 ships in two fleets of six battle squadrons each was decimated. Such units as the flagship Yamato flying the flag of Imperial Grand Admiral Eric von Brune being a total loss as was Kronprinz Humphry of Force-E, whilst the veteran Warspite, flagship of Force-C and the recipient of two first class Imperial Crosses, was sunk.'

In all, Charles produced 16 hand-drawn editions of *Mercurius Moronicus*, the last in 1985. He shared them with his friends. Dressing in costume, they held meetings to discuss the empire and the stories and battles that ensued. The obvious therapeutic benefit to Charles is clear and his wonderful eccentric newspaper an incredible feat of imagination.

The French author and art historian Laurent Danchin (1947–2017)[9] described Carlo Keshishian as a 'weaver of words', referring both to his work and his family's occupation as carpet and tapestry dealers. His painting *Picture Worth a Thousand Words* was displayed at the Outside In National Exhibition in 2009 at Pallant House Gallery. It took him 25 minutes to write each sentence and he planned the next sentence as he painted the one before. 'The messages in the painting, if any, are for myself to reflect on later in life.' And sometime after the painting was finished, Carlo returned to the work to 'extract the information' line by line, seemingly to discover the messages for his future self.

Carlo started his diary drawings in 2015; the first contains 3954 words and the last A4 diary drawing, finished between August 2020 to June 2021, contains 31,036 words. The drawings are 'filled with personal things, reflections of the

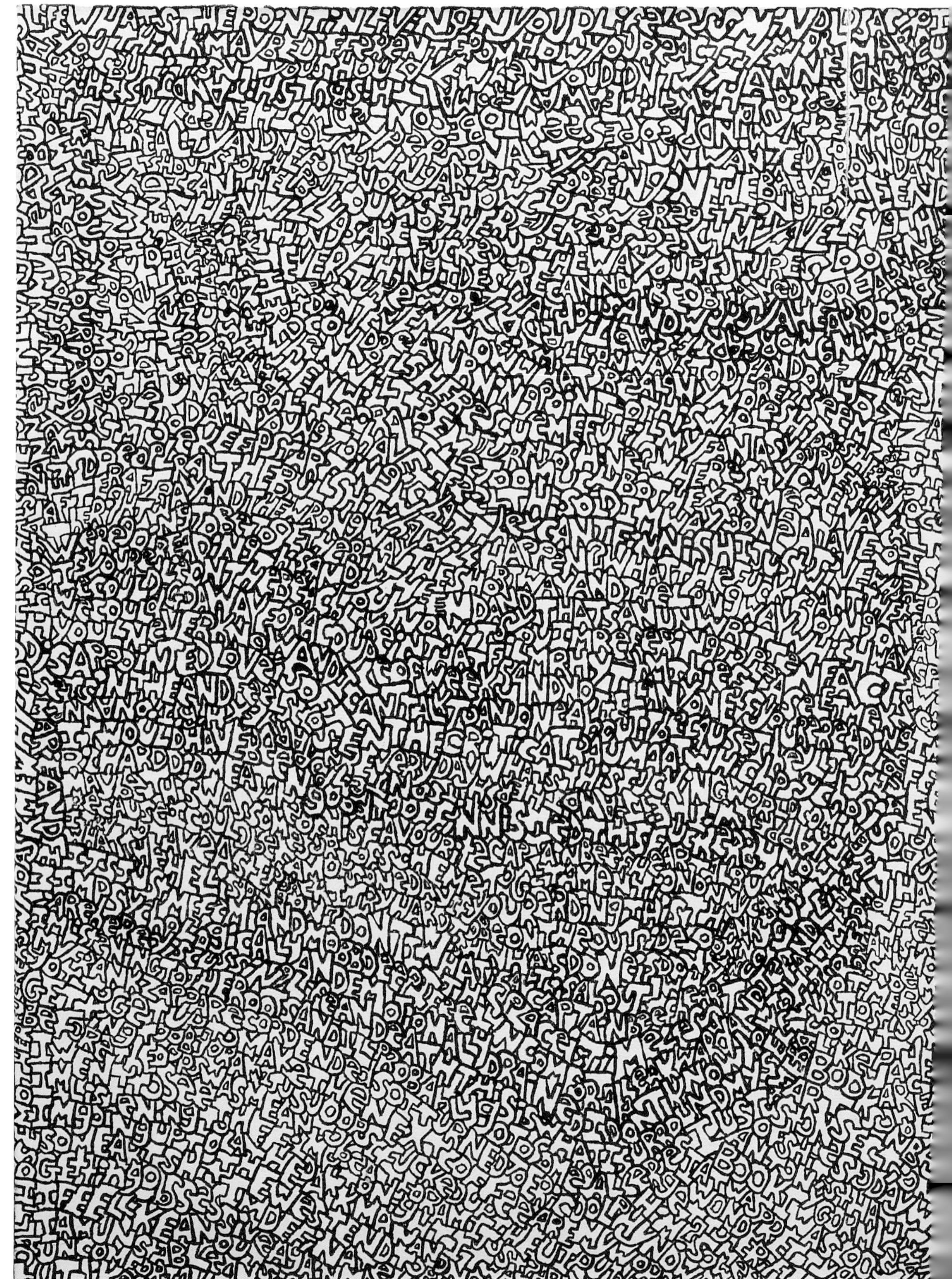

Carlo Keshishian
Picture Worth a Thousand Words
1998–9
Spray and gloss paint on canvas
151 × 116 cm

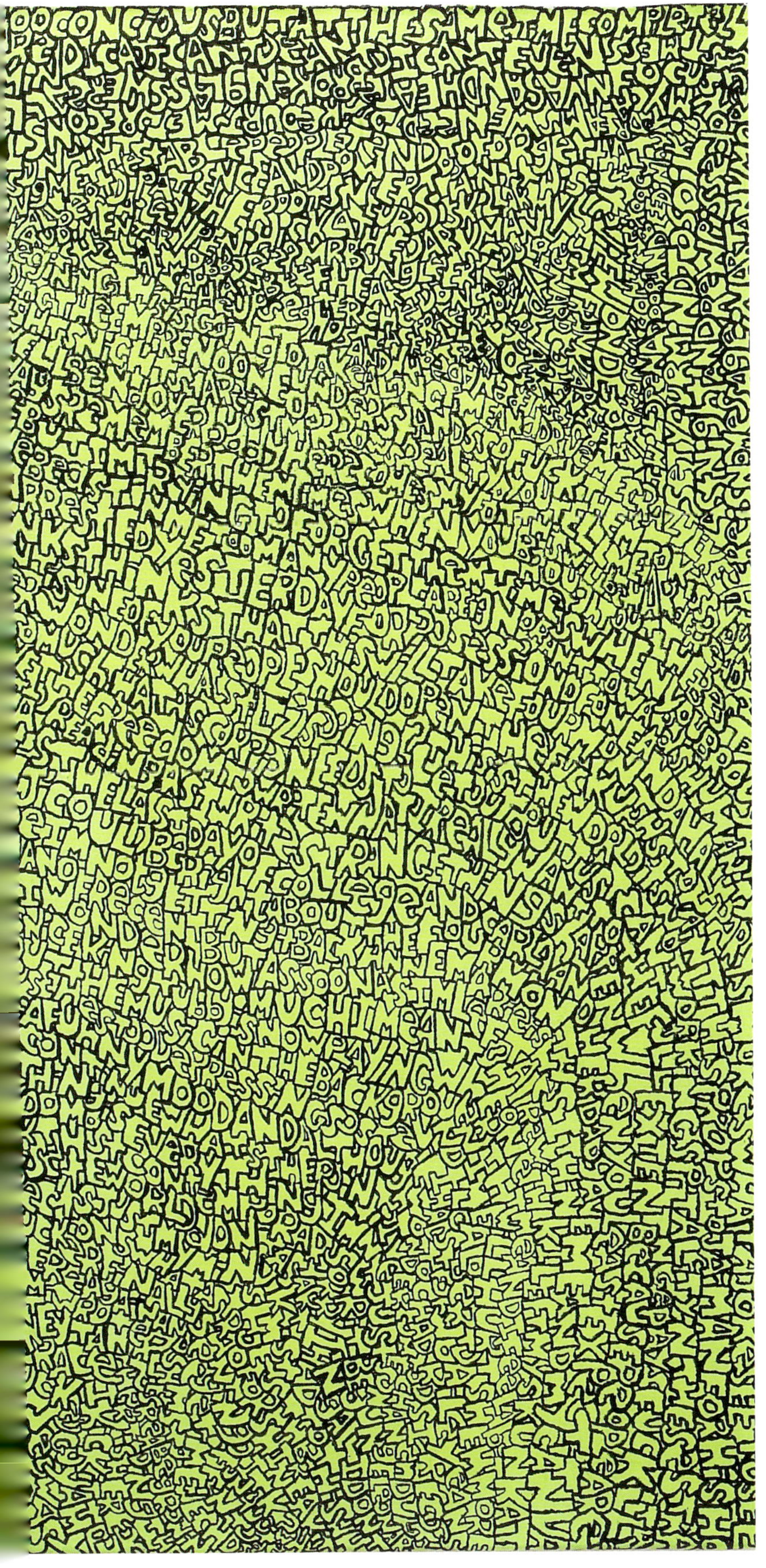

past, contemplations of the present and future, in relation to myself and the worlds around me, and further afield. I'm trying to capture all the mundane details and also what else is going on at the same time'. The diary drawings can take a long time to complete; one took around four and half years. Carlo said about his diary drawings that they 'could be interpreted as me wanting to share what I think, but at the same time, not wanting to share it. It is about ambivalence. Ambivalence is underrated. It makes me feel uneasy to think of other people reading it.'

To have an insight into someone's life might seem voyeuristic, maybe even a little uncomfortable. Being insightful might mean that we are able to share and learn from them. The *Oxford English Dictionary* definition of insight is 'the capacity to gain an accurate and deep understanding of someone or something'. The work in this chapter is important as it enables an understanding of, and develops compassion for, artists whose lives have been or continue to be challenging. The process of gaining and sharing insight can also challenge stigma and prejudice in a wider set of audiences, all too often lacking the courage or confidence to express or deal with these issues themselves. There is real bravery at work here, not just in the situations in which the artists have found themselves in their lives, but in their honesty in sharing their stories. As already observed, art does not always have to be beautiful or easy to look at. It can be difficult.

There is an important lesson in this type of work as it reveals the benefit of enabling creativity and its capacity to heal and help heal others, a tool which we all own, but often have forgotten to use. It reminds us that if we have something to share or express then it is important to do so, and that a connection with a lived experience can produce art of incredible strength and validity. The world would be a happier and healthier place if everyone could gain the benefits of living a creative life.

> 'The act of painting is about one heart telling another heart where he found salvation.'
> *Francisco Goya*

Carlo Keshishian
Diary Drawing
(31,036 words)
2020–21
Ink on card
29.7 × 21 cm

Interview with Grayson Perry

Grayson Perry, artist, writer and broadcaster, talks to Marc Steene, director of Outside In.

Marc Steene: This book explores and looks at artists who come from outside the recognised art world, including artists supported by the charity Outside In. It explores the reasons why they make their work, their use of unconventional practices and the settings in which the work is made. Making art is not necessarily about having a conventional artist studio or studying techniques. Often art produced by people on the periphery of the art world is driven by necessity, rather than methods taught in art school. This book looks at the subjects, techniques and skills which people have developed out of that need to create.

Grayson Perry: Yeah, it is certainly something that I think about a lot. We were hanging the show in Manchester that's come out of Channel 4's *Art Club* in which members of the public were encouraged to submit work. Everybody is included, from someone who hadn't done a painting since they were at primary school, at one end of the scale, to internationally known, established artists such as Antony Gormley at the other end of it. So, it was quite interesting when you hang them all in a room and give them all equal weight and nice frames and display them with space around them ... suddenly you need reminding which ones are the professional artists!

MS: It's so true though, isn't it?

GP: It is to a certain extent. I think one of the important parts of my practice has always been that when people come to an art gallery, they want to see something special, something that you wouldn't see anywhere else apart from in an art gallery. I don't really want to see something ordinary that's been dragged into the art gallery. Outsider art is something I have been studying all my professional life really ...

MS: I am really interested to know your thoughts on outsider art and the terminology that's used to describe it. What do 'outsider art' and 'outsider artist' mean now?

GP: Yes, it's a contested word isn't it. And I don't know if it's been sucked into the kind of 'woke', 'politically correct' thing now ... or even whether outsider art really exists? I mean, it still seems to have legs. My first encounter with outsider art was in 1979 in the *Outsiders* exhibition at the Hayward Gallery, London.

MS: I saw it as a student and it completely changed my world in terms of what I understood about art, and realising that there were other reasons why people make art. It was just groundbreaking. It completely transformed me, seeing that exhibition. Was it like that for you?

GP: It gave me permission to be more myself. I think when I was at art school, I wanted to be a good student. I mean, I always wanted to be a good student! And I think it gave me permission to be more my own sort of artist and not to worry about being a part of the art world or being part of art history. In art college they used to drum into you things like 'craft is dead' or 'decoration is a swear word'– the kind of orthodoxies of an over-intellectualised practice. When I saw that exhibition, I understood that these are people who just want to make things. They're not people who want to be an 'artist'. I always say to students: I'm not interested in people who want to be famous artists, I'm interested in people who want to make art. That was in 1979 and we're still using the 'outsider art' term now. 'Art Brut' seems a bit rude. 'Self-taught' I quite like!

'Self-taught' is quite a nice term but somehow it doesn't convey the spirit of it. 'Self-taught' could describe polite watercolours that someone has done. Whereas when you and I think of 'outsider art', we think of something a little bit deeper. It suggests someone who's embraced art as opposed to someone who is doing painting or craft because they've tapped into some kind of wellspring of what it is to be an artist. That's what I look to outsider art for, that kind of deep need to communicate through images.

MS: Yes, I agree.

GP: I'm continually fascinated by outsider art and it feeds into my practice constantly for the kind of permission it gives. It gives me permission to be a bit obsessive and to disregard the snobberies and rules that I've absorbed from the art world. I was making a piece recently and it was taking me right back to when I made Airfix models when I was a kid. I was making this sculpture of a car. It was literally model-making again and I thought 'fuck is this a bit self-indulgent?' It was interesting that there was a barrier in my head telling me I couldn't make a model. But with my car sculpture, I was giving myself permission, realising that I'm allowed to do that.

How do we encourage people to make things, satisfying things, as opposed to 'artistic' things. I'm conscious of the issue of art materials and what things are made of. We need to make things that are durable because quite often the materials that people use can be a bit shit. People need to be given good stuff to work with.

MS: But then doesn't that defeat the object?

GP: I don't necessarily mean that they have to be cast in bronze or something.

MS: But that is what the trouble is. People think, 'Oh, what artists need is a studio and an easel and good-quality paints and a canvas'. But actually, an artist might have developed a practice over ten years using the back of a cornflakes packet and felt-tips, which actually resulted in something really interesting.

GP: Yes, I agree with you there. I think I just have a problem with what I call the 'paint box', where you've got ten colours and you feel you have to use all the colours. Or you've got some collage materials in your bag bought from a collage materials shop specifically for making collages ... It's the opposite of what you're talking about, in a way. How do you encourage people to get away from what they think they should be doing? That's the thing.

MS: One group, based in Darlington, does stand out and they produce the most amazing work. Laurence Ward, who supports them, is very skilled. They've produced some of the most beautiful work I've seen. I remember when you were judging our National Exhibition in 2019, you made a comment about the work of Alan Payler, the award winner. 'Oh God,' you said, 'they've done it all in felt-tip!' You thought that all the mark making – because it was done with felt-tip – would probably fade to nothing with time. I felt, 'fuck art materials! Why is it always about needing quality materials?' I liked its impermanence.

GP: I remember that I loved them! And also, because the artists became good at what they were doing, they learned skills. They become good at drawing or painting or sculpting or whatever. I remember that brilliant exhibition of Japanese outsider art!

MS: Oh yes, at the Wellcome Collection in London.

GP: Oh, that was so good! There were such fantastic things in that show, and so skilful. I think what is brilliant to me as an artist, is that the aesthetic sense always comes through, it drives through all those other layers of creativity. It also drives through age, it drives through mental ability, it drives through skill. I have a feeling that the first thing those people made was probably pretty good. But by the time they made the next piece, they probably had something – and were off and running.

MS: Completely. There is something about that sort of intuitive making, where there's a lack of inhibition which allows you to work in a way which is truly your own.

GP: I don't think it's necessarily a mystical thing that you have from birth. I think it's more likely that people are unconsciously conditioned.

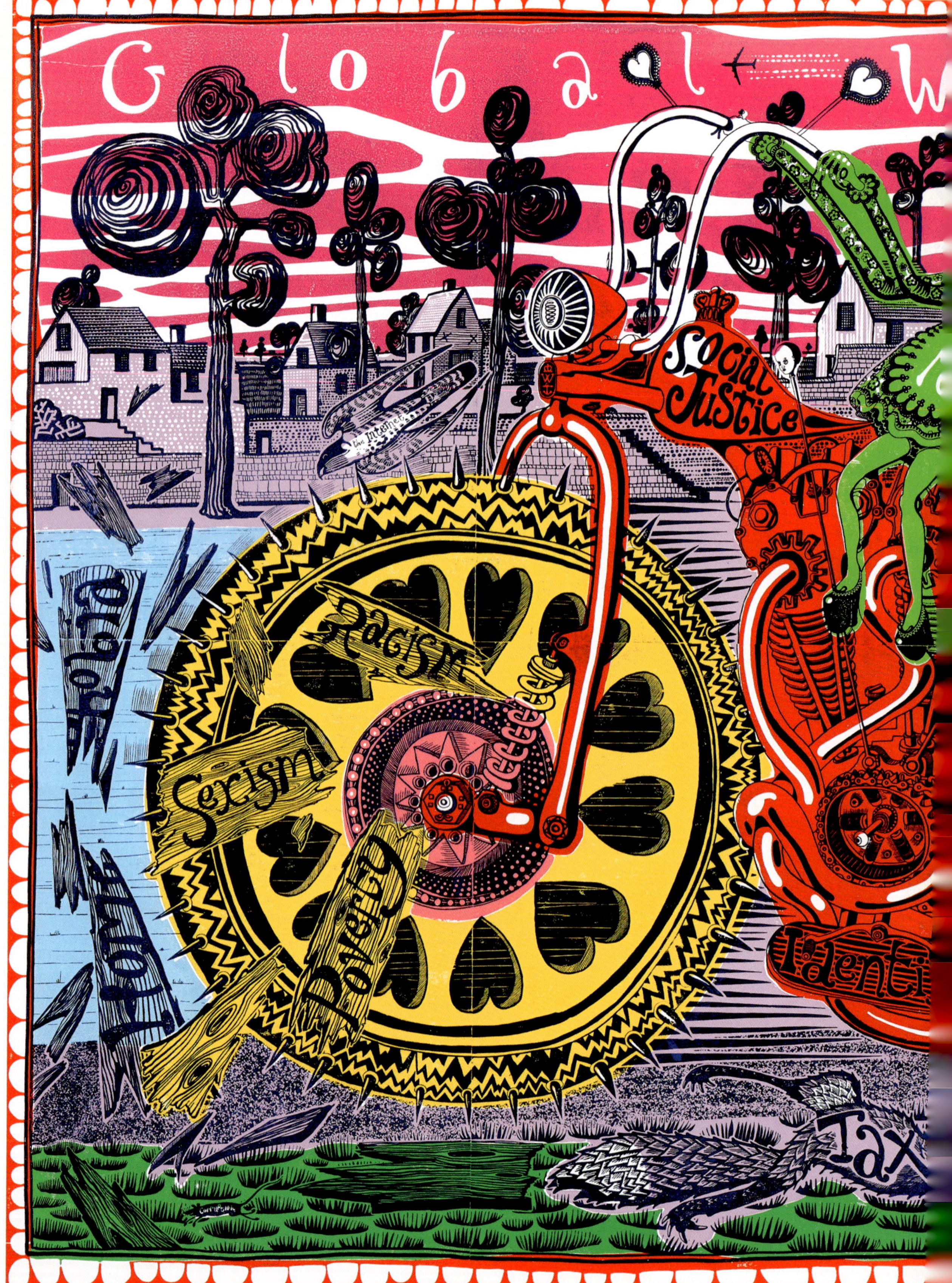

Grayson Perry
Selfie with Political Causes
2018
Woodblock print
Edition of 15 plus 2 artist's proofs
196 × 293 cm
(sheet size)

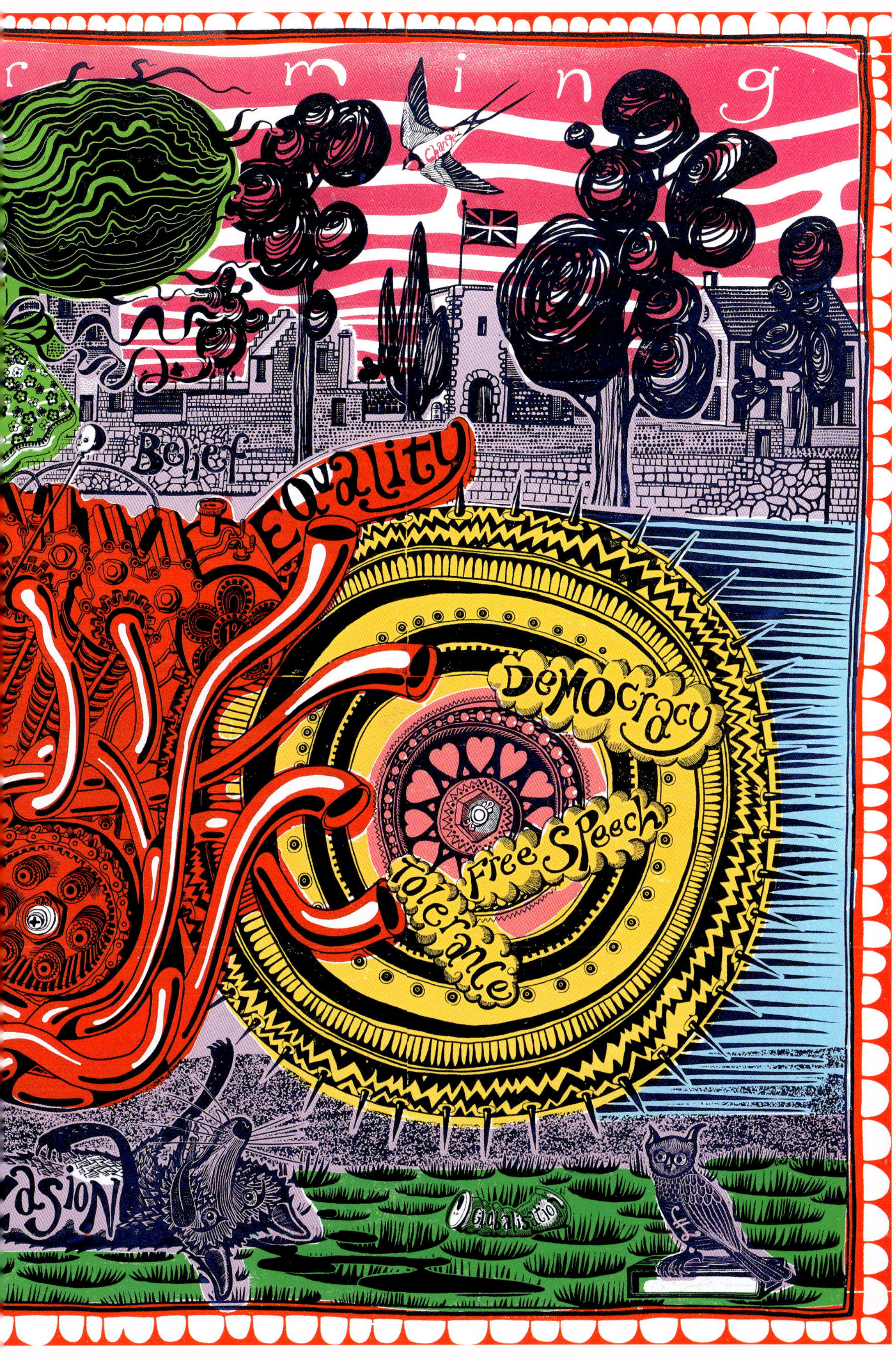
Change
Belief
Equality
Democracy
Free Speech
Tolerance

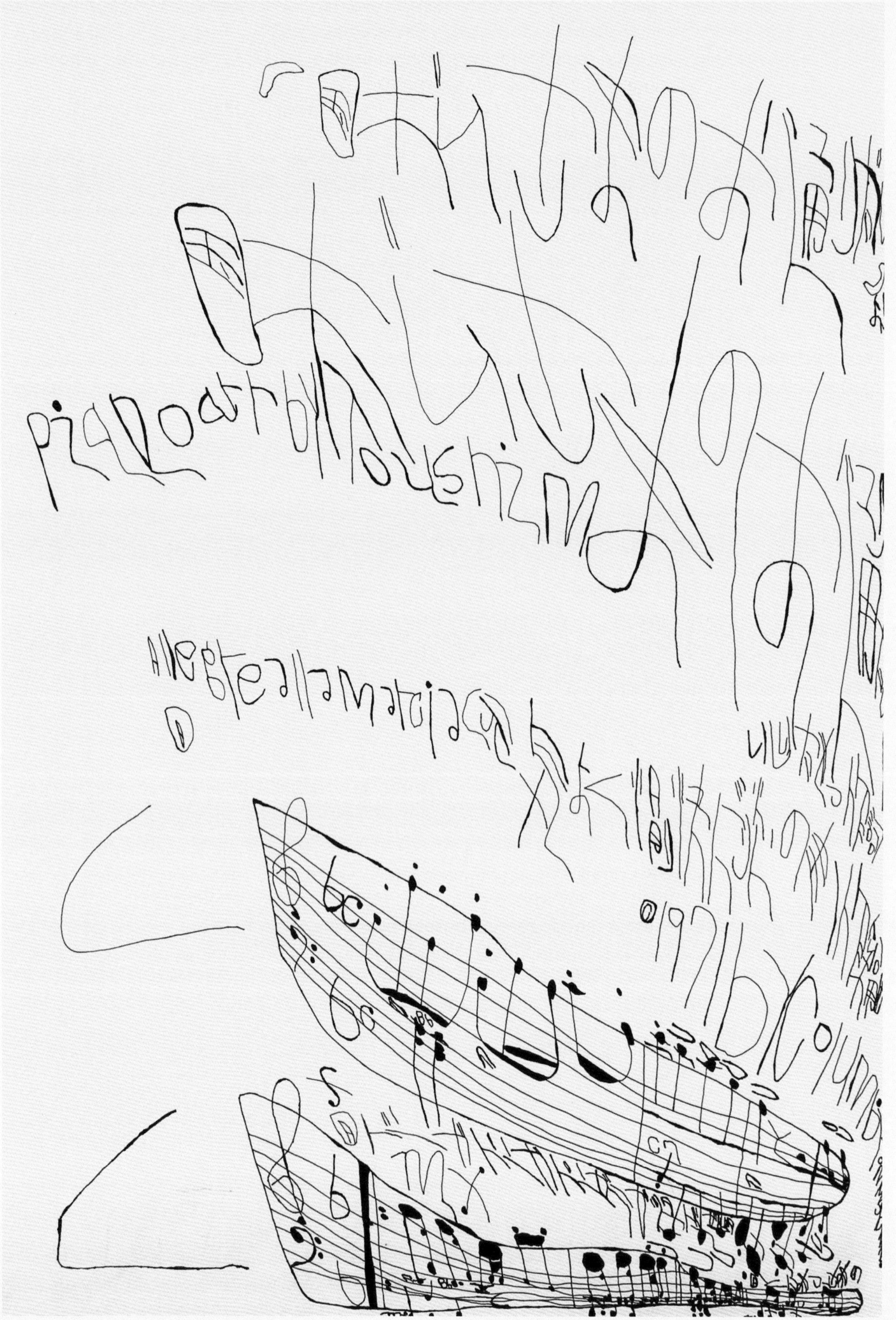

Koji Nishioka
Untitled
2016
Pen on paper
54 × 38 cm

Outsider artists are very sensitive people, so their receptors are out there and then they're exposed by conditioning to something that triggers an aesthetic joy or whatever. And they love putting things together, colours together, shapes together, textures together, etc. They are playing. Because art is play and nowhere is that more apparent than in outsider art – it's fun. I think that about my own practice and the outsider artists I love. What's so beautiful about it is that people are just having a conversation with themselves and saying 'well that red stick looks brilliant with that green stick. I'm going to put the black blob on top of it' and that's great.

MS: It's brilliant – my neighbour on the road where I live in Brighton, had an uncle and she'd tell me these stories about him and how he had made these German Second World War airplanes, Messerschmitts, out of cornflakes boxes because he had seen them fly over during the war. And they sounded like quite naive but beautiful things, and I said, 'Oh God that sounds amazing, I'd love to see them!' And when he died, I said to my neighbour, 'Don't forget to let me see them'. I could imagine this massive squadron of planes, but they destroyed the lot of them. Because they were embarrassed! They were embarrassed by what they thought were these crap airplanes made out of cardboard boxes. I wonder how much work is destroyed because people don't see it as art.

GP: Let me tell you about someone I visited the other day who reminded me of an outsider artist, although he's the absolute opposite of an outsider artist: Harry Hill, the comedian.

MS: Oh yes!

GP: He does wood carvings, but it's quite like outsider art. He carves these little statues and then he paints them. I think what really brings them alive is that he's found this enamel that they use in fairgrounds, called something like Craftsman Enamel and it's super glossy and super thick. The result is that they almost look glazed. And he paints these quite crude wood carvings and they're brilliant. If you asked me if these were outsider art I would say, yes they are, definitely.

MS: Does he know that? Is he aware?

GP: Yes. He's super aware.

MS: So, is he doing it with a sort of faux *naïveté*?

GP: No, he's coming from a knowledgeable starting point. He's got paintings up all round his studio that are quite good. So then he went into wood carving, and he wasn't so good at wood carving and that's what made them look like outsider art.

MS: Yeah, that's it, isn't it!

GP: It's all about the recipe isn't it? If you can't draw but you do it right to the edges and spend 50 hours on it, it's art.

MS: Yes, a labour of love.

GP: Right, totally. It's been a delight talking to you Marc.

Grayson Perry is an internationally celebrated English artist, writer and broadcaster. He is known for his ceramic vases, tapestries and cross-dressing, as well as the social commentary which is incorporated into his art. Perry's vases have classical forms and are decorated in bright colours, depicting subjects at odds with their attractive appearance. There is a strong autobiographical element in his work, in which images of Perry as 'Claire', his female alter ego, and 'Alan Measles', his childhood teddy bear, often appear.

Outside In Artists

Wherever possible, Outside In supports its artists to write their own artist statements, enabling them to self-define as artists in their own words. Some of these statements vary in length and comprise of quotes from the artists and others that have been put together by carers or support organisations. Where it has not been possible to gain a photograph of the artist, an image of their artwork has been used in its place.

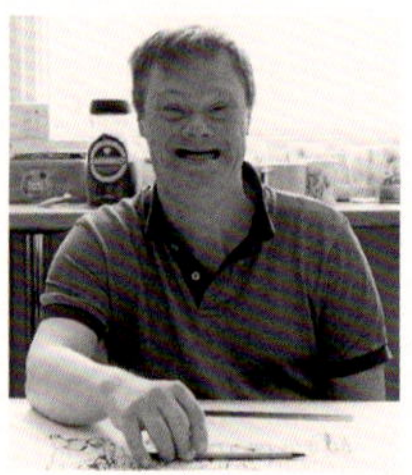

Matthew Beadon (b.1961)
Matthew attends the Community Art Project in Darlington. He describes his drawings as 'pictures of houses' and they usually contain architectural details and sometimes other recognisable elements such as figures, embedded in complex geometric patterns and structures.

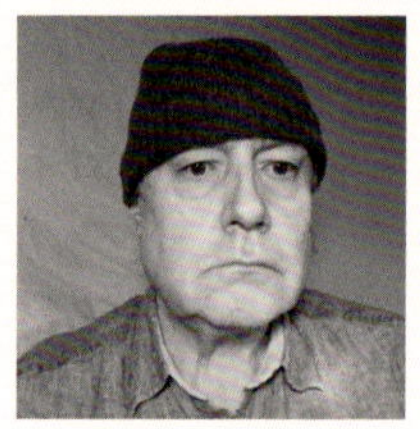

David Beales (b.1954)
'I am 68 years old, and I have been painting and drawing since I was a child. In 1975 I applied to Croydon School of Art and was accepted but could not get a grant for housing. After staying in squats for a few months I left the School of Art in spring 1976. I retreated to my parents but became withdrawn, then disturbed. In September 1976 I was admitted a psychiatric ward attached to Farnborough hospital, near Orpington. I was in and out of various psychiatric hospitals where I attended art therapy when I could and learnt to use art as a coping strategy. I have stayed out of hospital since 1992. In the community I have continued to draw and make prints, mainly informed by my own experiences and observations.'

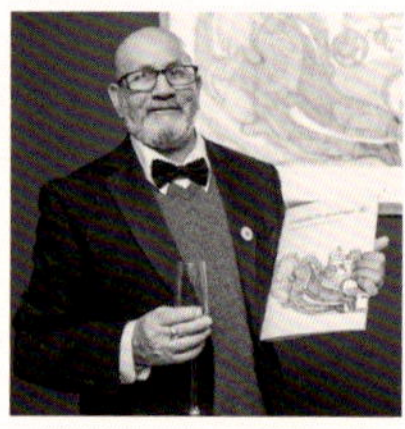

Manuel Bonifacio (b.1947)
'Being a part of Outside In has been life-changing in an emotional aspect and has had a positive impact on my life. It fills me with joy that someone appreciates my work. Outside In have helped me become a global artist and have my dream of being recognised come true. I am always producing more work to be displayed in museums around the world. I want to meet members of the Royal Family and travel around the world to see my work in museums though sadly I can't afford to travel.'

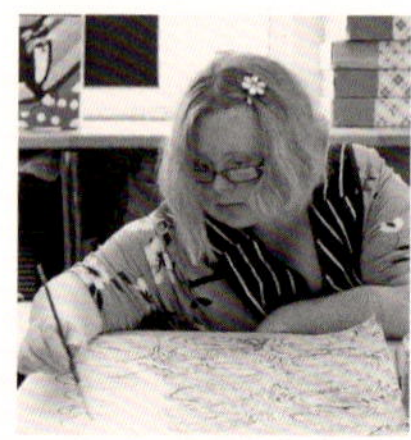

Victoria Bowman (b.1984)
Victoria attends the Community Art Project in Darlington. 'Art means a lot to me. I like to take my time and concentrate. I do think of myself as an artist. My sister was a good artist and she inspired me as well as my auntie.'

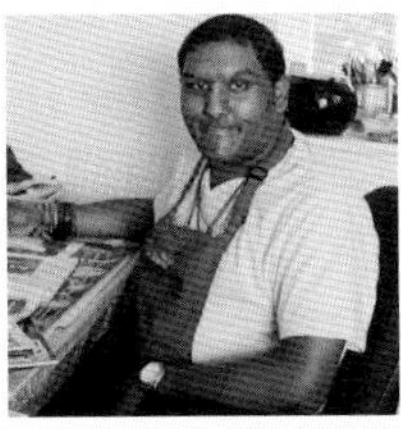

Rakibul Chowdhury (b.1987)
Raki was born in Petersfield, where his father ran a restaurant, and attends Art Invisible in Emsworth. 'I look at lots of magazines, *Empire*, *Stardust*, *You*, *Heat*, *Film*, *Hello! Fashion*, *Metro*, *Cosmopolitan* etc. I read the daily newspapers. I watch *EastEnders*, *Coronation Street*, *Strictly Come Dancing*, *The X Factor*.'

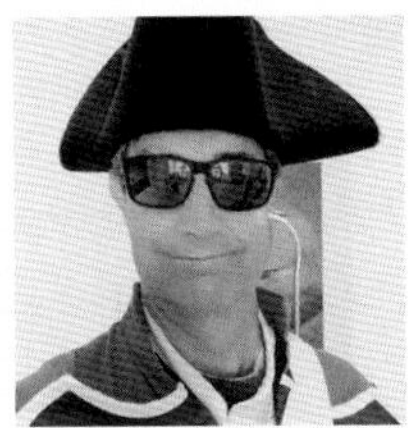

Charles Devus (b.1962)
'I was born into a volatile and dysfunctional bohemian family. My parents were painters, my grandfather a playwright, my paternal grandmother one of the hangers-on in the Bloomsbury set and my great-grandfather a successful author and journalist. There is a long line of actors and music hall comedians including Jimmy Nervo, famous for his times as a member of the Crazy Gang in the 1940s. I have the distinction of a bloodline that includes several convicts and peer of the realm and can now trace my ancestry back to some truly ancient poets.'

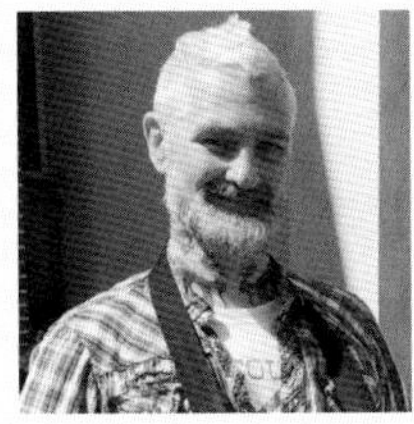

Drew Fox (b.1965)
'Born in 65, left school at 16 with no qualifications due to dyslexia which wasn't recognised at the time. Worked in factories and menial labour until 21 when I began living in a travelling off-grid anarchist commune for nine years, became a single parent in '94 for 18 years, again working in menial labour until I returned to university in 2004. I began working in health and social care in 2009. Cardiac business in 2012, lost job and made homeless. I continued to work menial jobs until ill health forced me to quit in 2019 and I moved to Sussex where I continue with my photography.'

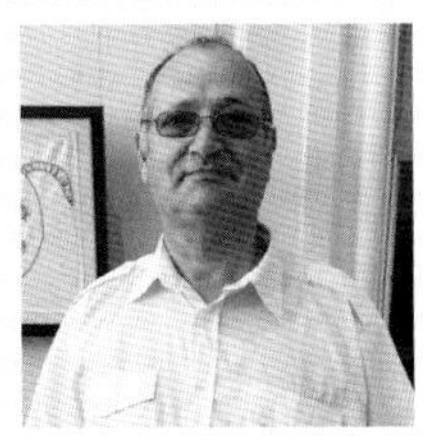

James Gladwell (b.1952)
James is supported by Barrington Farm in Norfolk where he has been making art since 1987. 'If I get things in my head, I start drawing. Some of my work is from my dreams. If I dream something I've got to put it down on the cloth right away. I have the cloth on my lap with a lamp and my music on. I keep the gypsy way of life going in my needlework. I'd be lost without doing the sewing.'

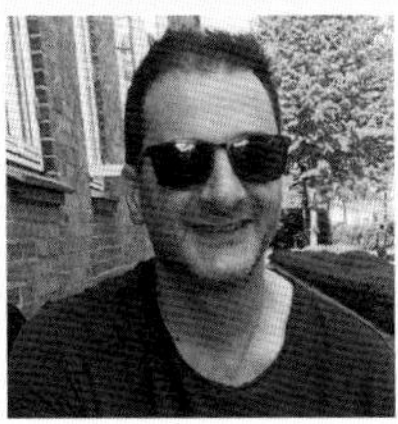

Andrew Hood (b.1967)
'I am interested in the space that's around me, particularly inside my home. I see space as fractured dimensions that can be free and open or closed and restricting. The internal and external world merge and flip in space and become reality. It feels like I am unravelling these spaces and merging into another state of consciousness.'

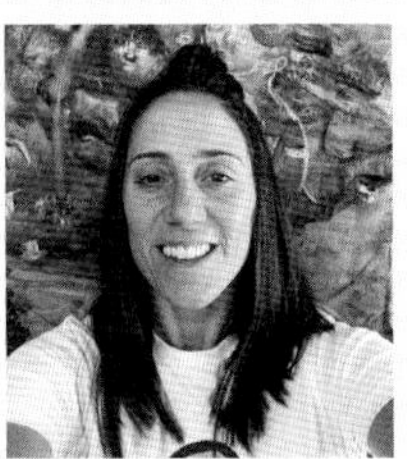

Dannielle Hodson (b.1980)
Dannielle was educated at Central Saint Martins, London (BA Womenswear Fashion Design, MA Fine Art) and is a graduate of the Turps Banana studio painting programme.

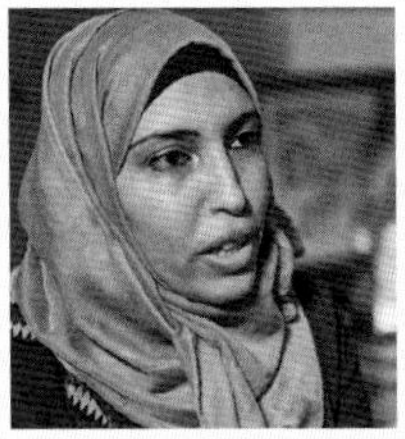

Laila Kassab (b.1985)
Laila is a Palestinian artist. She was raised in a Rafah refugee camp and attended UNRWA school. She has a degree in psychology from Al-Aqsa University in Gaza, Palestine. Laila is a member of the Gaza Art Association and has exhibited her work at the City Hall, Gaza.

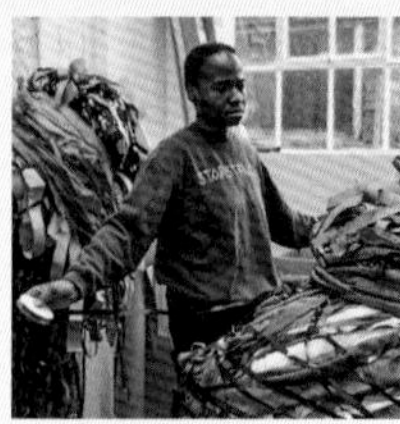

Nnena Kalu (b.1966)
Nnena has developed her artistic practice at ActionSpace's studio in Studio Voltaire since 1999. Over 20 years, Nnena has created a significant body of work and has exhibited nationally and internationally, including three major solo exhibitions.

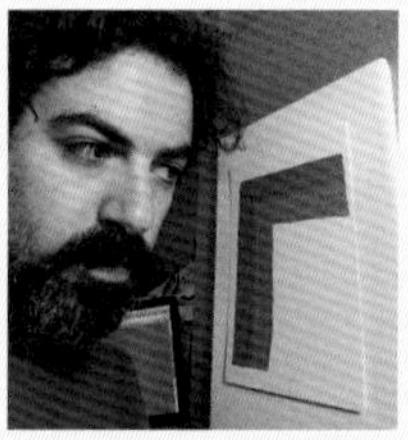

Carlo Keshishian (b.1980)
Carlo is a visual and sonic artist based in London. He works primarily with ink and paint, mostly focusing on a series of text-based diary drawings that capture his engagement with what he considers the illusory nature of time. He uses the creation process to reinforce or reimagine memories.

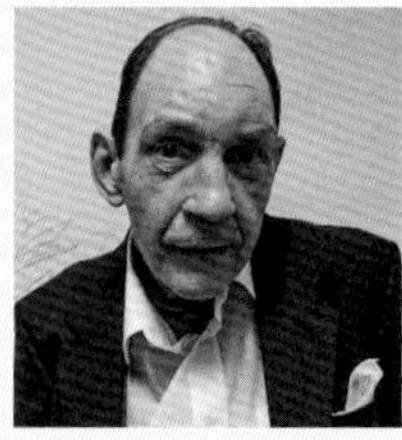

Nigel Kingsbury (1949–2016)
Nigel worked at the ActionSpace studio at Studio Voltaire in Clapham from 2004 to 2015. When he was younger, he spent a lot of time in hospital and drew artistic inspiration from the nurses there.

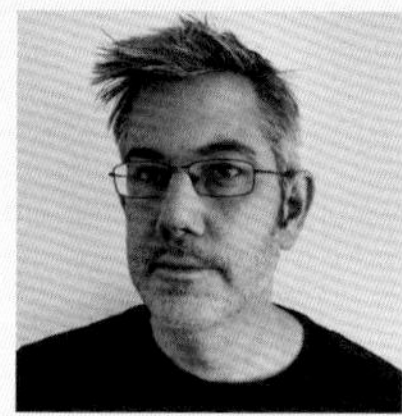

James Lake (b.1974)
'I am a sculptor. I work with cardboard for its immediacy, ease of availability and low environmental impact. My disability and dyslexia have also influenced my choice of material and the way I create my sculptures. For over 20 years I have created life-size three-dimensional portraits of people. I have also made animals, anatomical models, furniture, and other large-scale work for commission. I believe in art for all, art beyond race, gender, age, ability and disability. My work has appeared in the world-renowned Lucca Biennale and in local primary schools, as well as arts centres and exhibition spaces locally and nationally.'

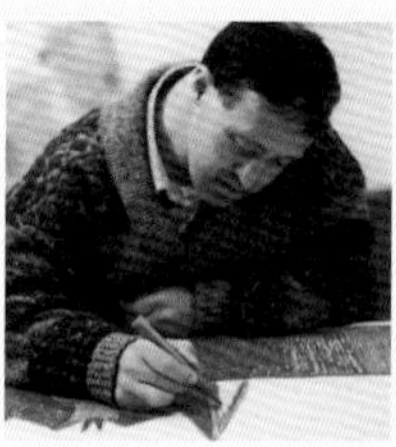

Alan Liddle (1955–2019)
Alan attended the Community Art Project in Darlington for over 20 years. He was very prolific and seemed deeply content when engrossed in one of his intricate geometric drawings, exploring the possibilities of line and pattern with great skill and patience.

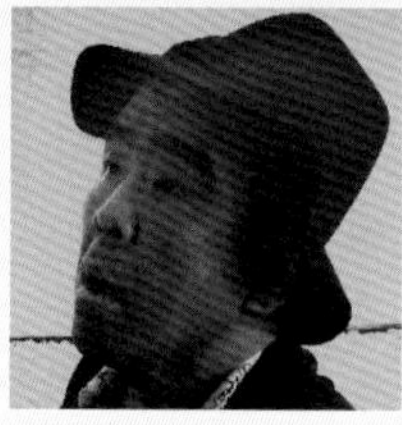

Koji Nishioka (b.1970)
Koji was born in Osaka, Japan, and is supported by Atelier Corners in Japan. Koji produces his drawings from existing music scores. He avoids distraction when creating by not listening to music, but he will hum songs as he draws. It seems there is always music in his head. As Koji's astigmatism worsens in his left eye, the compositions of his musical score drawings move further to the right.

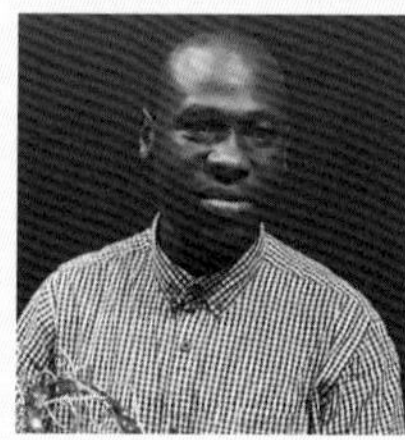

Andrew Omoding (b.1987)
Andrew is a young Ugandan-British artist supported by ActionSpace in London. He uses found materials and objects to create sculptural forms, binding them together, wrapping and layering with an implicit knowledge of shape and construction. Initially creating one-off sculptures, he now creates collections of pieces that are arranged together to tell stories, which are written down and sewn into banner-sized 'books' to accompany the work.

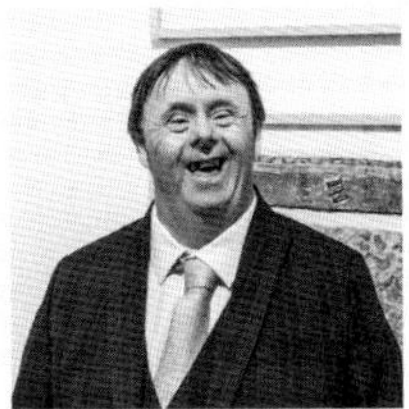

Alan Payler (b.1970)
Alan attended the Community Art Project in Darlington for two years, creating a distinctive body of work often featuring large expanses of colour with small objects or figures placed within them. He works with great patience – working his way slowly across the picture surface, filling large areas with carefully applied small marks, stopping every now and then to look at his picture and contemplate his next steps.

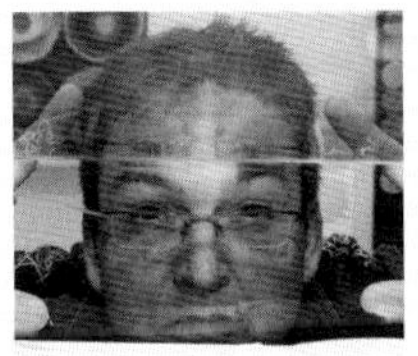

Neal Pearce (b.1967)
'I was born in Dorking on 12th April 1967. I changed my name to Neal Salvatore Pearce in December 2013. I added this middle name because I wanted to recognise a long-held belief that I came here as cosmic emissary/ messiah figure to inspire and enlighten Mankind in a bid to avert its apparently fated trajectory towards extinction. My art is simple and yet meticulous. I've been using what is one of the most ubiquitous writing instruments (the Bic biro) for 30 years now. My codex - Terra Computatrum as it came to be known – and mandalas were inspired by Douglas Adams' portrayal of the Earth and all its life as being part of a computational matrix devised to answer the ultimate question of life the universe and everything.'

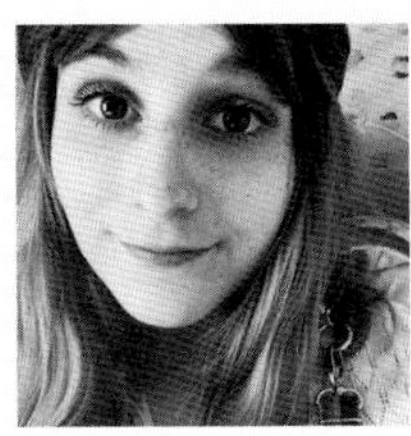

Corinne (b.1990)
'I'm Corinne, a disabled queer self-portrait artist. My struggles with severe mental illness confine me to bed. From here with the help of my imaginary and only childhood friend named Daisy I create photographic self-portraits as a form of therapy.'

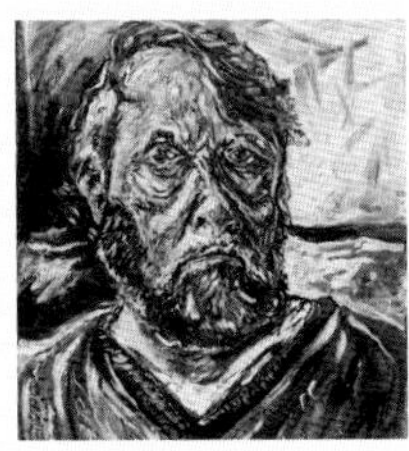

Jonathan Pettitt (b.1952)
'I was born in 1952, exactly 500 years to the year that Leonard da Vinci was born. In 1968 age 16 I was awarded first prize for highest graded O Level in Art at my school. In 1970, I moved to Eastbourne, East Sussex, and went to art school there and studied printmaking and illustration. I was the only one in my year to fail the illustration course. In 1972, I was awarded most meritorious student of the year for my printmaking. In 1974, I was awarded vocational certification in printmaking and illustration. That year I went to Byam Shaw School of Art. I had to work in a factory, twelve hours a day seven days a week during college holidays.'

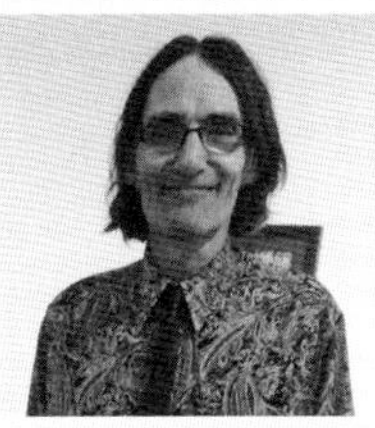

Martin Phillimore (1960–2017)
'My art was an outlet to start with and a way to express how I was feeling at the time. I include themes of nature with an organic feel in my work. My art gave me focus and I was happy when I was doing it.'

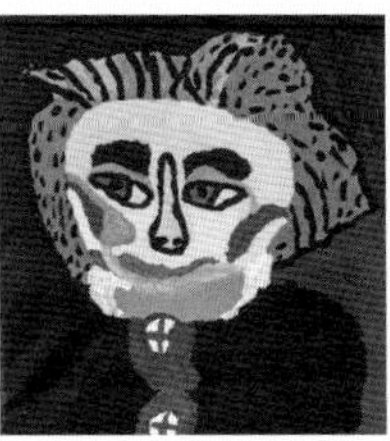

Keith Purcell (birth date not known)
Keith attended the Grace Eyre Foundation for a number of years and was a prolific painter. He is also a medal-winning weightlifter.

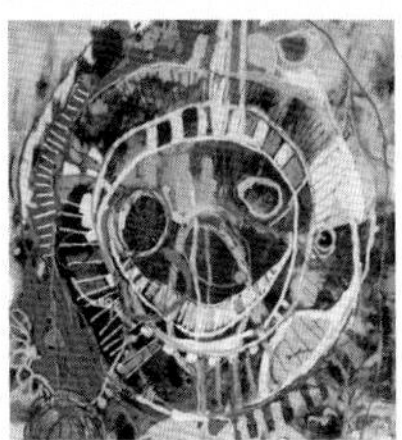

David Puttick (b.1963)
'I take a sketchbook wherever I go and have my pens in my bag, so I am creating all the time, it has been part of my life for a long time. I am a paranoid schizophrenic diagnosed at 20 and I am now 59. Life is very challenging, and I find creativity has been a constant tool to help my diagnosis.'

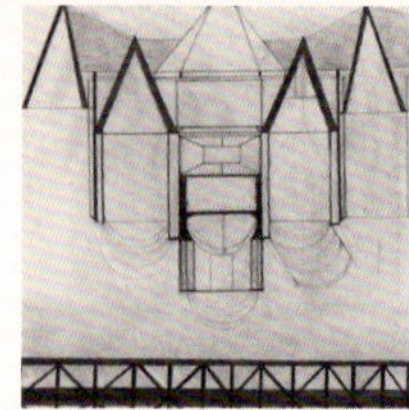

Albert Rackett (b.1962)
'I like to work with my hands. I've drawn for years on and off, even as a child I was always scribbling something, but I didn't take it seriously until I came to Bethlem[1] where I was encouraged by the staff to take it further. I draw to pass the time and it helps to get rid of my depression, especially when they go right, I like to draw buildings which I could imagine living in, they are safe, warm spaces with fences around them.'

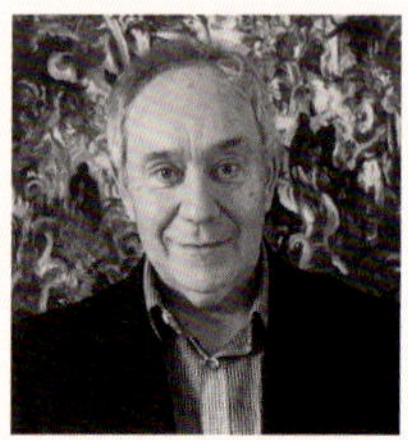

Ian Sherman (b.1961)
'My work is a response to being alive, its wonders and absurdities in a complex and beguiling world. The assemblages I create are usually made from diverse found objects and materials, initially in the workshop and later the kitchen.'

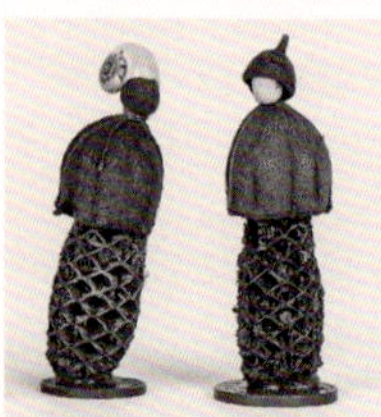

Joanna Simpson (b.1959)
'Inspired by materials available, the work is always created in response to the environment, with love for my own four children and compassion for all the lost children of the Stolen Generations, Australia, and globally.'

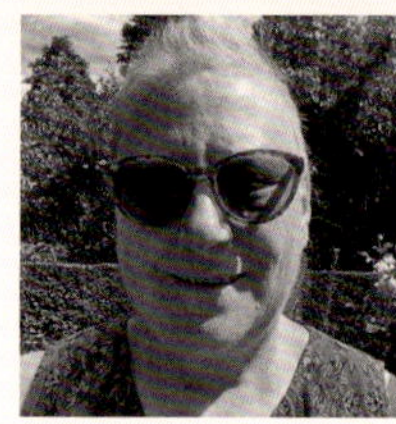

Tess Springall (b.1965)
'I first heard about Outside In through Creative Response and entered some work in 2009 to a competition that led to an exhibition at Pallant House Gallery. I have always loved art. I have worked as a potter at Amberley Chalk Pits Museum, a silversmith at R.L.S. Silversmiths and later in life took a National Diploma in graphic design and illustration at Northbrook College that led on to doing a degree at University of Portsmouth in Art Design and Media and Communication Design which I graduated from in 2001 with a 2:1. I was first ill in 2007 when I was sectioned and again in 2008. I was in hospital for about three months on both occasions and was diagnosed with bipolar. I enjoy painting, drawing, sculpture and experimenting with various media. Art is a great healer.'

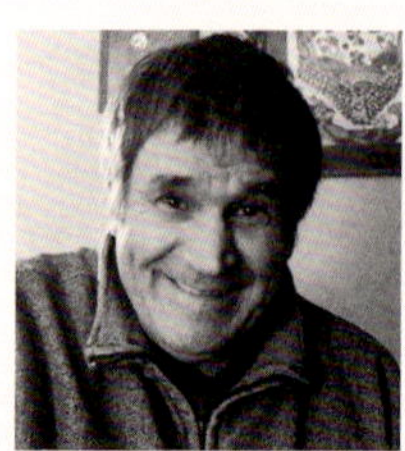

Chaz Waldren (b.1950)
'I use colouring pens and biros and felt-tip pens as I find I can have much more control over detail in my pictures. I really don't think I could do the same with a brush and paint. I'm just not that good an artist so I usually keep to what I can do. Two things have stayed with me over the years. One is my music and the other is the Church, which has always been a source of support and encouragement.'

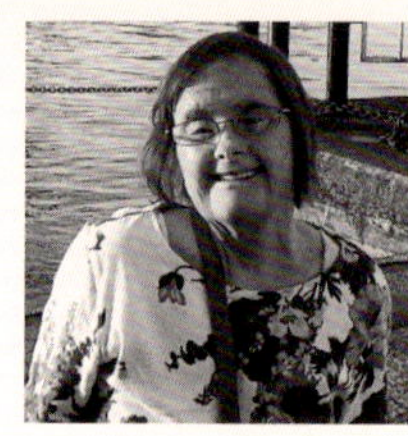

Joan Wilkinson (1946–2020)
Joan Wilkinson (née Jeffrey) was born in 1946 in Haverton Hill near Billingham. She attended the Community Art Project in Darlington for several years, producing a body of distinctive artwork which mixed humour, charm and intense concentration. Joan sadly passed away in October 2020 and her personality and presence is much missed but fondly remembered.

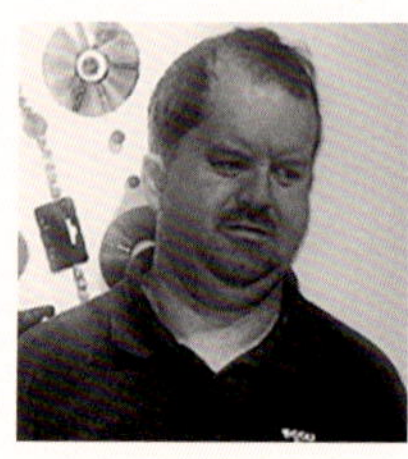

Gary Williams (b.1957)
Gary attends the Aldingbourne Trust in West Sussex.

Notes

Foreword

1. Outside In is a member of the European Outsider Art Association and Marc Steene is the Vice President.

Preface

1. Herbert, Martin, 'The Joys of Looking at Art Outside "the Artworld"', *ArtReview*, July 2022, https://artreview.com/the-joys-of-looking-at-art-outside-the-artworld.
2. Lakin, Max, 'The Enduring Appeal of the Self-Taught Artist', *The New York Times Style Magazine*, 7 July 2022, https://www.nytimes.com/2022/07/07/t-magazine/self-taught-artists.html.

Introduction

1. Pallant House Gallery is located in Chichester and holds one of the most important collections of Modern British Art in the country.
2. Arts Council England (ACE) Relationship Framework, 2018, p.5, https://www.artscouncil.org.uk/sites/default/files/download-file/NPO_2018-22_Relationship_Framework.pdf.

Chapter One – Intuition

1. Picasso, Marina, *Picasso: My Grandfather*, Vintage, New York, 2001.
2. Parr, Hester, 'Mental Health, the arts and belongings', *Transactions of the Institute of British Geographers*, June 2006, p.162.
3. *Raw Vision*, no.83, autumn 2014.
4. Leo Steinberg selections, http://www.artchive.com/theory/steinbrg/steinbrg.htm
5. Weidinger, Albert and Lachmayer, Herbert, 'The master of erotic theatre: Gustav Klimt', 1 May 2008, https://www.tate.org.uk/tate-etc/issue-13-summer-2008/master-erotic-theatre.
6. Matisse, Henri, *Jazz*, Tériade, Paris, 1947.

Chapter Two – Introspection

1. Bettelheim, Bruno, *The Uses of Enchantment, The Meaning and Importance of Fairy Tales*, Penguin, London, 1991, p.107.
2. Luchsinger, Katrin et al, *Extra-ordinary! Unknown Works from Swiss Psychiatric Institutions around 1900*, Scheidegger & Spiess, Zurich, 2018, p.224.
3. Prinzhorn, Hans, *Bildnerei der Geisteskranken* (*Artistry of the Mentally Ill*), Verlag Von Julius Springer, Berlin, 1922.
4. English, Charlie, *The Gallery of Miracles and Madness*, Harper Collins, New York, 2021.
5. Diary entry, January 1912, no.905, quoting his 'Munich Art Letter' in the journal *Die Alpen*.
6. Hill, Adrian, *Art Versus Illness. A Story of Art Therapy*, G. Allen and Unwin, London, 1945, p.30.
7. A collection of 5500 objects (paintings, drawings, ceramics, sculptures, and works on stone, flint and bone) created between 1946 and 1981.
8. Foucault, Michel, *The History of Madness*, Routledge, Abingdon, 2001.
9. The Graylingwell Heritage Project was a community-based heritage and arts programme focusing upon the history of the Graylingwell Hospital (formerly the West Sussex County Asylum) and the people associated with it from 1894 to the present day. The project was a partnership between Chichester Community Development Trust, Pallant House Gallery, West Sussex Record Office and the University of Chichester.
10. Dr Brian Vawdrey was a well-respected psychiatrist who was the Senior Registrar and then Consultant at Graylingwell Hospital from 1954 to 1985. He trained as a Jungian psychotherapist and was one of the earlier exponents of art therapy.
11. Vawdrey, Brian Dr, 'Art in Analysis', MD thesis, University of Cambridge, 1953.
12. ibid.
13. Blinko, Nick, *The Primal Screamer*, PM Press, New York, 2011.
14. *Pallant House Gallery magazine*, No.24, 2011.
15. Durcan, Graham Dr, 'The future of prison mental health care in England, A national consultation and review', Centre for Mental Health, 2021, https://www.centreformentalhealth.org.uk/publications/future-prison-mental-health-care-england.
16. Hieronymus Bosch (c.1450–1516) was a Dutch painter from Brabant, famous for his fantastical paintings.
17. Spengler, Andreas, 'Julius Klingebiel and his Cell, a new chapter in psychiatric art history', in *Outsider Art: Interdisciplinary perspectives of an art form* (Bogaczyk-Vormayr, Małgorzata, Neumaier, Otto eds.), Lit Verlag, Vienna and Münster, 2017, pp 79–96.
18. ibid. p.84.
19. Jones, Raya A., 'A Discovery of Meaning: The case of C. G. Jung's house dream', Working Paper 79, 2007, School of Social Sciences, Cardiff University.
20. Friedrich Stowasser (1928–2000), better known by his pseudonym Hundertwasser, was an Austrian visual artist and architect who also worked in the field of environmental protection.
21. Cardinal, Roger, Carolin, Clare and Grayson, Richard, *A Secret Service: Art, Compulsion, Concealment*, Hayward Publishing, London, 2006.
22. Sherwood, Harriet, 'Blue plaque to honour Yorkshire woman who was locked in asylum for calling vicar a liar', the *Guardian*, 8 November 2020, https://www.theguardian.com/lifeandstyle/2020/nov/08/blue-plaque-to-honour-yorkshirewoman-who-was-locked-in-asylum-for-calling-vicar-a-liar.
23. https://forgottenwomenwake.com/our-women/mary-frances-heaton/
24. 'The Voynich manuscript is an illustrated codex handwritten in an otherwise unknown writing system, referred to as "Voynichese". The vellum on which it is written has been carbon-dated to the early 15th century (1404–38), and stylistic analysis indicates it may have been composed in Italy during the Italian Renaissance.' https://en.wikipedia.org/wiki/Voynich_manuscript
25. David Puttick, Artist of the Month, Outside In, June 2022, https://outsidein.org.uk/news/artist-of-the-month-june-2022-david-puttick/.
26. Oliver, Charlotte, 'The man behind the masks', *The Jewish Journal*, 2016, https://www.thejc.com/culture/features/the-man-behind-the-masks-1.61135.
27. Bettleheim, Bruno, *The Uses of Enchantment: The Meaning & Importance of Fairy Tales*, Penguin, London, 1991, p.109.

Chapter Three – Insight

1. https://en.wikipedia.org/wiki/Aktion_T4
2. *Merriam-Webster's Encyclopaedia of Literature*, Merriam-Webster, Springfield, Massachusetts, 1995, p.217.
3. Fundamental Principles of Disability: Being a Summary of the Discussion Held on 22nd November 1975 and Containing Commentaries from Each Organisation, Union of the Physically Impaired Against Segregation, UPIAS/Disability Alliance, 1976.
4. https://www.shapearts.org.uk/Blogs/arts blog/reflections-on-the-disability-arts-movement
5. Dubois, Heather, 'Confessional art: Working through conflict in constructed female identity', dissertation for BA (Hons) in Visual Culture, 2015.
6. Laila Kassab, application form for co-commission, 2018.
7. ibid.
8. *To Death and Back*, a film by Drew Fox, https://www.youtube.com/watch?v=YE7Zt982fUs
9. https://rawvision.com/blogs/obituaries/news-laurent-danchin-1947-2017

Outside In Artists

1. Bethlem Royal Hospital is a psychiatric hospital in London.

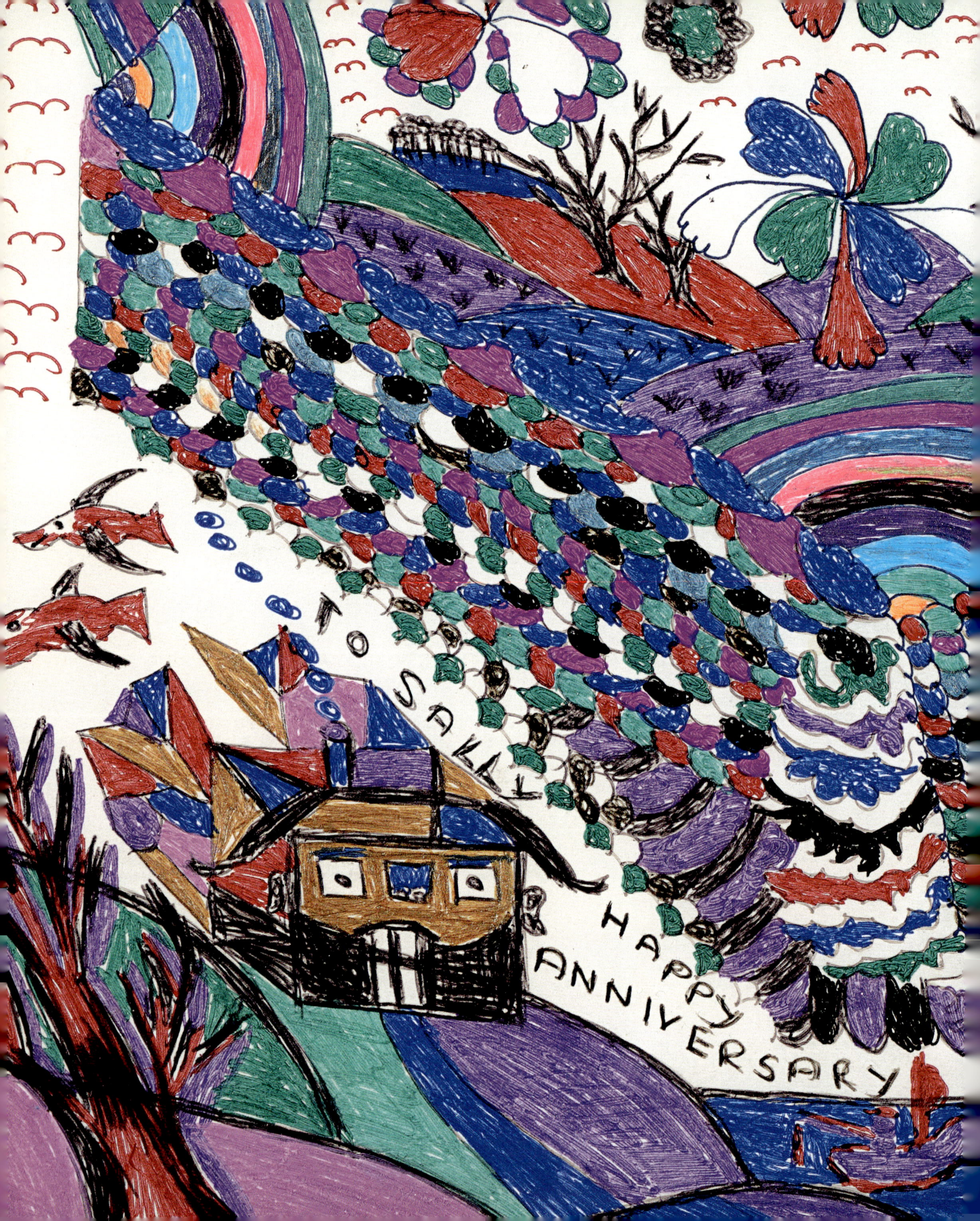
TO
HAPPY
ANNIVERSARY

Endnote

Working to help create a fairer art world has been a sometimes difficult and challenging journey. The world was a very different place when the idea first emerged to establish Outside In in 2006. Diversity and inclusion were not the drivers for change they are now. The Disability Discrimination Act and the Equality Act had not yet come into force. The Black Lives Matter movement was yet to happen and prejudice and stigma were very much real and felt. Progress has been made, as evidenced by the Royal Academy's inclusion of a more diverse range of artists in their Summer Exhibition and Project Art Works being shortlisted for the Turner Prize, but there is still so much to do. Too many doors remain closed and it is too easy to be seen to be doing the right thing rather than actually delivering lasting change.

We are yet to see truly representative programming in the most important art spaces and galleries, nor in the wider collecting of works of art. The arts workforce is still not truly diverse or representative. While the voices and experiences of a wider set of creators and artists remain unheard, nothing will change. Without such steps towards inclusion and diversity, the art world is not realising its full potential.

Outside In's purpose is to address and challenge these barriers to inclusion by working in partnership with artists, arts organisations and wider society. Building on its hubs in the South, Midlands and North West, and its website hosting 4000 artists' work, it has developed a two-fold strategy of creating new interactive digital spaces and establishing further hubs in areas of need.

If we are to create a permanent shift in the arts landscape and create a genuinely representative arts sector, we need to rethink how we define art and culture. Without a shift we are in danger of creating an elitist ghetto of those in the know which has little relevance to society more broadly. Creativity is vital for a healthy society. It should be an individual's right, not to be determined by others, but for each of us to discover and own ourselves. This is the important and lasting change that Outside In seeks to deliver.

Chaz Waldren
Jesus loves the weird and wonderful (detail)
2008
Pen on paper
29.7 × 21 cm

Outside In – Selected Exhibitions

Outside In has held over 50 exhibitions, the most important of which are listed below.

2007

Outside In Open Pallant House Gallery

2009

Outside In National Exhibition Pallant House Gallery

Outside In West The Brewhouse, Taunton;

Outside In Central Compton Verney;

Outside In East Angela Ruskin University, Cambridge;

Outside In North East Woodhorn Museum, Northumberland;

Outside In North West Tullie House, Carlisle; and

Outside In Scotland Aberdeen Art Gallery and Project Ability, Glasgow.

2012

Art from the Margins Outside In National Exhibition, Pallant House Gallery

Outside In London Café Gallery Project

Outside In Milton Keynes MK Gallery

Outside In Bethlem Bethlem Gallery, London

2013

Outside In: On Tour The Museum of East Anglian Life, Stowmarket; Royal Brompton and Harefield hospitals; Salisbury Arts Centre; and the Public, West Bromwich.

Outside In South East Hastings Museum & Art Gallery

Gold Run: Remix The Lightbox, Woking; Chapel Arts Studios, Andover; Pallant House Gallery Chichester; and Shape Arts, London.

2014

Intuitive Folk Masao Obata, Shinichi Sawada, Chaz Waldren and Jason Pape at Pallant House Gallery.

2015

Radical Craft Outside In National, Pallant House Gallery, in partnership with Craftspace. Tour: Oriel Davies Gallery and Aberystwyth Arts Centre, Wales; Tullie House Museum & Art Gallery, Carlisle; and the Barony Centre, West Kilbride.

Intuitive Visions: Shifting the Margins HOUSE arts festival, Phoenix Art Space, Brighton.

2016

Home Away From Home Outside In and HOUSE Co-commission, Regency Town House, Brighton.

Nama Āto: Japanese Outsider Art Southbank Centre, London, and Attenborough Arts Centre, Leicester.

2017

HOUSE Biennial Outside In and HOUSE Co-commission, Andrew Omoding and Anthony Stevens, Phoenix Art Space, Brighton.

James Gladwell: The Dreams 2015 National Exhibition award-winning artist exhibition, Pallant House Gallery.

Alternative Visions: Undiscovered Art in the South West Bristol Museum & Art Gallery; Falmouth Art Gallery; the Wilson, Cheltenham; and Poole Museum.

2018

Journeys Outside In launch exhibition, Sotheby's London.

Colliding Worlds Outside In and Pallant House Gallery Co-Commission, Laila Kassab and Greg Bromley, Pallant House Gallery.

2019

Realm Residency and exhibition by Outside In with artists Richard Downes, Mr X and Hazel Brill at Café Gallery Projects (CGP) London and Bethlem Gallery, London.

Hard Wired Touring exhibition by Outside In and Chrysalis Arts Development: North Bridlington, Catterick, Whitby and Chorley Libraries.

The Outside and Inside Outside In and the Ingram Collection exhibition curated by Marc Steene at the Lightbox, Woking.

Environments Outside In National Exhibition, Kings Place, London.

2020

All Souls Outside In and Pallant House Gallery Co-Commission, artist Julia Oak, Pallant House Gallery.

2021

Strange Relations Outside In and Fabrica exhibition of artists Simon Le Boggit and Carys Reilly, Fabrica, Brighton.

2022

Kindred Spirits Outside In and Jerwood Collection exhibition at Harley Gallery, Nottinghamshire, curated by Outside In artists trained through the Step Up Programme.

Under a Blue Sky 2019 National award-winning artist Alan Payler alongside works by the Community Art Project, Darlington, at Phoenix Art Space, Brighton.

Taking Flight Works from the Outside In Collection curated by Outside In artist Corinne at Paradise Row, London.

Unlocking the Extraordinary Kelvingrove Art Gallery and Museum, Glasgow, and Project Ability, Glasgow.

Recollections May Vary Mental Health Museum, Wakefield.

Looking to the Light Glenside Hospital Museum, Bristol.

2023

Humanity Outside In National Exhibition at Sotheby's London; Project Ability, Glasgow; and Brighton Museum & Art Gallery.

Virtual exhibitions

Community and Friendship Works from the Outside In Collection curated by trustee Frances Christie.

Art and Activism Works from the Outside In online galleries curated by Helen Wewiora, director of Castlefield Gallery, Manchester.

Layers of Creativity Works from the Outside In Collection curated by Jo Baring, director of the Ingram Collection.

The Dove – A Symbol of Peace and Hope An exhibition of work inspired by the acclaimed Ukrainian artist Maria Prymachenko (1908–97) in partnership with the European Outsider Art Association.

Another Space Within An exhibition of works and research created by Outside In artists produced during the Patient Artwork project in partnership with Glasgow Museums; the Mental Health Museum, Wakefield; and Glenside Hospital Museum, Bristol.

The Outside In Collection

Outside In has a growing collection of artwork made by non-traditional and excluded artists. The collection is the first of its kind in the UK and aims to become a lasting legacy for future generations and to provide a fairer and more inclusive definition of our culture.

Further Reading

Beales, David, *The Road to The Asylum*, Kindle, 2016

Blinko, Nick, *The Primal Screamer*, PM Press, New York, 2011

Cardinal, Roger, Carolin, Clare and Grayson, Richard, *A Secret Service: Art, Compulsion, Concealment*, Hayward Publishing, London, 2006

Cardinal, Roger, *Outsider Art*, Studio Vista, London, 1972

English, Charlie, *The Gallery of Miracles and Madness*, Harper Collins, New York, 2021

Jay, Mike, *This Way Madness Lies – The Asylum and Beyond*, Thames & Hudson, London, 2016

Luchsinger, Katrin et al, Extra-ordinary! Unknown Works from Swiss Psychiatric Institutions around 1900, Scheidegger & Spiess, Zurich, 2018

Maclagan, David, *Outsider Art: From the Margins to the Marketplace*, Reaktion Books, London, 2009

Maizels, John, *Raw Creation: Outsider Art and Beyond*, Phaidon, London, 2000

Prinzhorn, Hans, *Artistry of the Mentally Ill*, Martino Fine Books, Connecticut, 2019

Tromans, Nicholas, *Richard Dadd: The Artist and the Asylum*, Tate Publishing, London, 2011

Image Credits

Credits listed in page number order.

2 © David Puttick
7 © Carlo Keshishian. Photo: Mark Heathcote
8 © Alan Liddle. Photo: Outside In
9 Photo courtesy of private collection
11 © ADAGP, Paris and DACS, London, 2022. Bridgeman Images
13 © Keith Purcell. Photo : Outside In
13 © The estate of the Artist. Photo: Outside In
14 © Alan Payler. Photo: Laurence Ward
16-17 © Rakibul Chowdhury. Photo: © Pete Jones / www.pjproductions.co.uk
18 © The estate of the Artist. Photo courtesy of private collection
19 Photo courtesy of private collection
20 Acquired by Pallant House Gallery in 2017 with thanks to support from Art Fund (with a contribution from The Wolfson Foundation), the Arts Council England / Victoria & Albert Purchase Grant Fund, the Friends of Pallant House Gallery Acquisition Fund
21 © Angela Verren Taunt. All rights reserved, DACS 2022. © Kettle's Yard / Bridgeman Images
22 © Manuel Bonifacio. Photo: Outside In
23 © Manuel Bonifacio. Photo: Outside In
24 © Rakibul Chowdhury. Photo: © Pete Jones / www.pjproductions.co.uk
26-27 © Rakibul Chowdhury. Photo: Mark Heathcote
28 © Victoria Bowman. Photo: Laurence Ward
29 © Victoria Bowman. Photo: Laurence Ward
30 Courtesy of the artist and Creative Growth. Image © the Whitworth, The University of Manchester. Photo: Michael Pollard
31 © Andrew Omoding / ActionSpace. Photo: © Hydar Dewachi
32–33 Photo courtesy of Humber Street Gallery and the artist, 2019. Image © Jules Lister.
34 © James Gladwell. Photo: Mark Heathcote
35 © James Gladwell. Photo: Outside In
36–37 © Joanna Simpson. Photo: © Pete Jones / www.pjproductions.co.uk
38–39 © Gary Williams. Photo courtesy of family archive
40 © Joan Wilkinson. Photo: Laurence Ward
41 © Joan Wilkinson. Photo: Laurence Ward
42–43 © Chaz Waldren. Photo: Mark Heathcote
44 © Chaz Waldren. Photo: Outside In
45 © Nigel Kingsbury/ActionSpace. Photo: Outside In
46–47 © Martin Phillimore. Photo: Outside In
48 © Prinzhorn Collection, University Hospital Heidelberg.
49 Courtesy of Adamson Collection/Wellcome Collection
50 © Miss. B. M. Private Collection. Reproduced with permission of West Sussex Record Office
51 © Miss. B. M. Private Collection. Reproduced with permission of West Sussex Record Office
52 © Tess Springall. Photo: Mark Heathcote
53 © Tess Springall
54 Photo: Tate
55 © Albert Rackett. Photo: Mark Heathcote
56–57 © Nick Blinko. The Henry Boxer Gallery. Photo : Mark Heathcote
58–59 © Tyrome Jordan. Photo: Outside In
60 © Tyrome Jordan. Photo: Outside In
61 Copyright: Land Niedersachsen (State of Lower Saxony). Photo © Andreas Spengler
62 Copyright: Land Niedersachsen (State of Lower Saxony). Photo: Hans Starosta
63 © Matthew Beadon. Photo: Laurence Ward
64–65 © Matthew Beadon. Photo: Laurence Ward
66 © Prinzhorn Collection, University Hospital Heidelberg.
67 © Prinzhorn Collection, University Hospital Heidelberg.
68 Photo: Mental Health Museum, object reference: SR2015.323.
69 Photo: Mental Health Museum, object reference: SR2015.323.
70 © Neal Pearce
71 © Martin Phillimore. Photo : Outside In
72 © Martin Phillimore. Photo: Outside In
73 © David Puttick
74 © Jonathan Pettitt. Photo: © Pete Jones / www.pjproductions.co.uk
75 © Madge Gill. Private Collection. Photo: Outside In
76 © Madge Gill. Private Collection. Photo: Outside In
77 © Madge Gill. Private Collection. Photo: Outside In
78 Photo: Jan Baldwin
79 © Friedrich Nagler. Photo: © Pete Jones / www.pjproductions.co.uk
80 © Ian Sherman, Despotic Tribulator, 1999. Photo Jacqui Cavalier
81 © Ian Sherman. Photo: Mark Heathcote
82–83 © Dannielle Hodson. Photo: Roberto Garagaza
85 Photo: Metropolitan Museum of Art, NY.
86 © Dannielle Hodson. Photo: Outside In
87 © Dannielle Hodson. Photo: Roberto Garagaza
89 © Dannielle Hodson. Photo: Roberto Garagaza
90 © Laila Kassab. Photo: Outside In
91 © James Lake. Photo: Andrew Hood
92 © Corinne
93 © Andrew Hood
93 © Andrew Hood
94 © Drew Fox. Photo: © Pete Jones / www.pjproductions.co.uk
95 © Drew Fox
96 © Prinzhorn Collection, University Hospital Heidelberg.
97 © Prinzhorn Collection, University Hospital Heidelberg.
98 © David Beales
98–99 © David Beales. Wellcome Collection. Photo, courtesy of the Bethlem Gallery
100 © Charles Devus
101 © Charles Devus
101 © Charles Devus
101 © Charles Devus
102 © Carlo Keshishian. Photo: Mark Heathcote
104–105 © Carlo Keshishian
108 © Grayson Perry. Courtesy the artist, Paragon |Contemporary Editions Ltd and Victoria Miro
110 © Koji Nishioka. Photo : Mark Heathcote
114 Photo : Courtesy Outside In
114 Image courtesy of the artist and ActionSpace.
114 Image courtesy of ActionSpace
114 Photo: Carlo Keshishian
114 Photo: Laurence Ward
114 Photo: James Lake
114 Atelier CORNERS
115 © Jonathan Pettitt. Photo: © Pete Jones / www.pjproductions.co.uk
115 Photo: Phoebe Wingrove
115 Photo: Outside In, with permission from Luc(e) Raesmith
115 Photo : David Puttick
115 Photo: Outside In
115 Photo: Corinne
115 © Keith Purcell. Photo : Outside In
116 © Joanna Simpson. Photo: © Pete Jones / www.pjproductions.co.uk
116 Photograph courtesy of the artist's family.
116 Photo: Courtesy of family
116 © Albert Rackett. Photo: Mark Heathcote
116 Photo: Tess Springall
116 Photo : Gary Shepherd
116 Photo: Outside In
118 © Chaz Waldren. Photo: Outside In

Index

Illustrations and captions are in *italic*.